Twelve

A TUSCAN COOK BOOK

Twelve

A TUSCAN COOK BOOK

TESSA KIROS

PHOTOGRAPHY
MANOS CHATZIKONSTANTIS

whitecap

First published by Murdoch Books Pty Limited in 2005

This edition published in Canada in 2005 by Whitecap Books, 351 Lynn Avenue.,
North Vancouver, British Columbia, Canada, V7J 2C4
www.whitecap.ca
Reprinted 2006, 2008.

Photography: Manos Chatzikonstantis
Food Styling and Illustrations: Michail Touros
Art Direction: Lisa Greenberg
Additional Design: Marylouise Brammer and Annette Fitzgerald
Cover Design: Marylouise Brammer
Editors: Joanna Warren and Gordana Trifunovic
Editorial Consultant: Raffaela Pugliese
Editorial Director: Diana Hill
Production: Janis Barbi

Chief Executive: Juliet Rogers
Publisher: Kay Scarlett

ISBN 978 1 55285 732 8

Printed by 1010 Printing International Limited. Printed in China.

IMPORTANT: Those who might be at risk from the effects of salmonella poisoning (the elderly, pregnant
women, young children and those suffering from immune deficiency diseases) should consult their GP with any
concerns about eating raw eggs.

www.twelve-tuscany.it

For Yasmine and Cassia and any other soul that may choose me as their mamma. This book is dedicated to everybody that I love. And to wanderlust — and the joy that stepping onto new territory and finding wonderful things brings.

Acknowledgements

My biggest thanks must go to Mario and Wilma Neri, who are wonderful, professional, dedicated cooks — and delightful, honest people. They patiently gave me most of the recipes, tasted my trials, and inspired me to begin my collection of Tuscan recipes. Giovanna Barellini, a splendid cook, taught me how to make jam and preserves from the fruit and vegetables that she sows and reaps herself. She rears chickens, rabbits and ducks for her family's needs and makes her own wine and olive oil from their plot of land, and has the energy of a child at her gentle age of 78.

My interest in food is a lifelong passion, so how can I not thank my family who showed me that quality begins with good ingredients. They gave me the tools I needed to realise this book. Thank you George, Sipi, Tanja and Nicolas.

I wonder if I can ever sufficiently thank the most colourful and creative people in my world: Michail Touros, Manos Chatzikonstantis and Lisa Greenberg, who took a flat concept and gave it life — and without whom, I wouldn't have had such fun.

A sincere thank you to my editor — Joanna Warren — for her solid, yet flexible enthusiasm and insight, and for lighting up and helping me reach those places that were beyond my grasp. There are those I would like to thank for their assistance, enthusiasm or recipe contribution. Without their assistance, this book might have remained just an idea. An enormous thank you to Hervé Pronzato, Paul Mattison, Luisa Moscucci, Luca Neri, Angela Maria Bertucci, Giacomo Neri, Giulianna Pagni, Marco Lunghetti, Francesca Baldesi, Giulietta Inglese, Kristen Bridge, Megan Payne, Kyoko Rokutanda, Gianluca Pardini and Serena Massari.

A very big thank you to Ketty Koufonichola Touros and Artemis Herodotou for the gracious use of their homes, and to Roberto Tuzzami, Jennifer Storey, Ana De la Cruz, Paola Mascagni, Sophia Mila, Daniela De Jesus and Barbara Rosi for their enthusiasm and support. But above all, I must tell Giovanni Neri, whose beautiful soul led me to all these people and, from whom I collected recipes and gathered advice, how very much this all has meant to me.

I would like to thank Kay and Murdoch Books for their open-hearted faith and their natural, professional enthusiasm in welcoming a visitor.

Contents

Introduction

This book is about ingredients and what I have seen people here do with them, and it is about the joy brought by each month with its new ingredients. It is about Tuscany, and even though all the dishes in the book are not Tuscan in origin they are all eaten here. Most of the recipes, however, have their roots firmly embedded in Tuscan soil. Year after year, as the months and ingredients change, so does the family table.

The trattorias serve what seasonal goods their suppliers offer and generally don't rely on expensive, out-of-season produce. People are accustomed to accepting the gifts that their surroundings offer. I once asked a local what he did when he wanted strawberries in December and he looked genuinely puzzled. His reply finally was that he wouldn't, because strawberries come in May. What is assumed by the homecook is supported by medical science it seems. A paediatrician suggested simply serving what the month has to offer as, she maintained, nature has taken care of us during the different seasons of the year. The earth gives as we need — oranges and their vitamin C come in winter and refreshing watermelons arrive in August.

Ingredients vary — not just seasonally but monthly — and sometimes subtly, sometimes dramatically. This is reflected on the canvas that is the Tuscan countryside. Each month that passes I notice a change in the land, a change in ingredients — from the young green of a tiny, new bud to a more insipid shade of hill brown. People are involved with their surroundings here, and respect them for what they have to give; many seem to choose a vegetable patch over a flower garden. The so-called peasants lovingly sow and reap all year — and naturally reap most in the summer months, when there is abundance. From that abundance, preserves are made, and the flavours of June may be recalled in December. The generosity of summer eventually wanes, but there are the vegetables that last a long time — potatoes, pumpkin and onions — and these are used deep into the months that render nothing. Some products are ever-present, such as carrots, celery, sage and rosemary, and they form the basis of most stews and casserole dishes that might appear at any time. Although the land provides great variety in fruit and vegetables, Tuscany is not a land of vegetarians, and to the bounty of the earth are added the catch off its seacoast and the annual hunts in the woodlands.

My aim in writing this book has been to share some of the delights that have been part of my life here. More than an informative guide, it outlines the basic goings-on taking place on stovetops in a place whose culinary fame is steadfastly rooted amongst the hills and within tradition.

First amongst the list of things I have appreciated is the quality of ingredients: an apparently ordinary piece of meat, grilled and transformed by lashings of olive oil; the apricot eaten off the tree after lunch; the gorgeous artichoke dipped in lemon juice and luminous green olive oil, and the tomatoes bursting with summer. The sensibility in knowing what to do with good ingredients is a strong point in Tuscan cuisine, such as the ability to deliciously vary the final taste with a change in the basic ingredient or addition of a new one at the last moment.

Hopefully as the reader, and especially a kitchen reader with this book propped up on the kitchen counter and surrounded by beautiful ingredients, you will come to appreciate all this on your own. Throughout the months of the year you will find the ingredients of Tuscany just as they become available to the Tuscans. In each month there are recipes for all the courses of an Italian meal — though as you will see in "The Italian meal", even an Italian doesn't eat all the courses all the time. In the spirit of beginning well, "The store cupboard" gives tips on filling your pantry with the right type of basic ingredients that are at the heart of these recipes, and the "Basics" section provides preparation instructions and recipes that Tuscan homecooks will have learned at their parents' and grandparents' side. Although it is my belief that with good ingredients anyone can cook a good Tuscan meal, I recognise that not everyone lives in Tuscany and so I have occasionally given alternatives for those harder-to-find ingredients. The rest, I trust you will shift, find, improvise and add to suit your personal space and marketplace.

My story begins in January.

The store cupboard

On examining an Italian's refrigerator and store cupboard, it is clear that one would never be found in a panic situation at the unexpected arrival of guests. A quick stock with pasta boiled in it or a pasta with onions, tomatoes and *pancetta*, or simply garlic, chilli and olive oil — generally served with grated Parmesan cheese — can always be thrown together in a matter of minutes.

Most houses are stocked with various homemade jams and preserves, including fresh tomato sauces. Bread, cheese, meat, fish, and fruit and vegetables are bought fresh every day or as needed. A window box with fresh basil, parsley, mint, sage, rosemary and thyme are commonplace and a wonderful addition to any meal. Carrots and celery are almost always in the refrigerator and are used with onions, garlic and parsley just about everywhere. Any special ingredients can be bought from specialist shops as they are needed.

Here is a list of shouldn't-be-withouts.

Olive oil
(Extra virgin and a lighter olive oil)

Vinegar (balsamic and white)

Salt and pepper

Sugar (caster and icing)

Honey   Coffee

Milk

Sweet biscuits

Cocoa powder

Butter

Wine
(suitable for cooking as well)

Beer

Onions

Garlic

Dried chillies

Potatoes

Tomatoes (tinned and fresh)

Lemons

Capers
Anchovies
Flour
(bread and cake)

Rice
(risotto, long-grain
and short-grain or pudding rice)

Dry pasta
(spaghetti, and a choice of short
pasta such as penne)

Semolina

Polenta

Parmesan cheese

Yoghurt

Prosciutto crudo

Pancetta

Salami
Dried herbs —
eg. oregano, bay leaves
and nutmeg

Eggs

The Italian meal

16 November
    the table was laid beautifully . . .
spaghetti with eggplant, tomato, and shiny black olives. Pan-fried endive, fennel, and marzolino cheese. Bread, tomato, beans, and olive oil. Pane co' santi. sweet red wine. Coffee. Things that say yes inside always, bells that chime in harmony with my inner being. A simplicity that I love and flavours I don't get tired of. Amongst the ancient buildings, washing lines, beautiful hills and between the fagiolini and rows of hanging salsicce, there is still more, even after the sweetness of Vin Santo has gone.

I have heard people complain endlessly that if they had to eat like they eat when they visit Italy, or like the Italians eat every day, they would be enormous.

Yet I find that the Tuscans, at least, have a rather balanced way of eating and by not haphazardly mixing up their foods all in one meal manage both to stay healthy and to look good. They often manage an *antipasto*, a first course, a main course, wine and a dessert followed by coffee. They often have a liqueur — an *amaro* (a bitter) after a meal to aid digestion, they say, and in fact many of their liqueurs contain fennel and other digestion-aiding ingredients.

The *antipasto* might be a simple artichoke or seafood salad or a small piece of bread with a topping (the well-known *crostino*). The *primo* (first course) consists generally of either a soup, a rice dish or a pasta. The *secondo* (main course) is often a piece of meat, fish or poultry generally not excessively large and served quite plain, more often with just a drizzle of olive oil — unless, of course, it is a stewed dish. There is often a *contorno* (side dish) of vegetables or salad. *Dolce* (dessert) may be a piece of cake, ice cream or some fruit. Cheese, rather than at the end of the meal, is often eaten during a meal in place of a first or second course.

To me, the Tuscans seem to have it in their blood — this natural knowledge of what goes with what. Generally speaking you wouldn't find an *antipasto* dripping with meat, followed by a pasta with meat sauce and then a roast meat. Rather, a roast meat would be preceded by perhaps a tomato pasta and before that a couple of olives and a slice of cheese. The combinations seem to be chosen with care and render a light, harmonious whole. The heavy combinations are often saved for special occasions. Those meals, which turn into hours at the dining-room table, would find their grace note in a small cup of Italian espresso.

Wine notes

To speak of Tuscan food without the accompaniment of the local wine, produced in the hills of this land so rich in tradition and history, would be a sign of not having understood, in total, the culture of a people.

Tuscan table wines have been purposely grown to be enjoyed with the local dishes in an absolutely original context of taste and flavours. Tuscan wines, dry and serious with decisive body and clear fragrances, are perfect for the light, lean and flavourful Tuscan cuisine, one made up of essential ingredients. Those basic ingredients that nature has put at the Tuscans' disposal, such as extra virgin olive oil, bread, veal, game and flavourful vegetables, excel on the tables of this region.

These wines historically accompany the local dishes, making them seem as if they have a natural affinity.

The Tuscan whites, those made from the trebbiano grape like the Val d'Arbia and the Vergine Val di Chiana, are best served cold with classic dishes such as *crostini neri* (a chicken liver-based appetiser), the sliced mixed cold meats, various soups and, best of all, with *panzanella* (bread, tomato and olive oil salad). These wines are also well-matched to the various fish dishes. The white wine par excellence, however, is the Vernaccia di San Gimignano, with its slightly bitter almond fragrance. It is tempting and penetrating, with a beautiful straw colour.

This is a good wine to accompany white meat dishes, such as rabbit stewed with herbs, or with tomato and olives. Above all it complements the various cold meats of the region: a two-year old *prosciutto*, fennel salami and Italian sausages. The abundance of fish in the nearby sea creates a use for this wine by pairing it with some of the classic fish dishes.

The wine which most characterises Tuscan territory is red wine — identified by the name Chianti. It is the wine most known to the world and also the most appreciated for its simple and comprehensible tasting qualities. It is considered a wine for all meals, and can be adapted to all the classic dishes of Tuscan cooking.

The base of this wine is the sangiovese grape, grown across most of Tuscany, although there are fundamental distinctions in quality and character determined by zone. The Chianti wine, bearing the DOCG mark which ensures a control over its origin, is the wine most popular in Tuscany. Of a distinct ruby colour, with a vinous, sweet-violet fragrance, it is made for early drinking. It is suitable for any meal: for pasta and risotto dishes with various meats and vegetable sauces, for boiled and stewed meats, and for roasted poultry and other white meats.

Of a higher standard and decisively superior quality is the Chianti Classico (also DOCG), produced in a legally defined area in the heart of Tuscany — between the provinces of Florence and Siena. Of an intense ruby colour and rich in fragrance, it is a wine suited to a light maturing process of two to three years, and calls for more complex dishes, such as fried foods, poultry and game, and mature cheeses. The Tuscan territory is rich in tradition, but also rich in wines. In the neighbouring town of Siena — a city of antiquity steeped in history and artworks — some of the world's most important wines are cultivated.

The Brunello di Montalcino offers an intense, ruby colour with a tendency toward purple as it ages, an ethereal smell and dry flavour. It is warm, robust and vivacious — a little tannic, yet harmonious.

Once on the table, a Brunello immediately becomes the protagonist of the meal, especially when combined with its most complementary dishes: game, mixed braised meat dishes and mature cheeses. It is an ideal companion, too, for meditating on those cold winter evenings.

The other Siennese wine is the Nobile di Montepulciano — born in a land of saints, popes, artists and poets who as early as the year 1000 decanted this nectar, as documents found in ancient archives reveal. It is without a doubt the oldest wine known to Tuscan territory, presenting a fairly deep purple colour, which tends to become a reddish-brown as it ages. It has a delicate, sweet-violet fragrance, with a dry, slightly tannic flavour. It is a grand wine for roasts and red meats, game, poultry and mature cheeses. It is the perfect wine to enjoy with a grilled Florentine T-bone steak.

Tuscany is rich in wine-growing establishments, and has many other eminent wines. An example is the Carmignano, which takes its name from the area where it originates, between Florence and Pistoia, in the hills of Montalbano. It is a wine of a ruby colour, tending toward purple as it ages, with a persistent fragrance of sweet violets. It marries well to the roast meat, game and poultry dishes.

Our tour has ended, but as chroniclers, we must also note a few other wines, not distant from the traditions of this region.

Whites: Bianco di Valdinievole, Bianco di Pitigliano, Bianco di San Torpé, Candia Bianco, Elba Bianco, Parrina, Pomino.
Reds: Montescudaio, Morellino di Scansano, Montecarlo Rosso, Elba Rosso, Rosso di Montalcino, Rosso di Montepulciano, Nipozzano.

The Vin Santo of Tuscany, the only dessert wine, deserves a special note. It is extracted from the fermentation of generally white grapes, which are dried on trellises, or mats made from vines or bamboo, in appropriate places. These sites are usually well ventilated and not at all humid, to prevent the bunches of grapes from becoming mouldy. The concentration of sugar that develops throughout drying encourages the process. After three to four years of ageing in small vats called *caratelli*, a bright amber-coloured wine emerges, loaded with fragrance and flavour, and an alcohol content of 17 per cent. It is well suited to the more dry desserts, such as the Cantuccini (almond biscotti), Panforte, and the Pinolata.

Mario Neri, professional chef and sommelier

JANUARY

The fields are dry now, the corn a pale shade of straw. The brick, thatch and rust tiles blend beautifully into their brown, monotoned background of hills, which stand silently and patiently, knowing that they shall one day bear their gifts. It is January.

The snow of last week is fading, exposing the countryside once again. Everywhere there are logs stacked up, fireplaces waiting each evening to be lit. People are indoors, so it is natural to assume that so are the crops. Many of the long-lasting vegetables from months before — pumpkins, potatoes, onions and carrots — are cooked and eaten with various meats. There is cavolo nero, a dark green type of cabbage that provides satisfying meals. The hunting season continues until towards the end of this month and still provides a lot of meat — pigeon, wild boar, pheasant and guinea fowl.

It is bitterly cold and humid, and freezing wet outside, the coldest it ever gets. Many people grill meat in their open fireplaces at home. It is such a beautiful thing — I've never seen huge steaks cooking over woodfires in people's living rooms before.

Crostini di polenta con gorgonzola

Polenta crostini with gorgonzola

Cooked polenta is a cold-weather favourite. Here, this simple ingredient is made more elegant by its combination with the sharpness of a blue cheese. Serve a couple of polenta squares or triangles per person as an antipasto.

Serves 6–8

1.3 litres (5 cups) water

250 g (9 oz) polenta

a little olive oil

about 125 g ($4^1/2$ oz) gorgonzola cheese

To wash the pot you make polenta in, leave it filled with warm water to soak for a couple of hours, and the polenta will just peel away.

Put the water into a large pot with 1 teaspoon of salt. When it comes to the boil, pour in the polenta in a thin steady stream, whisking continuously with the other hand to prevent lumps forming. Lower the heat and cook the polenta for about 30 minutes, stirring often to prevent it sticking. It will begin to appear very smooth and thick.

Lightly grease a large baking sheet with a little olive oil. Pour the cooked polenta out onto the baking sheet and spread it out with a wooden spoon to a thickness of about 1 cm ($1/2$ in). Leave it to cool completely.

Heat a chargrill (griddle) pan and turn on the oven grill (broiler), as well. Cut the polenta into squares of about 7 or 8 cm ($2^3/4$ or 3 in). Brush the top side with a little olive oil and when the pan is hot, cook the polenta pieces until grill marks appear on the undersides. Turn over and cook the other side. The idea is to form a crust, so you can also cook it under the oven grill or on a barbecue. Divide the gorgonzola between the polenta squares and transfer to an oven dish. Put the polenta squares under the hot grill for a few minutes to melt the gorgonzola slightly. Remove from the oven. Cut each square diagonally in half and serve immediately.

Torta di porri

Leek tart

Vegetable tarts are served either as an antipasto or as a light main meal. You can substitute any other vegetable for the leeks here. Onions, artichokes, green beans, silverbeet (Swiss chard), spinach and mushrooms are a good choice. Estimate that you will need 2 full cups of the sliced and cooked vegetable. You can add fresh herbs and seasonings of your choice.

Makes one 26 cm (10$^{1}/_{2}$ in) tart

$^{1}/_{2}$ the quantity of savoury pastry*
(see page 389)

3 leeks, about 800 g (1 lb 12 oz) in total

3 tablespoons olive oil

250 ml (1 cup) white wine

3 eggs

150 g (1$^{1}/_{2}$ cups) freshly grated Parmesan cheese

nutmeg

125 ml ($^{1}/_{2}$ cup) cream

Make your pastry and leave it to rest in the refrigerator for about an hour before rolling it out.

Preheat the oven to 180°C (350°F/Gas 4). Using a loose-bottomed tart case with 2.5 cm (1 in) high sides, follow the instructions for rolling out the pastry and baking it (partially) blind.

Strip away any damaged tough parts and the top extreme ends, and chop the leeks into thin slices of about 3 mm ($^{1}/_{8}$ in). Put them into a bowl of cold water and swish them with your hands to ensure they are well rinsed. Scoop them up and transfer to a colander to drain.

Put the olive oil into a saucepan to heat and add the leeks. Sauté gently to soften, and season with salt and pepper. When the leeks become very lightly golden, add the wine and continue cooking until most of it has evaporated. Add about 250 ml (1 cup) of water and sauté for another 10 minutes or so, until the leeks are soft and there is only a little liquid left in the pan. Remove the saucepan from the heat.

Lightly whip the eggs in a bowl. Stir in the slightly cooled leeks, mixing to make sure you don't produce an omelette. Add the Parmesan cheese, a good grating of nutmeg and the cream. Adjust the seasoning if necessary and pour the mix into your baked tart case, shifting the leeks evenly with a spoon. Return the tart to the oven for about 20–30 minutes, until the top is lightly golden and set. Cool before removing from the tart case and slicing into portions. Serve slightly warm or at room temperature.

Ribollita

Thick bean and dark cabbage stew

Serves 8

300 g (10¹/₂ oz) dried cannellini (or other white) beans, soaked overnight

5 tablespoons olive oil

2 medium red onions, peeled and finely chopped

2 stalks celery, trimmed and finely chopped

500 g (1 lb 2 oz) silverbeet (Swiss chard), washed, trimmed and finely sliced

800 g (1 lb 12 oz) *cavolo nero*, washed, trimmed and finely sliced

¹/₂ small red dried chilli, crumbled

1 tablespoon tomato paste (purée)

250 g (9 oz) white, country-style bread, cut into 5 mm (¹/₄ in) slices

extra virgin olive oil, to serve

Traditionally, this soup is prepared ahead of time and portions are heated up in a saucepan or pot with extra olive oil, as needed. Hence its name, "reboiled".

This is a thick vegetable, bean and bread soup with a soft texture. *Cavolo nero* is a dark green cabbage very typical of Tuscany, but can be substituted with kale or Savoy cabbage.

Drain the soaked beans and put them into a large saucepan. Cover with plenty of cold water and bring to the boil. With a slotted spoon, remove any scum that comes to the surface. Lower the heat slightly and cook for at least an hour or until the beans are tender. Add more water when necessary to keep the beans well covered. Season with salt halfway through.

Meanwhile, in a stockpot, heat the olive oil. Add the onion and the celery and sauté until they have softened.

Add the silverbeet and *cavolo nero* and sauté for a little longer, until they have softened and are reduced.

Cover with 3 litres (12 cups) of water and bring to the boil. Season with salt and pepper, and add the chilli and tomato paste. When it comes to the boil, lower the heat and simmer for about 1¼ hours.

Put the bread slices onto an oven tray and dry them in a hot oven. Remove from the oven when they are quite dry and keep aside.

Drain the cannellini beans, keeping about 250 ml (1 cup) of their cooking water. Purée half of the beans with this water, leaving the rest of the beans whole. Add both to the stockpot in the last 10 minutes of the cooking time. Put a ladleful of the thick soup into a large soup dish. Add a couple of the bread slices, then another ladleful of soup. Continue, until you have used up the soup and bread. Leave it to stand for a few minutes for the bread to soften, and the flavours to blend, before serving. If it seems too thick adjust the consistency with a little hot water. Serve warm, in large soup bowls, generously drizzled with extra virgin olive oil.

Ribollita

Risotto alla Toscana

Tuscan risotto

Serves 6

1.5 litres (6 cups) meat
stock* (see page 388)

20 g (3/4 oz) dried
mushrooms

250 ml (1 cup) warm water

200 g (7 oz) chicken livers

2 tablespoons olive oil

1 medium red onion, peeled
and finely chopped

1 garlic clove, peeled and
finely chopped

150 g (5½ oz) minced
(ground) beef

1 Italian sausage, about
80 g (3 oz), skinned and
crumbled

250 ml (1 cup) red wine

500 g (1 lb 2 oz) risotto rice

50 g (1¾ oz) butter

50 g (½ cup) freshly grated
Parmesan cheese plus
extra for serving

a small handful chopped
parsley

While this wintery risotto uses rich, tasty ingredients, it is not
a heavy dish and could be served before a simply cooked
main course.

Make the stock and keep it warm on the stovetop.

Soak the mushrooms in the cup of warm water for about
10 minutes. Strain the water and set aside. Chop the mushrooms.
Clean the livers, removing any bits of bile or little filaments, and
chop the liver into pieces of about 1 cm (½ in). Heat the olive oil
in a large saucepan suitable for making risotto.

Add the onion and sauté until it has softened. Add the
garlic, the beef and the sausage meat, and sauté until golden
brown. Add the wine and cook until it has evaporated. Add
the strained mushroom water and the mushrooms together with
the rice and the chicken livers, and stir for a couple of minutes to
coat the rice. Add a ladleful or two of hot stock and lightly season
with salt and pepper, to taste.

Lower the heat and continue cooking, stirring the risotto
every few minutes. Add another ladleful of stock to the pot as it
is absorbed by the rice. After about 20 minutes taste the rice;
it should be soft yet firm and the texture should be creamy and
slightly liquid. (You may have to continue cooking it for a few more
minutes.) When your rice has achieved this consistency, stir in the
butter and the Parmesan cheese. Serve immediately, sprinkled with
a little chopped parsley and extra Parmesan cheese.

Pappardelle alla lepre

Pappardelle with hare

Serves 6

1 medium hare, cleaned, deboned and cut into small pieces, about 1.2 kg (2 lb 10 oz) deboned weight

1.5 litres (6 cups) vegetable stock* (see page 389)

6 tablespoons olive oil

1 large onion, peeled and very finely chopped

1 celery stalk, washed, trimmed and very finely chopped

1 medium carrot, peeled and very finely chopped

4 tablespoons chopped parsley

2 Italian pork sausages, about 80 g (3 oz) each, skinned and crumbled

200 g (7 oz) minced (ground) pork

250 ml (1 cup) red wine

250 ml (1 cup) tomato passata

4 fresh bay leaves

a few juniper berries

1 quantity, about 650 g (1 lb 7 oz), fresh pasta* (see page 372)

120 g (1 1/4 cup) freshly grated Parmesan cheese, to serve

This is a very classic, antique Tuscan recipe. It is traditionally made with the whole hare, of which part was minced to dress the pasta as a first course and larger pieces were cut and served on the bone as a second course. It is also possible to buy ready-prepared portions of hare for pasta. If you are using a whole hare which your butcher is deboning for you, keep a couple of the bones and add them to the stockpot — there could still be quite a bit of cooked meat afterwards to scrape into the hare sauce. Normally, the heart and the liver are also chopped up and cooked with the meat. Duck is also very often cooked in this way and eaten with fresh pasta.

If the hare has a very strong smell, rinse it in a little vinegar and cold water. Make your stock, or if it is ready, keep it warm on the stovetop.

Heat 3 tablespoons of the olive oil in a wide saucepan, and add the chopped onion, celery, carrot and parsley. Sauté until the vegetables are softened and lightly golden.

Meanwhile put the remaining olive oil into another saucepan, add the sausage and pork, and sauté for a few minutes before adding the hare. Stir the meat with a wooden spoon to prevent it from sticking. Continue stirring until it is lightly browned. Season with salt and pepper.

Add the sautéed vegetables to the meat saucepan or vice versa, and pour in the wine. Continue cooking until the wine has almost evaporated. Add the stock and the tomato passata, and when it comes to the boil, lower the heat, cover and simmer for 1½–2 hours. Add the bay leaves and juniper berries halfway through and stir the sauce now and again. The end result should be a thick, soft mass of small bits of meat with a little thickened liquid. If it seems too watery, cook for a little longer — uncovered to reduce it. If it seems like it needs a little more liquid, add a little hot water.

While the hare is cooking, make the pasta dough following the instructions and leave it to rest, covered, for about 30 minutes in a cool place.

Roll out the pasta dough following the instructions and cut into pappardelle. Roll up the strip of dough along its longest part and cut the pasta with a sharp knife at 3 cm (1¼ in) intervals. Keep the cut pasta on a lightly floured tray until you are ready to cook them.

Cook the pappardelle in boiling salted water for 4–5 minutes, testing it to check if it is ready. It should be soft, yet with a slight resistance to the bite. Cook longer if necessary. Drain and put into individual pasta bowls. Dress with a few tablespoons of the hare sauce, sprinkle with Parmesan cheese and serve immediately.

Bollito misto con salse

Mixed boiled meats with herb and anchovy sauces

Serves 6–8

¹/₂ a boiling hen or chicken, about 700 g (1 lb 9 oz), cleaned and rinsed

400 g (14 oz) deboned shoulder of veal, trimmed of fat

400 g (14 oz) piece silverside (or similar) beef

400 g (14 oz) veal tongue, skinned

3 small tomatoes, quartered

2 carrots, peeled

2 small onions, peeled

2 small celery stalks

1 veal trotter, cleaned

1 pre-cooked zampone (stuffed pig's trotter) or cotechino (pork) sausage (available from Italian delicatessens)

lentils, cooked, to serve (recipe follows)

250 ml (1 cup) *salsa verde** (see page 378)

250 ml (1 cup) *acciugata** (see page 379)

Although this recipe uses six different types of meat, in Italy it is also very common to boil only one type of meat — either beef or chicken — and to serve pasta in the stock as a first course with grated Parmesan cheese. The boiled meat is eaten as a second course accompanied by *salsa verde** (see page 378) and *acciugata** (see page 379). A different variety of meats may be used in a reduced quantity, as well.

The mixed boiled meats can be served on a plate with the sauces and some lentils — or in a big bowl, splashed with some of the stock.

Put the hen, veal, beef and tongue into a large saucepan. Add the tomatoes, carrots, onions and celery to the pan (cutting them into large chunks if necessary). Cover generously with about 4 litres (16 cups) of cold water. (If your saucepan isn't large enough, add more water when the stock reduces.) Season with salt and pepper and bring to the boil, skimming the surface with a slotted spoon to remove any scum. Lower the heat and continue cooking for about 2¹/₂ hours until all the meats are very tender.

At the same time, put the trotter into a small, separate saucepan, cover with cold water and bring to the boil. Skim the surface, lower the heat and continue cooking for about 2 hours, topping up with hot water if necessary.

Towards the end of this cooking time, put the *zampone* sausage into a third saucepan, cover with cold water and bring to the boil. It will need about 20 minutes on medium heat. If it is not pre-cooked it will need up to 3 hours.

Make the sauces while the meats are boiling and put them into separate bowls.

Remove the pots from the heat. Transfer the hen, beef, chicken and tongue to a cutting board, and strain stock through a fine strainer to serve with the meat. Cut the hen into small pieces with a pair of poultry shears. Cut the beef, veal and tongue into fairly thick slices and distribute amongst large individual soup plates. Transfer the sausage and the trotter to a cutting board.

Discard the cooking water. Cut the sausage into fairly thick slices and add a slice to each plate. Remove the soft, gelatinous meat from the hard bone of the trotter and put a piece into each bowl. Cover each portion with a ladleful of hot stock and serve immediately with a small, separate bowl of lentils, and a serving of herb sauce and anchovy sauce for each person.

Bollito misto con salse

Lenticchie

Lentils

These are almost always served alongside a *bollito misto*, but can also accompany any other main course.

Serves 4–6

300 g (10½ oz) green or brown lentils

4 tablespoons olive oil

1 medium onion, peeled and chopped

2 garlic cloves, peeled and chopped

about 1.5 litres (6 cups) water

extra virgin olive oil

Rinse the lentils and discard any odd, hard bits.

Heat the olive oil in a pot and add the onion. Sauté for a few minutes to soften, then add the garlic and the lentils. Stir through. Cover with the water, season with salt and pepper and bring to the boil. Lower the heat slightly, cover, and cook for about 30 minutes, or until the lentils are soft and most of the water has been absorbed.

Add a little more water, if necessary, during the cooking time to prevent the lentils from drying out, and stir from time to time to prevent them sticking. Transfer to a serving bowl with a slotted spoon. Serve hot or at room temperature, drizzled with extra virgin olive oil.

Spezzatino di cinghiale

Wild boar stew

Serves 6

1.2 kg (2 lb 10 oz) deboned wild boar, from leg or shoulder, cut into cubes of about 3 cm (1¼ in)

6 tablespoons olive oil

1 large onion, peeled and finely chopped

2 garlic cloves, peeled and chopped

2 medium carrots, peeled and finely chopped

1 stalk of celery, washed, trimmed and finely chopped

200 g (7 oz) minced (ground) beef

2 bay leaves

2 whole cloves

a few juniper berries

½ teaspoon ground cinnamon

500 ml (2 cups) red wine

250 ml (1 cup) tomato passata

1.5 litres (6 cups) vegetable stock* (see page 389)

polenta (recipe follows)

In Tuscany, wild boar is a common choice for making ragù and slow-cooked stews. It is also made into sausages, dried and preserved in oil. You may substitute pork here, or even beef or veal. However, the cooking times may differ, and should be cooked as for a stew, until the meat is very tender.

Washing the wild boar in a little vinegar can help to remove its wild gamey smell if it is very strong. If not, rinse the wild boar in water and pat dry.

Heat 5 tablespoons of olive oil in a large stockpot. Add the onion, garlic, carrot and celery and sauté until they have softened. Add the beef and sauté until lightly golden.

Heat 1 tablespoon of olive oil in a separate saucepan on a high heat. Add the wild boar meat and season with salt and pepper. Add the bay leaves, cloves, juniper berries and cinnamon. Cover the pan with a lid and cook for about 10 minutes or until juices form. Pour away this liquid and add the meat to the vegetable stockpot. Pour in the wine and when it has evaporated, add the tomato passata.

Add the hot stock and simmer, uncovered, on a low heat for 1½–2 hours, until the meat is tender. Add a little more stock or water, if necessary, to keep the meat moist and for extra sauce to serve with the meat. Serve hot with polenta.

Polenta

This porridge type of polenta — which is like a thick potato purée — is often served with stews, but also goes well with mushrooms, gorgonzola cheese, a meat or tomato sauce, or simply with grated pecorino cheese and butter.

Serves 6

2.5 litres (10 cups) water

400 g (14 oz) polenta

100 g (3^1/$_2$ oz) butter

120 g (1^1/$_3$ cup) grated pecorino cheese

To wash the saucepan you make the polenta in, leave it filled with warm water to soak for a couple of hours and the polenta will just peel away.

Boil the water in a large saucepan with 1^1/$_2$ teaspoons of salt. When it comes to the boil, pour in the polenta in a thin, steady stream, whisking continuously with the other hand to prevent lumps forming. Lower the heat and cook the polenta for about 30 minutes, stirring often to prevent it sticking. The polenta will begin to appear smooth and soft, and will start coming away from the sides of the pan if you scrape it down with a wooden spoon.

Stir in the butter and the grated pecorino cheese. Add a grinding of black pepper and serve immediately.

Scottiglia

Mixed meat stew

Serves 6–8

500 g (1 lb 2 oz) deboned shoulder or leg of lamb, trimmed of fat

500 g (1 lb 2 oz) deboned veal shank, trimmed

1.5 kg (3 lb 5 oz) pork ribs, halved horizontally through bone and trimmed of excess fat

4 tablespoons olive oil

1 large onion, peeled and finely chopped

1 large carrot, peeled and finely chopped

1 stalk celery, trimmed and finely chopped

3 garlic cloves, peeled, 2 chopped and 1 left whole

250 ml (1 cup) red wine

800 g (1 lb 12 oz) tin peeled tomatoes (with juice), puréed

6 sage leaves

2 bay leaves

$1/2$ small red dried chilli, crumbled

6 thick slices, country-style white bread

This is a mixed meat stew, simmered in tomato until all the meats are very tender. You can use any combination of meats for this recipe. You could add different cuts of pork, beef, chicken, pigeon, turkey or guinea fowl. It is the mixed combination of meats that gives this dish its special flavour.

Cut the lamb and veal into fairly large chunks. Divide the pork ribs between the bones leaving them attached in twos.

Heat the olive oil in a large stockpot and sauté the meats until they are browned on all sides. Season with salt and pepper. Transfer the browned meat to a plate, and add the onion, carrot, celery and chopped garlic to the pot, adding another drop of olive oil, if necessary. Sauté for a few minutes until they have softened, seasoning lightly with salt and pepper.

Return the meat to the pot and add the wine. Cook until a lot of it has evaporated, then add the tomatoes, sage, bay leaves and chilli. Add 1 litre (4 cups) of water and simmer on a low heat in the covered pot for 2–$2^1/2$ hours more, until the meats are very tender. (If you are using poultry, the cooking time will be slightly less.) Adjust the seasoning if necessary. There must be an abundant amount of sauce to serve with the meat, so add another cup or so of water during the cooking time, if necessary.

Grill (broil) the bread on both sides. Rub one side of each piece with the peeled garlic clove. Put a piece of bread into each large individual soup bowl. Spoon the stew over the bread and serve immediately.

Teglia di patate con cipolle

Oven-baked potato and onion slices

This is a wonderful and very versatile wintery dish that is good to accompany roast meats and stews. You can create many variations depending on the season, using chopped prosciutto, slices of tomato, fresh herbs, mushrooms or gorgonzola and many other ingredients. A few slivers of truffle slipped between potato slices and baked in this manner are excellent.

Serves 8–10

8 medium potatoes, about 1.5 kg (3 lb 5 oz), peeled

4 medium white or red onions, peeled

50 g (1³/4 oz) butter, plus a little extra for greasing

4 bay leaves (fresh or dried)

60 ml (¹/4 cup) white wine

60 ml (¹/4 cup) water

4 tablespoons olive oil

Preheat the oven to 200°C (400°F/Gas 6). Slice the potatoes into rounds of about 3 mm (¹/8 in) and the onions into even thinner rounds.

Generously butter a round 26 x 5 cm high (10¹/2 x 2 in high) oven dish, and lay flat half of the potatoes on the bottom. Season with salt and pepper. Cover with the onion slices and bay leaves, then add the rest of the potatoes to the dish, and season. Add the wine and the water. Drizzle over the olive oil and dot with the butter. Cover the oven dish with aluminium foil and put into the hot oven. Bake for 40 minutes.

Remove the aluminium foil and cook for another 30 minutes or until the top is lightly golden and crispy. Serve in squares.

Torta di riso

Rice tart

Serves 10

Tart

1 litre (4 cups) milk

250 ml (1 cup) water

150 g (5$^{1}/_{2}$ oz) pudding or short-grain rice

100 g (3$^{1}/_{2}$ oz) caster (superfine) sugar

50 g (1$^{3}/_{4}$ oz) butter

4 tablespoons Vin Santo or good-quality brandy

1 teaspoon vanilla essence

grated zest of $^{1}/_{2}$ a lemon and $^{1}/_{2}$ an orange

70 g (2$^{1}/_{2}$ oz) candied citrus peel, chopped

3 eggs, separated

Caramel

220 g (1 cup) sugar

a few drops of water

This dessert — something between a pudding and a cake — is also ideal as a snack, or even for breakfast. You can vary the flavouring, or just make it plain. If you don't use candied fruits, add about 40 g (1$^{1}/_{2}$ oz) more sugar to the mixture.

Make it in a round, non-stick cake tin — 28 cm (11 in) in diameter with sides of about 5 cm (2 in).

Put the milk and water into a saucepan on the stovetop and boil. As soon as it comes to the boil, add the rice and turn down the heat slightly. Cook uncovered for 20–30 minutes, stirring often to prevent it sticking, until the rice is cooked and has absorbed most of the liquid. Remove from the heat and stir in the sugar, butter, liqueur, vanilla, grated zest and citrus peel. Leave to cool slightly.

Preheat the oven to 180°C (350°F/Gas 4).

Meanwhile, to make the caramel, put the sugar with a few drops of water into a small, heavy-bottomed saucepan on a medium–high heat. As soon as the sugar begins to turn golden, turn down the heat to low, swirling the pan around to distribute the heat. Watch the sugar carefully as it only takes a second for it to turn from a rich, golden colour to a burnt mixture.

When the caramel is a deep golden colour, remove it from the heat and immediately pour it into the cake tin. Holding the tin with a cloth, swirl it to cover the bottom completely with the caramel and a little way up the sides.

Lightly whip the egg yolks in a bowl and stir into the slightly cooled rice mixture. Whip the whites to soft peaks and fold thoroughly into the rice mixture. Pour onto the caramel and bake it in a bain-marie in the preheated oven for about 35 minutes, until the rice is lightly golden on top. Remove from the oven and let it cool for 5–10 minutes before gently loosening the sides and inverting onto a serving plate. If the tart is left too long before inverting it may stick to the tin. Serve in slices, warm or cold.

Budino di semolino

Semolina pudding

Serves 10–12

100 g (3¹/₂ oz) sultanas

4 tablespoons Marsala or port

1 litre (4 cups) milk

250 ml (1 cup) water

150 g (5¹/₂ oz) fine semolina

150 g (5¹/₂ oz) caster (superfine) sugar

50 g (1³/₄ oz) butter, plus a little extra for greasing

grated zest of 1 small lemon

4 eggs, separated

fine breadcrumbs for lining the cake tin

200 g (7 oz) good quality, unsweetened dark chocolate

125 ml (¹/₂ cup) cream

This is a very homely, satisfying winter dessert, which you can make even simpler by leaving out the sultanas and liqueur. Also, you can serve this plain without the chocolate, slightly warm and cut into squares or diamond shapes.

Preheat the oven to 180°C (350°F/Gas 4). Soak the sultanas in the Marsala in a small bowl.

Put the milk with the water into a saucepan to boil. Just as it comes to the boil, add the semolina in a thin steady stream, mixing continuously with a wooden spoon to prevent lumps forming. Add the sugar, the butter and lemon zest, and cook on a medium heat, stirring regularly.

When the semolina has absorbed most of the liquid and has the consistency of not-too-stiff porridge, remove it from the heat. This should take less than 10 minutes. Mix in a pinch of salt and the sultanas and Marsala. Leave it to cool slightly.

Whip the egg yolks lightly and add to the semolina, mixing in quickly to avoid scrambling them. Whisk the whites to soft peaks and fold thoroughly into the semolina.

Butter a 28 x 5 cm (11 x 2 in) round or square cake tin. Sprinkle with the breadcrumbs to line the tin, shaking away excess. Pour in the semolina mix. Bake in a bain-marie for 30–40 minutes, until the top is lightly crusty and golden. Remove from the oven and let it cool slightly before turning out and flipping over again onto a plate.

Cut chocolate into slivers and add to the cream in a small saucepan set over a larger saucepan of simmering water, mixing with a wooden spoon to melt. Working quickly, spoon the melted chocolate over the surface of the cooled cake, spreading it evenly over the top and slightly down the sides.

Budino di semolino

FEBRUARY

Carnival time. Everywhere is full of people disguised in bright costumes — even tiny blue werewolf and pink bear babies in prams. The energy is wonderful and so are the sugar-dusted cenci piled up everywhere.

The fields, less dressed, have given little. We rely on the richer months, when abundance was beautifully preserved — and on the simplicity of the rosemary and sage bushes which never leave us without. And there still are the orange and citrus colours which brighten up things a bit, and some winter vegetables, like broccoli and cauliflower, that last throughout the season.

Pane al rosmarino e olio

Bread with rosemary and olive oil

This is a variation on the unsalted white Tuscan bread generally made here. You can also make small individual bread rolls if you prefer. You might want to make more than these quantities and even freeze the loaves for future use.

Makes 1 large or 2 small loaves

about 25 g (1 oz) rosemary sprigs

25 g (1 oz) fresh yeast

a pinch of sugar

310 ml (1¼ cups) tepid water

500 g (1 lb 2 oz) bread flour

60 ml (¼ cup) olive oil

Strip the rosemary leaves off the stems and discard the stems. Put the yeast into a bowl with the pinch of sugar. Stir in the water and leave it to activate.

Put the flour into a large, wide bowl or onto your work surface. Add the yeast, most of the rosemary, half a tablespoon of salt and most of the olive oil, and mix well to incorporate. Knead the dough for about 10 minutes, or until you have a smooth, compact, elastic ball. Add a few more drops of water or a little more flour if necessary to achieve this consistency.

Put the dough into a bowl, cover and leave to rise in a warm place for about 1½ hours, or until it has doubled in size.

Dust your work surface lightly with flour. Divide the dough into halves or leave whole, and shape into ovals or rounds. You can also make small, individual rolls by breaking off chunks of the dough and rolling them into balls. Sprinkle the tops with the remaining rosemary and drizzle with the remaining oil.

Dust a baking tray with flour and put the bread loaves onto the baking tray, allowing for some space between each loaf for spreading. Use two trays if necessary, and cover the bread loosely with a cloth. Leave in a warm place for 30 minutes to an hour until the loaves have risen.

Meanwhile, preheat the oven to 200°C (400°F/Gas 6). Put the baking tray into the hot oven and bake for about 35 minutes, until the top is golden. The bottom of the loaves should be golden and sound hollow when tapped.

Remove to a rack to cool slightly before serving. When cool, the bread can be wrapped in plastic wrap and frozen for future use.

Finocchiona all' aceto balsamico

Fennel salami in balsamic vinegar

Serve this warm as an unusual antipasto, cut up into strips with the pan juices spooned over. You can substitute the fennel salami with another type available. The fennel salami in Tuscany is about 10 cm (4 in) in diameter. If your salami is smaller, allow for a few more slices. The warm balsamic vinegar mingles with the juices in the pan and becomes quite syrupy.

Serves 4–6

1 tablespoon olive oil

4 slices fennel salami, sliced 5 mm (1/4 in) thick

4 tablespoons balsamic vinegar

Heat the oil in a saucepan. Add the salami slices and pan-fry on a high heat for about a minute on each side to colour lightly. Add the balsamic vinegar and heat through until it bubbles up and reduces a little. Serve immediately.

Zuppa di ceci

Chickpea soup

Chickpeas are used mainly in soups in Tuscany, but are also ground into a flour and used to make a flat savoury tart.

Serves 6–8

500 g (1 lb 2 oz) dried chickpeas, soaked overnight in cold water

1 medium onion, peeled and chopped

2 medium carrots, peeled and chopped

1 large celery stalk, trimmed and chopped

2 garlic cloves, peeled

4 tablespoons olive oil

2 sprigs rosemary

1 small red dried chilli, left whole

100 g (3^1/$_2$ oz) silverbeet (Swiss chard), trimmed and finely sliced

2 ripe tomatoes, skinned and puréed or 150 g (5^1/$_2$ oz) tin of peeled tomatoes, puréed

6 thick slices white, country-style bread

extra virgin olive oil, to serve

Drain the soaked chickpeas and put them into a large stockpot. Add the onion, carrot and celery. Cover with 3.5 litres (14 cups) of cold water (add the rest later if it doesn't fit), and bring to the boil. Skim the surface to remove any scum. Lower the heat slightly and cook, uncovered, for about 1^1/$_4$ hours, or until the chickpeas are tender. Season with salt and pepper in the last half hour of the cooking time. Purée two-thirds of the chickpeas with their cooking liquid, leaving the remainder whole. Return all to the pot. Add a little hot water if it seems too thick.

Chop one of the garlic cloves. Heat the olive oil in a saucepan. Add the chopped garlic, rosemary sprigs and the chilli. When you begin to smell the garlic, add the silverbeet. Sauté on a medium heat for a couple of minutes before adding the tomato. Season with salt and pepper and continue cooking for about 5 minutes until the tomato has melted into a sauce and seems cooked. Remove the rosemary sprigs and discard. Add the tomato mix to the chickpea pot and simmer for another few minutes to blend the flavours. Check the seasoning and adjust with salt and pepper, if necessary.

Toast or grill (broil) the bread slices on both sides. Rub one side with the whole clove of garlic and drizzle with the olive oil. Put the soup into large individual bowls with a splash of extra virgin olive oil and a grinding of black pepper. Serve with the garlic bread.

Penne alla senese

Penne with sausage, walnuts and cream

This is a rich, filling pasta which seems to leave a delicious subtle sweet lingering taste.

Serves 6

20 g (³/4 oz) butter

3 Italian sausages, about 80 g (3 oz) each, skinned and crumbled

100 g (³/4 cup) shelled walnuts, chopped finely

50 g (1³/4 oz) *prosciutto crudo*, finely chopped

3 tablespoons good brandy

250 ml (1 cup) thick (single) cream

500 g (1 lb 2 oz) penne or similar short pasta

about 120 g (1¹/4 cups) freshly grated Parmesan cheese

Melt the butter in a non-stick saucepan. Add the sausage meat and walnuts. Sauté for about 5 minutes or until the mixture is golden, breaking up the sausage into little pieces with a wooden spoon.

Add the prosciutto and sauté for another minute. Add the brandy and when it has evaporated, add the cream. Season according to the saltiness of the prosciutto and sausages. (Remember, Parmesan cheese will be added later, so extra seasoning may not be necessary.) Cook for a couple of minutes.

If you find the sauce is a little too thick, add a bit of meat stock, if available, or later, add some of the pasta cooking water.

Cook the penne in boiling salted water. Drain and add to the saucepan. Add the Parmesan cheese, toss thoroughly to coat and serve immediately.

Orecchiette ai broccoli

Orecchiette with broccoli

This is a classic, wonderful and healthy combination. Anchovies are often used in sauces and are particularly well suited to broccoli and cauliflower. You can use Parmesan cheese instead of the mature ricotta cheese in this recipe.

Serves 6

1.2 kg (2 lb 10 oz) broccoli

6 tablespoons olive oil

2 garlic cloves, peeled and crushed

1 small dried red chilli

100 g (3^1/2 oz) salted anchovies, cleaned and filleted (about 5 whole anchovies or 10 fillets in olive oil)

500 g (1 lb 2 oz) orecchiette or similar dry pasta

about 120 g (^{1}/2 cup) grated dried ricotta cheese

Wash the broccoli and trim away the hard outer stem. Cook in a large saucepan of boiling, salted water for about 10 minutes, or until tender. Transfer the broccoli to a bowl, using a slotted spoon, and reserve the cooking water in the pan.

When cool enough to handle, cut away the stem part of the broccoli and cut this into smaller pieces. Return these pieces to the pan of water. Divide the rest of the broccoli into florets.

Heat the olive oil in a large frying pan. Add the garlic, the chilli and anchovies. Sauté, until you smell the garlic and the anchovies melt into the oil, mashing them up with a wooden spoon. Add the broccoli florets and cook for a few minutes more for them to absorb the flavours. Season with pepper and a little salt, depending on the saltiness of the anchovies.

Boil the pasta in the reserved broccoli water with the stems, following the packet instructions. Drain, reserving about 250 ml (1 cup) of the water and toss into the broccoli sauce with the water, mixing quickly to coat all the pasta evenly. Sprinkle with the grated ricotta cheese, mix through and serve immediately.

Orecchiette ai broccoli

Arista

Roast rack of pork

Serves 6–8

125 ml (¹/₂ cup) herbed
olive oil* (see page 377)

1 rack of pork loin with
bones, about 1.8 kg (4 lb)

finely grated zest of
1 lemon

150 g (5¹/₂ oz) finely sliced
unsmoked *pancetta*
(belly bacon)

2 tablespoons olive oil

1 onion, peeled and roughly
chopped

1 carrot, peeled and
roughly chopped

1 celery stalk, trimmed and
roughly chopped

250 ml (1 cup) white wine

This is a rack of pork, seasoned, often wrapped in unsmoked *pancetta* (belly bacon), and roasted. It is cooked with the bones intact and a few vegetables in the oven dish for flavour. Even if your butcher cuts right through the individual chops leaving them attached by a small piece of bone, you will have trouble cutting through to serve, unless you are equipped with a professional cleaver. In this case, give one clean hack through each and serve with the bone. If not, ask your butcher to carve the meat away from the bone, leaving the meat slightly attached on the bottom. When the meat is cooked, you can cut it completely away from the bone and slice it into boneless chops to serve. You can also cut the meat into many more thinner slices.

Preheat the oven to 200°C (400°F/Gas 6). Prepare the herbed oil if you don't already have any, even just estimating with a couple of sprigs of rosemary, sage, and a clove of garlic all chopped up and mixed into just less than half a cup of olive oil.

Season the meat lightly with salt and pepper, depending on whether your herbed oil is seasoned or not. Rub the herbed oil all over the meat and scatter the grated lemon zest on top. Wrap the pancetta around the meat to cover it and tie up with kitchen string, securing the meat and pancetta to the bones. Drizzle the olive oil into a roasting dish and add the rack of pork. Scatter the vegetables around the meat and put into the oven.

Brown the meat, it should take 10–15 minutes each side, and then add the wine. Lower the heat to 180°C (350°F/Gas 4) and continue cooking for another hour. When the wine begins to bubble up and reduce a little, add about 375 ml (1¹/₂ cups) water. Baste the meat with the pan juices and turn the meat over now and then during the cooking time. If the pancetta seems like it's crisping up too much, continue cooking with the bones, not the pancetta, facing upwards.

The meat should be tender and completely cooked through. Remove from the oven and remove the string. Cool slightly. Carve the meat into boneless chop portions or thinner slices. Serve with the pan juices.

Faraona ripiena

Stuffed guinea fowl

Serves 6

10 g (¹/₄ oz) dried porcini mushrooms or 40 g (1¹/₂ oz) Swiss Brown mushrooms

2 thick slices of white bread

about 125 ml (¹/₂ cup) milk, for soaking the bread

200 g (7 oz) minced (ground) lean pork or veal, or mixed

1 Italian sausage, about 80 g (3 oz), skinned and crumbled

1 egg, lightly beaten

Ask your butcher to debone the whole guinea fowl keeping the skin intact or do it yourself if you know how. You can add a couple of the bones directly into the roasting dish around the guinea fowl or into the stockpot.

Preheat the oven to 180°C (350°F/Gas 4).

Soak the mushrooms in 125 ml (¹/₂ cup) of warm water for 10 minutes to reconstitute them, then chop them up. If using Swiss Brown mushrooms don't soak them, simply chop them up.

Soak the bread in the milk to soften, squeezing out the excess with your hands. Mix the bread in a bowl with the minced meat, the sausage meat, the egg and Parmesan cheese. Add the mushrooms. Season with salt and pepper, and mix well to incorporate.

3 tablespoons freshly
grated Parmesan cheese

a little butter for greasing

1 free-range guinea fowl,
about 1.2 kg (2 lb 10 oz),
deboned and interiors
removed, about 800 g
(1 lb 12 oz) when deboned

4 tablespoons olive oil

250 ml (1 cup) white wine

about 250 ml (1 cup)
vegetable stock*
(see page 389)

Lay out a sheet of aluminium foil on your work surface and grease the centre with the butter. Lay the guinea fowl down flat, skin side down. Spread the stuffing onto the guinea fowl, leaving a generous border all round. Roll up the guinea fowl enclosing the stuffing, and roll up the foil tightly around it to hold the shape. Crunch up the sides, like a giant sweet wrapper, to seal and tuck sides down to fit into your roasting pan.

Drizzle the olive oil into your roasting dish, put in the guinea fowl, and cook in a hot oven for about 20 minutes. Turn the meat over and add the wine to the dish. When the wine has evaporated, add the stock and continue cooking for another hour. There should be enough liquid in the pan to serve as a thickened sauce with the meat. If not, add a little more stock or water.

Remove from the oven and carefully remove the aluminium foil. Return the guinea fowl to the oven for another 15 minutes or so, turning to brown on all sides. Remove from the oven and let it cool slightly before cutting into 1 cm ($^1/_2$ in) slices and serving with the pan juices.

salsicce e fagioli

Salsicce e fagioli

Sausages and beans

Tuscans are well known for their love of beans, and this rustic recipe is one of their favourites.

Serves 6

500 g (1 lb 2 oz) dried cannellini (or other white beans), soaked overnight in cold water

3 garlic cloves, peeled

2 sprigs of sage

2 tablespoons olive oil

6 large Italian pork sausages, about 100 g (3 1/2 oz) each

400 g (14 oz) tin peeled tomatoes, with their juice, chopped

Rinse the beans and put them into a large saucepan. Cover with cold water and bring to the boil. Skim the surface of the scum with a slotted spoon. Add 2 whole garlic cloves and one of the sage sprigs. Cook for 1–1 1/2 hours or until the beans are tender. Season with salt and pepper in the last half hour of the cooking time.

In a separate large saucepan, heat the olive oil. Prick the sausages in a couple of places with a fork and add them to the pan. Fry on a medium-high heat to brown on all sides. Add the remaining garlic clove and the sage, and as soon as it begins to sizzle, add the tomatoes. The sausages should provide enough seasoning; if not add a little salt and pepper. Simmer for about 15 minutes or until the tomatoes have melted into a sauce.

Drain the cooked beans, reserving a little of the cooking liquid and add the beans to the sausage pot. Check the seasoning and add salt and pepper, if necessary. Simmer for 10 minutes more, adding about 125–250 ml (1/2–1 cup) of the reserved water to thin it out a little. Serve warm.

Spiedino misto di maiale

Mixed pork skewers

Serves 6–8

about 150 g (5½ oz) caul fat (available from the butcher's)

500 g (1 lb 2 oz) pork liver

3 tablespoons breadcrumbs

1½ tablespoons dried wild fennel flowers (or fennel seeds), crushed

400 g (14 oz) pork fillet

6 Italian pork sausages, about 80 g (3 oz) each

2 thick slices fresh unsmoked *pancetta* (pork belly), about 140 g (5 oz) each

6 slices white country-style bread, about 1.5 cm (⁵/₈ in) thick

20–30 fresh bay leaves

4 tablespoons extra virgin olive oil

Pork is a very popular meat in Tuscany and is featured in most menus in a variety of ways. This recipe, which incorporates various forms of pork, should make about 12 skewers. The pork liver bundles (*fegatelli*) can be put onto separate skewers with the pork fillet as they take less time to cook than the rest, and may otherwise harden during the cooking. The pieces of pork liver are seasoned with dried wild fennel flowers and wrapped in caul fat to make little bundles, which when grilled are deliciously moist, yet slightly crispy.

Pork sausage and fresh, uncured pork belly (*pancetta fresca*) are put onto the skewers with bread pieces (which absorb the flavour of the meat) and fresh bay leaves. They are then grilled. I have seen this dish made in November with a handful of just-picked olives thrown into the oven dish before grilling.

Soak the caul fat in salted water for about 15 minutes. Drain and pat dry. Lay out the large piece of caul fat onto your work surface and cut roughly into 12 cm (5 in) squares.

Preheat the grill (broiler) while you are preparing the meat. Carefully clean the liver, removing any membrane covering it and any little filaments. Cut into pieces of about 3 x 2 cm (1¼ x ¾ in). Make a mix on a flat plate with the breadcrumbs, the fennel flowers (or crushed fennel seeds), and salt and pepper. Roll the liver pieces into this mix, then lay each piece onto a separate caul fat square. Begin rolling up, tucking the sides in, then continue rolling to enclose the liver completely in separate bundles.

Cut the pork fillet into chunks, slightly smaller than the liver bundles, and season lightly with salt and pepper. Cut each sausage into halves. Cut each piece of pancetta into about six pieces. Cut each bread slice into three or four, depending on its original size they should be more or less in proportion with the pieces of meat.

Thread a liver bundle onto a skewer, then a bay leaf. Add a piece of bread, then a piece of fillet. Add another bay leaf, then another piece of bread. Continue with another skewer until the liver bundles and fillet are finished.

Put a piece of sausage onto another skewer. Add a piece of bread, then a piece of pancetta. Add a bay leaf, another piece of sausage, bread, then pancetta onto the same skewer. Continue making more skewers like this until all the ingredients are used up.

Put the skewers into an ovenproof dish, drizzle with the olive oil and put under the hot grill. The liver bundles and fillet skewers will need about 15 minutes on each side. The mixed skewers will probably need slightly longer on each side to brown and cook through, depending on the heat of the grill. Take care that the skewers are not too near the grill, as the bread may burn.

Remove the liver skewers from the oven and transfer to a plate while you finish cooking the sausage skewers. Check the sausage skewers to see if they are done as they could take less than the indicated time.

You can serve a couple of skewers per person, or remove all the meat and bread from the skewers and pile them up onto a serving dish for everyone to help themselves. This is ideal served with roast potatoes and perhaps some simply boiled greens (spinach, silverbeet or Swiss chard, chicory, etc.) dressed with olive oil and lemon juice.

Patate arrosto

Roast potatoes

Instead of the herbed oil here, you can add about 2 peeled, crushed garlic cloves with 2 sprigs each of rosemary and sage, and a little extra olive oil to the ovenproof dish before roasting.

Serves 6

about 1.5 kg (3 lb 5 oz) potatoes

2 tablespoons herbed olive oil* (see page 377)

4 tablespoons olive oil

Preheat the oven to 200°C (400°F/Gas 6). Peel the potatoes, rinse and cut them into chunks about the size of an unshelled walnut. Put them into an ovenproof dish and add the herbed oil and olive oil. Mix well to coat all the potatoes and put into the hot oven.

Roast for 45–60 minutes, tossing them over a couple of times. The potatoes should be golden and crispy outside and soft inside. Remove from the oven and scatter with a little salt and pepper. Serve immediately.

Cipolline in agro-dolce

Cipolline in agro-dolce

Sweet sour baby onions

In Tuscany, sweet and sour implies that vinegar, salt and sugar have been used in the preparation of the dish. Many vegetables are preserved in this way, in particular onions, capsicums (red peppers), carrots, zucchini (courgettes) and cauliflower. These oven-baked onions can be served as an antipasto, or as an accompaniment to a second course.

Serves 6

1 kg (2 lb 4 oz) fresh, baby onions, peeled and rinsed

2 bay leaves

50 g (1³/4 oz) butter

125ml (¹/2 cup) white wine vinegar

50 g (1³/4 oz) caster (superfine) sugar

Preheat the oven to 190°C (375°F/Gas 5). Bring a large saucepan of salted water to the boil, then add the onions and boil for about 10 minutes to soften them. Remove from the heat, drain and discard the cooking water.

Put the onions into an ovenproof dish in a single layer. Add the bay leaves, 250 ml (1 cup) water, and dot with the butter. Season with a little black pepper. There should be enough salt from the boiling water, if not add a little.

Bake for 20 minutes. Remove from the oven and splash with the vinegar. Sprinkle with the sugar and mix through. Return to the oven for another 20–30 minutes, or until the onions are soft, golden and the sugar begins to lightly caramelise. Serve hot.

Crêpes al torroncino

Crêpes with pastry cream and praline

Crêpes always seem to be popular — and this elegant recipe
is well worth the effort.

Crêpes are often eaten just with some melted chocolate spread over them and folded up into quarters, but they are equally delicious with a little jam.

Makes 10–12 crêpes

50 g (1³/4 oz) caster (superfine) sugar

a pinch of salt

50 g (1³/4 oz) butter, melted, plus a little for frying

3 eggs

50 g (1³/4 oz) plain (all-purpose) flour

about 250 ml (1 cup) milk

1 cup of praline* (¹/4 of the recipe, see page 395)

¹/2 the quantity of pastry cream*, about 600 ml (2¹/2 cups) (see page 394)

400 ml (14 fl oz) thick (single) cream

a little Vin Santo or brandy, or other liqueur of your choice

Put the sugar, salt and butter into a bowl, and mix together. Add the eggs and whip. Add the sifted flour, then the milk and whisk to make a smooth, fairly liquid batter. Cover with a cloth or plastic wrap, and leave the batter to rest for about 30 minutes.

Meanwhile, make the praline and keep it aside in a jar or bowl. Make the pastry cream and leave it aside to cool completely.

Heat a 20 cm (8 in) crêpe pan or a non-stick frying pan on a medium heat. Grease the bottom with a little butter and pour enough batter in it to cover the bottom of the pan when you swirl it around. Cook until the crêpe is golden on the underside, then flip it over with a spatula to cook the other side. Stack them on a plate as you fry them.

Whip the cream to form soft peaks and fold it gently into the pastry cream. Put a crêpe onto each individual serving plate and spoon on about 2 tablespoons of the cream. Sprinkle with praline and roll up or fold over into quarters. Splash a teaspoon of liqueur onto each crêpe, sprinkle with a few more praline bits and serve.

Cenci

Cenci or chiacchere

Deep-fried pastry ribbons

These ribbons of pastry suddenly appear out of nowhere amongst the costumes and masks of February, and are found unevenly stacked up in every shop and every home.

The pastry strips may also be rolled out in a pasta machine to the final setting, and cut. They can be eaten plain or served with ice-cream or with crème anglaise and fruit.

If you will be serving them with crème anglaise (see page 393) and fruit, prepare those first so the dish can be served as soon as the cenci are ready.

Makes about 35 strips

280 g (2¼ cups) plain (all-purpose) flour

2 tablespoons caster (superfine) sugar

2 eggs

2 tablespoons butter, melted

grated zest of ½ a lemon and ½ an orange

1 teaspoon vanilla essence

2 tablespoons Vin Santo or port

light olive or sunflower oil for frying

icing (confectioners') sugar for sprinkling

Sift the flour, a pinch of salt and the caster sugar into a wide bowl or onto your work surface. Make a well in the centre and add the eggs. Begin mixing with a fork to incorporate the eggs into the flour. Add the butter, the zest, vanilla and Vin Santo. Begin working the dough with your hands, kneading until it is smooth, adding a little more flour if it seems too wet.

It should be a soft, workable dough. Dust your work surface with flour. Divide the dough into 4 equal parts and beginning with one, roll it out with a rolling pin to a thickness of about 2 mm (less than ⅛ in). Cover the dough you are not using with a cloth to prevent it drying.

Cut into strips of about 10 x 5 cm (4 x 2 in). Keep them on a lightly floured tray while you roll out the rest.

Pour enough oil into a saucepan to come about 3 cm (1¼ in) up the sides of the pot. Heat the oil on a medium heat and when it is quite hot, fry the cenci on both sides until they are crisp and golden. They should not become too brown, so lower the heat if it seems necessary. With a slotted spoon, transfer them to a plate lined with kitchen paper to absorb the excess oil.

Sprinkle with icing sugar and put a few onto a serving plate with a small pile of orange salad to eat with the *cenci* and a small bowl of crème anglaise to dip the *cenci* into. Alternatively serve them plain as they are.

Arance macerate

Orange salad

While the 'blood oranges' of southern Italy are particularly striking in colour, you can use any type available, or even substitute another fruit in season. You can add more or less sugar here, depending on the sweetness of the oranges.

Serves 4

1/2 the quantity of crème anglaise* (see page 393)

6 sweet, juicy oranges

4 tablespoons caster (superfine) sugar

2 tablespoons Vin Santo

Make the crème anglaise. If you are making it ahead of time, refrigerate it when it has cooled until you will be serving it.

Slice off the top and bottom of the oranges. Put the oranges onto a wooden board. With a small sharp knife, cut downwards to remove the skin and pith. Cut the orange into its segments in between the white pith and remove the pips. You should be left with an orange skeleton — which you can discard. Put the segments into a bowl. Add the sugar and Vin Santo and mix gently. Leave to macerate in the refrigerator for about an hour before serving portions to accompany the *cenci*, along with a bowl of the crème anglaise.

MARCH

The sudden pink and white blossoms are swaying nonchalantly in the winds of unpredictable March, as though they had always been there.

When will we taste their cherries and almonds? The colours are such a surprise, finally, after a seemingly drawn-out winter.

There are definitely some warmer days, and the first daisies and violets have pushed their way up through the grasses to survey the setting.

Although the table is still dependent on the winter fresh produce, there is the welcome and exciting arrival of green garlic and asparagus. And even in the wooded countryside, there is the atmosphere of a treasure hunt, as people make their way back to their cars, their hands full of the long thin stalks of the first wild asparagus.

In the main squares of the city, there is a certain air of festivity when fried, crispy, sugar-dusted rice balls are sold mid-March for the annual festival of San Giuseppe.

Focaccia con cipolle

Flat bread with onions

This very popular bread is made all over Tuscany with varying ingredients and sold in squares in every bakery. It can be eaten on its own as a snack, or served in place of regular bread, and is lovely filled, for a picnic sandwich.

Makes one 30 x 40 cm (12 x 16 in) oven tray

25 g (1 oz) fresh yeast

310 ml (1¼ cups) tepid water

a pinch of sugar

500 g (1 lb 2 oz) bread flour

2 tablespoons olive oil, plus extra for drizzling

1 large red onion, thinly sliced

In a bowl, combine the yeast, water and sugar and leave it to activate.

Put the flour and a teaspoon of salt into a large, wide bowl or onto your work surface. Add the yeast mixture to the flour and mix in with a fork to incorporate. Add the 2 tablespoons of oil and begin kneading with your hands for about 10 minutes, until you have a compact smooth dough. Add a little more flour or water if necessary. You can also make the dough in a mixer using a dough hook.

Cover the bowl of dough with a cloth and leave to rise in a warm place for about 1½ hours, or until it has doubled in size.

Using your fingertips, spread out the dough into a lightly oiled oven tray with sides 3 cm (1¼ in) high, pulling it towards the sides of the tray to cover the bottom. Scatter the onions on top. Drizzle the surface with a little olive oil and sprinkle with salt and pepper. Leave in a warm place for another 30–60 minutes, covered lightly with a cloth, until it has risen.

Meanwhile, preheat the oven to 200°C (400°F/Gas 6). Bake in the hot oven for about 30 minutes, until the onions are soft, cooked and golden, and the focaccia too is golden. Cut into serving pieces and serve warm.

Crostini con asparagi

Crostini with asparagus

The *crostino* holds a solid place in Tuscan cuisine — and is quite simply a slice of bread (or polenta) with a topping, which could include smoked salmon, or a thick chicken liver sauce* (see page 346), or a couple of bits of anchovy with a few capers* (see page 346). The possibilities are endless. When entertaining, offering a small crostino together with a drink always seems to be appreciated. This larger crostino can also be served as a first course.

Serves 6

12 thin-stemmed asparagus

4 eggs

3 tablespoons milk

2 tablespoons freshly grated Parmesan cheese

6 thick, large slices white country-style bread, halved

1 tablespoon butter

Rinse the asparagus well to get rid of any sand. Trim away the woody ends.

Tie them up into a neat bundle with kitchen string, and boil the asparagus in lightly salted water for about 10 minutes, or until tender — but not too soft — testing the spear to check for readiness. Drain and cut off about 1/3 of the end of each asparagus and chop this.

Whip the eggs lightly in a bowl with the milk, season with salt and add the Parmesan cheese and the chopped asparagus. Grill the bread slices on both sides and put 2 slices onto each individual serving plate.

Melt the butter in a saucepan and add the eggs. Cook on a medium heat and stir with a wooden spoon to scramble them for a couple of minutes, leaving them slightly creamy. Spoon the eggs over the bread slices, top with the asparagus spears and add some black pepper. Serve immediately.

Asparagi con uova

Asparagus with poached eggs

This can be served as a first course or as a light main course.

Serves 6

1.2 kg (2 lb 10 oz)
asparagus, woody, ends
trimmed

6 thick, large slices white
country-style bread

1 tablespoon vinegar

6 eggs

6 tablespoons butter,
slightly softened

100 g (1 cup) Parmesan
cheese shavings or very
thin slices

Rinse the asparagus well to get rid of any sand. Tie up the asparagus into neat bundles with kitchen string. Boil them in lightly salted water for about 10 minutes until they are tender but still firm. Test the spear to see if the asparagus is ready. Drain well and divide them between individual serving plates.

Grill (broil) the bread slices on both sides and keep them warm, if possible.

Meanwhile, bring a saucepan of lightly salted water to the boil with the vinegar. Break one egg into a small ramekin or bowl and slide it carefully into the water. Lower the heat to medium, and cook for 2–3 minutes, until it turns white and opaque. The inside must remain soft. Slide in the other eggs, one by one. It will probably be easier if you do two at a time.

Remove the eggs with a slotted spoon and put them gently onto the asparagus. Top each asparagus pile with one tablespoon of butter. Scatter with the Parmesan cheese shavings, a grinding of black pepper and a little salt, if necessary. Serve with the grilled bread slices.

Risotto agli asparagi

Risotto with asparagus

This risotto has the gorgeous gold colour of saffron, and the creaminess of a soft light cheese that is added at the last moment.

Serves 6

1 kg (2 lb 4 oz) green medium-thick asparagus

2 tablespoons fresh marjoram, chopped

2 large French shallots (eschalots), peeled

3 tablespoons olive oil

500 g (1 lb 2 oz) risotto rice

250 ml (1 cup) white wine

1 teaspoon saffron threads (or powder), dissolved in a little warm water

60 g ($2^{1}/_{4}$ oz) butter

170 g (6 oz) robiola cheese (or a mild, light cream cheese substitute)

80 g (1 cup) grated mature pecorino cheese

freshly grated Parmesan cheese, to serve

Soak the asparagus in several changes of cold water to remove any sand. Trim off the extreme woody end of the asparagus and discard. Cut the asparagus into three sections. Put the ends into a pot and cover with about 2 litres (8 cups) of water. Add the marjoram, one of the French shallots, and season with salt and pepper. Bring to the boil, then simmer for 30 minutes to make the stock for the risotto. Strain and discard the solids. Keep the stock warm in a saucepan on the stovetop.

Chop the other french shallot and the asparagus middle parts. Heat the olive oil in a saucepan suitable for risotto and sauté the french shallot and chopped asparagus for about 5 minutes or until softened.

Add the rice and cook for a couple of minutes more to coat each grain, stirring with a wooden spoon.

Add the wine, and when it has evaporated begin by adding one ladleful of the stock at a time. When it has been absorbed, add another ladleful, stirring to prevent the risotto sticking.

The total cooking time should be 20–25 minutes. Halfway through, add the spear parts of the asparagus, in halves or quarters if they are very thick. Add the dissolved saffron. Check the seasoning and add salt and pepper if necessary.

The risotto should be creamy and a little liquid. A couple of minutes before it is ready, add the butter, the robiola and the pecorino cheeses. Stir in and serve with grated Parmesan cheese.

Asparagi con uova

Pasta e fagioli

Pasta with beans

These two favourite Tuscan ingredients are simply combined with a few fresh herbs to produce this dish so appreciated by all generations.

Serves 6

300 g (10¹/2 oz) dried cannellini or other white beans, soaked overnight in cold water

1 medium carrot, peeled and chopped

1 stalk of celery, trimmed and chopped

1 medium onion, peeled and chopped

200 g (7 oz) ditalini or other similar small pasta

6 tablespoons olive oil

3 garlic cloves, peeled

2 sprigs of rosemary

1 small dried red chilli, crumbled

1 tablespoon tomato paste (purée)

extra virgin olive oil, to serve

Drain the soaked beans. Put them into a saucepan, cover abundantly with cold water and bring to the boil. Skim the surface of any scum, lower the heat and add the carrot, celery and onion. Cook for about 1 1/2 hours, or until the beans are soft. Add more water during the cooking time, if necessary, to keep the beans well covered and, towards the end, season with salt and pepper. Remove from the heat and leave the beans in their cooking water.

Cook the pasta in boiling salted water, following the packet instructions. Drain and put into a bowl with a little olive oil to prevent the ditalini sticking together.

Heat the olive oil on a medium heat in a separate large pot. Add the garlic, the whole rosemary sprigs, the chilli and the tomato paste. Sauté gently to flavour the oil until the garlic is lightly golden. Remove the garlic and rosemary branches and discard.

Pass half of the cooked beans through the fine-holed disc of a food mill, or purée in a blender and add to the saucepan with the flavoured oil. Add the whole beans as well and about 1 litre (4 cups) of their cooking water. Return to the heat and simmer for a few more minutes to mix the flavours.

Add the cooked pasta and stir through. It should have the consistency of a thick, creamy soup. Add a little more hot water if it seems too thick. Serve hot, drizzled with extra virgin olive oil.

Fusilli con cavolfiore

Fusilli pasta with cauliflower

Very often cauliflower is served as a side dish, simply boiled and dressed with an anchovy sauce* (see page 379), which is certainly worth trying. Here cauliflower is combined with pasta and given a definite character with the addition of chilli oil at the end.

Serves 6

900 g (2 lb) cauliflower florets

5 tablespoons olive oil

2 garlic cloves, peeled and finely chopped

a handful of freshly chopped parsley

3 salt-packed anchovies, rinsed and filleted or 6 fillets in olive oil

1 tablespoon tomato paste (purée)

500 g (1 lb 2 oz) short pasta, such as fusilli, penne, shells

about 120 g (1¼ cups) freshly grated Parmesan cheese

chilli oil* (see page 242) or crushed dried chilli with extra olive oil, to serve

Bring a large saucepan of lightly salted water to the boil. Add the cauliflower and when the water comes back to the boil, cook for 5 or 10 minutes, or until the cauliflower has softened. Transfer it to a bowl with a slotted spoon and leave it aside. Reserve the water to cook the pasta.

Heat the olive oil in a large saucepan and add the garlic, half the parsley and the anchovy fillets. As soon as it starts to sizzle, and the anchovies begin to melt, add the cauliflower, breaking them up a little with a wooden spoon. Dilute the tomato paste in 125 ml (½ cup) of hot water and add it to the saucepan. Simmer for a few minutes to blend the flavours.

Meanwhile, cook the pasta in the reserved boiling water, following the packet instructions. Drain and toss into the sauce with the remaining chopped parsley. If it seems dry, add a little of the pasta water to the sauce. Serve immediately with the Parmesan cheese and a good drizzle of chilli oil — or alternatively, a sprinkling of dried chilli and a drizzle of olive oil.

Agnello in fricassea

Lamb stew with egg and lemon sauce

As Easter approaches, lamb makes a regular appearance on the Tuscan menu. The egg and lemon sauce is a popular Mediterranean feature, which combines beautifully with this meat.

Serves 6–8

2 tablespoons olive oil

1.5 kg (3 lb 5 oz) deboned shoulder or leg of lamb, trimmed and cut into chunks of about 5 x 3 cm (2 x 1¹/₄ in)

2 spring onions (scallions), finely sliced

2 sprigs rosemary

2 bay leaves

250 ml (1 cup) white wine

about 1 litre (4 cups) vegetable stock* (see page 389) or water

3 eggs

the juice of 2 lemons

a small handful of chopped parsley

Heat the olive oil in a large stockpot. Add the lamb and brown lightly on all sides. Add the spring onions and sauté for a little longer to soften. Add the rosemary sprigs and the bay leaves, and season with salt and pepper. Pour in the wine and cook until it has evaporated; then add the warm stock or water. Lower the heat and cook, uncovered, for 45–60 minutes or until the lamb is very tender. Add more hot stock or water, if necessary, to maintain about 2 cups of sauce in the saucepan at all times.

Lightly whip the eggs in a bowl. Add a little of the sauce from the lamb to the eggs, and whisk to prevent them from scrambling. Whisk in the lemon juice. Mix in a little more sauce and whisk. Make sure the lamb is on the lowest possible heat and add the egg mixture to the lamb pan and stir, with a wooden spoon.

Check the seasoning and adjust, if necessary. Heat through for a couple of minutes, stirring with a wooden spoon to thicken the sauce, taking care not to cook the eggs. Remove from the heat, stir in the parsley and serve.

Trippa alla toscana

Tuscan-style tripe

Serves 6

1 veal trotter, cleaned

1.3 kg (3 lb) prepared bleached tripe

6 tablespoons olive oil

1 medium onion, peeled and finely chopped

1 celery stalk, trimmed and chopped

2 medium carrots, peeled and finely chopped

3 Italian pork sausages, about 80 g (3 oz) each, skinned and crumbled

250 ml (1 cup) white wine

650 g (1 lb 7 oz) tin peeled tomatoes with their juice, puréed

1 small dried red chilli, crumbled

about 120 g (1 1/4 cups) grated Parmesan cheese

Although this is not everyone's favourite dish, it certainly has its loyal supporters who are always delighted at the presentation of a bowl of tripe.

A calf's trotter is added for its gelatinous consistency which keeps the tripe slightly creamy and holds it together. It is not, however, essential to the taste, so you can leave it out if you prefer. Buy cleaned, bleached and partly-cooked tripe for this, which is often how it is sold. If it is not partly cooked, the cooking time will be about 3 hours.

Put the trotter into a saucepan, cover with water and boil for about 2 hours, until the meat is soft. Remove the meat from in between the bone part of the trotter and keep aside, discarding the bone part. Slice up the meat into pieces.

Wash the tripe in hot water with a little salt and a splash of vinegar. Drain and slice into thin strips.

Heat the olive oil in a saucepan on a medium heat and add the onion, celery and carrot, and sauté until the vegetables have softened. Add the sausage meat and cook until lightly golden, breaking it up with a wooden spoon.

Add the prepared tripe and the trotter meat. As it begins to cook, splash with the wine and cook until it evaporates. Add the tomato and the chilli, and season with salt and pepper. Cook on a medium heat, covered for 30–40 minutes, adding a little more water, if necessary. The tripe should be slightly creamy but still slightly firm in texture.

Serve hot sprinkled with the grated Parmesan cheese.

Serves 4

8 free-range quail, cleaned, and insides removed

4 Italian sausages, about 80 g (3 oz) each, skinned and crumbled

8 garlic cloves, peeled

about 12 sage leaves

7 tablespoons olive oil

125 ml (¹/₂ cup) white wine

250 ml (1 cup) vegetable stock* (see page 389)

Quaglia arrosto con salsicce

Roast quail stuffed with Italian sausages

This dish, consisting of a couple of quails served on soft potato cakes with the pan juices spooned over, looks and tastes quite splendid.

Preheat the oven to 200°C (400°F/Gas 6). Rinse the quails in cold water and pat dry with kitchen paper. Rub a little salt and pepper into the cavity of each quail and sprinkle onto the outsides as well.

Divide the sausage meat equally between the cavities. Add a whole garlic clove and a sage leaf into each.

Secure the thigh openings together with a toothpick to ensure that the stuffing remains in the cavity, and tuck back the wings to hold them in place.

Sprinkle 5 tablespoons of the oil into a roasting dish and put the quails into the dish. Drizzle the remaining oil over the quails and put into the hot oven. Roast for about 15 minutes, to brown the quails lightly all over, then add the wine. When most of it has evaporated, lower the heat to 180°C (350°F/Gas 4) and add the stock. Continue cooking for about 40 minutes more, turning over at least once to brown on all sides. If the pan seems dry during this time, add a few more drops of stock — or just enough to provide a thickened sauce to spoon over the quails.

Remove from the oven. Serve with the pan juices and mashed potato cakes (recipe follows) if you like.

Polpette di patate

Mashed potato cakes

500 g (1 lb 2 oz) potatoes

2 tablespoons olive oil

100 g (1 cup) mature pecorino cheese, grated

Wash the potatoes, leaving on the skins, and cook them in lightly salted, boiling water for 20 minutes or until they are soft. Drain, and, when cool enough to handle, peel them. Pass them through a food mill into a bowl or simply mash them up with a fork. Add the olive oil, the pecorino cheese and season with salt and pepper.

Using your hands, form small log shapes, of about 6 cm (2^1/$_2$ in) in length. Flatten them slightly and arrange a couple onto a serving plate. Serve the quails on top with some of the pan juice.

Gobbi rigirati tre volte

Thrice cooked thistle

The thistle is a member of the artichoke and cardoon family and can be cooked in a variety of ways. This recipe may require a bit of organisation, but is certainly worth the effort. An alternative vegetable for this dish is artichoke or celery.

Serves 6–8

1 kg (2 lb 4 oz) thistle stalks, washed with tough outer stem and fibres stripped away

juice of 1/2 a lemon

3 or 4 eggs

about 125 g (1 cup) flour for dusting

about 125 ml (1/2 cup) light olive oil for frying

about 30 g (1 oz) butter

500 ml (2 cups) fresh tomato sauce* (see page 382) or 500 ml (2 cups) ragù* (see page 384)

about 60 g (2/3 cup) freshly grated Parmesan cheese

Divide each thistle stalk lengthways into 6 cm (21/2 in) pieces. As you finish cutting them, soak the stalks in water mixed with the juice of half a lemon to avoid discolouration. Leave aside until you are ready to cook them.

Drain, put them into a saucepan and cover with cold water. Add a little salt and bring to the boil. You can cover the surface of the thistle in the saucepan with a cloth to make sure they are all covered by the water and do not discolour. Boil for about 20 minutes to soften, then drain well and discard the water. Leave them to cool slightly.

Preheat the oven to 180°C (350°F/Gas 4). Lightly whip the eggs in a bowl. Put the flour onto a flat plate. Dust the thistle pieces in flour on all sides and dip them into the beaten eggs.

Heat enough olive oil in a pan to come about 2 cm (3/4 in) up the sides. Fry the pieces in batches until golden all over. Transfer to a plate lined with paper towels to absorb the excess oil.

Liberally butter an oven dish and arrange the fried thistle pieces in a single layer. Cover with the meat or the tomato sauce and sprinkle with the Parmesan cheese. Bake in the hot oven for 10–15 minutes to gratinée before serving.

Sformato di cavolfiore

Baked cauliflower pie

Pastry-less baked vegetable pies are very common and are made with various vegetables depending on the season, such as green beans, artichokes, and spinach* (see page 362). You can also use broccoli in place of cauliflower.

Makes one 30 cm (12 in) loaf tin

Serves 6

1 medium cauliflower, about 700 g (1 lb 9 oz)

500 ml (2 cups) béchamel 2* (1/2 the quantity, see page 380)

2 eggs, lightly beaten

50 g (1/2 cup) freshly grated Parmesan cheese

nutmeg

a little butter

about 2 tablespoons fine breadcrumbs

Preheat the oven to 180°C (350°F/Gas 4). Wash the cauliflower and trim away the hard stem. Put it into a pot of boiling salted water and boil for about 10 minutes, or until it has softened.

Meanwhile, make the béchamel sauce and keep aside. Drain the cauliflower and chop it up finely or roughly purée it. Put into a bowl and mix in the eggs, the béchamel, Parmesan cheese, a grating of nutmeg (depending on how much you have used in the béchamel) and salt and pepper to taste, adjusting if necessary. Mix well with a wooden spoon.

Butter an oven dish or loaf tin and sprinkle with half of the breadcrumbs to line the tin, shaking away the excess. Pour in the mixture and sprinkle the surface with the remaining breadcrumbs. Bake for 30–40 minutes in the hot oven, until the top is golden and slightly crusty. Serve slightly warm in thick slices, or at room temperature.

Torta al cioccolato

Chocolate cake

It is always useful having a good, simple chocolate cake recipe in your repertoire that can be referred to often.

Makes one 24 cm (9$^{1}/_{2}$ in) cake

200 g (7 oz) good quality unsweetened, dark chocolate

6 tablespoons milk

100 g (3$^{1}/_{2}$ oz) butter

4 eggs, separated

150 g (5$^{1}/_{2}$ oz) caster (superfine) sugar

50 g (1$^{3}/_{4}$ oz) cake flour

1$^{1}/_{2}$ teaspoons baking powder

Preheat the oven to 180°C (350°F/Gas 4). Butter and flour a 24 cm (9$^{1}/_{2}$ in) springform cake tin.

Break up the chocolate into small pieces and melt it together with the milk and the butter in a small saucepan, set over a larger saucepan of simmering water. Whip the egg yolks with the sugar in a bowl until thick and creamy. Scrape in the melted chocolate, whisking quickly to prevent the egg mixture from cooking.

Whisk in the sifted flour and baking powder. Whip the egg whites to soft peaks and fold them gently into the batter, incorporating well.

Pour into the cake tin and bake in the preheated oven for about 35 minutes or until a skewer inserted comes out clean. The cake should be soft and moist, and will slightly indent in the middle when cool.

Serve dusted with a little icing sugar, or with a little pile of fruit and whipped unsweetened fresh cream.

Tiramisu

Mascarpone dessert

This popular dessert is easy to make and, as its name implies, is a quick fix — a 'pick-me-up' with a shot of coffee and sugar. Although this recipe calls for Marsala, you can use another liqueur, if you prefer.

This makes about 10 small cup moulds, or 1 large deep dish of about 25 x 35 cm (10 x 14 in).

Serves 10

6 eggs, separated

125 g (4^1/2 oz) caster (superfine) sugar

500 g (1 lb 2 oz) mascarpone

375 ml (1^1/2 cups) strong coffee

4 tablespoons Marsala

about 30 Savoiardi (finger) biscuits or 1 quantity sponge* (see page 397)

unsweetened cocoa powder or chocolate shavings, to serve

Whip the yolks in a bowl with the sugar until they are very thick and creamy. Add the mascarpone and whisk until it is well blended, the mixture is thick and ribbons form with the whisk. Whisk the egg whites to soft peaks and gently fold them into the mascarpone mixture to blend.

Put the cooled coffee into a bowl and mix in the Marsala. Dip the biscuits into the liquid mixture and line individual cup moulds or a large dish. Break the biscuits up if necessary to make a closely packed layer. If you are using sponge cake, cut the sponge to fit into your individual cups or dish. Put a layer into the cups and brush with the coffee mixture. Cover with the mascarpone mixture, spreading it gently if necessary, to completely cover the biscuits. If you are using small moulds that are quite tall, you might like to make two layers each of biscuits and mascarpone cream.

Refrigerate for at least a couple of hours before serving. Dust generously with sifted cocoa powder or scatter with chocolate shavings, and serve in the individual moulds, or dish out from the larger container in squares or dollops.

Frittelle di riso

Fried rice balls

These make a sudden appearance towards the middle of March for San Giuseppe's (St Joseph's) day and are sold in the main piazzas everywhere. They then disappear, though you might spot them for another year in the kitchens of some devotees. This quantity will make about 75 rice balls.

Serves 10–12

500 g (1 lb 2 oz) pudding or short-grain rice

2 litres (8 cups) water

zest of 1 small lemon

90 g (3¼ oz) plain (all-purpose) flour

light olive oil for frying

about 100 g (3½ oz) caster (superfine) sugar

about 100 g (3½ oz) icing (superfine) sugar

Put the rice into a saucepan and cover with the cold water. Add a pinch of salt and the lemon zest, and bring to the boil. Cook on a medium heat for 20–30 minutes, stirring frequently, until the rice has absorbed the liquid. Remove from the heat and cool. Cover and refrigerate for 24 hours.

About three hours before frying the rice balls, remove the mixture from the fridge. Mix with a wooden spoon, then mix in the flour, making sure it is well absorbed.

Pour the light olive oil into a pot suitable for shallow-frying to come about 3 cm (1¼ in) up the sides.

Working with 2 teaspoons, form small balls with the rice mixture — each about the size of a small, unshelled walnut. Heat the oil, and begin adding a few rice balls at a time. Fry them until they are golden and crispy all over, making sure that the oil isn't too hot. With a slotted spoon, transfer them to a plate lined with paper towel to absorb the excess oil.

Mix the two types of sugar together on a plate. Put the rice balls onto a serving platter and sprinkle with the sugar mixture, or roll the rice balls in the sugar mixture. Serve immediately.

APRIL

The weather has changed. Flowering trees have become the norm. Their beautiful colours reveal their imminent peach and plum secrets. What you sow now, you will reap in the following months, so people are planting energetically on their verandas or gardens. There is still some reluctance about completely packing winter away, and small piles of pullovers are left on stand-by, while the umbrella stands drip.

The hills have reached their summit of green, and bicycles are beginning to weave their way through them. There is tarragon, rocket, and the wonderful arrival of stunning strawberries — which are said to help the body in throwing off winter-accumulated toxins, with their slightly astringent qualities.

This month is spring-cleaning. It is also the Easter month, which goes with lamb, accompanied by artichokes which are now in the fields. Their tall, solid, lilac-crowned stalks stand in smart lines — as if realising their own splendour.

Filetti di baccalà fritti e marinati

Fried and marinated salt cod fillets

Serves 10

185 g (1½ cups) plain
(all-purpose) flour, plus
about 125 g (1 cup) for
dusting

60 g (½ cup) cornflour
(cornstarch)

1 teaspoon baking powder

500 ml (2 cups) cold water

1 kg (2 lb 4 oz) fillet of salt
cod, soaked, skinned,
cleaned and all bones
removed

light olive oil or sunflower
oil for deep frying

Marinade

2 sprigs rosemary, leaves
stripped off stalk

2 garlic cloves, peeled and
chopped

1 small dried red chilli,
crumbled

60 ml (¼ cup) olive oil

125 ml (½ cup) red wine
vinegar

This is a beautiful antipasto or even main-course dish which
can also be prepared a couple of days ahead and served cold
from the refrigerator. *Baccalà* is generally widely available.
It is unsmoked cod, which has been preserved with salt. It
therefore needs to be thoroughly soaked and rinsed repeatedly
to eliminate the salt (usually for about two days) before
cooking. It is also possible to find ready-soaked *baccalà* —
in which case, omit the soaking process.

Put the 185 g (1½ cups) of flour, the cornflour, baking powder
and a little salt into a bowl. Add the water and mix through to
obtain a fairly thin batter. Leave it to rest for about 10 minutes.
Cut the fish into 5 x 2 cm (2 x ¾ in) pieces and pat them dry
with paper towels.

Pour enough oil into a non-stick frying pan to come about
3 cm (1¼ in) up the sides. Heat the oil. Dust the fish pieces in
flour and dip into the batter. Fry in the hot oil on a medium heat
on both sides until the fish is crispy, lightly golden and cooked
through. Do not overcrowd the pan. Remove and transfer to a
plate or tray lined with paper towels to absorb the excess oil.

To make the marinade, chop up the rosemary leaves and
put into a bowl, adding the garlic, chilli, olive oil and vinegar, and
season with salt. Put the still warm fish into a large serving bowl,
splash with the marinade and mix through carefully and thoroughly.
Adjust any seasoning to taste.

This can be served immediately or left to marinate for a
while — even up to a few days — in the refrigerator.

Frittata di ortica

Green nettle frittata

This may be served hot or cold in wedges, as part of an antipasto or as a light meal. Nettle has healing properties as well as good taste. The leaves are collected in spring and are rich in vitamins and minerals. Nettle should be picked with gloves. Choose the tips of the plant as they are softer. Strip the leaves off the stalk and discard the stalks. The sting is extinguished in its washing water, so handle with gloves before and while washing it. Once cooked, the leaves become really soft. If all this seems too daunting, you can substitute it with spinach or silverbeet (Swiss chard).

Serves 6

about 600 g (1 lb 5 oz) young nettle leaves, or 200 g (7 oz) cooked weight

8 eggs

about 40 g (1 1/2 oz) freshly grated Parmesan cheese

30 g (1 oz) butter

lemon juice, to serve

Wash the nettle leaves and plunge them into a saucepan of boiling, lightly salted water for a couple of minutes. Drain well and chop finely.

Preheat an oven grill (broiler). Whip the eggs lightly in a bowl. Season with salt and pepper, and add the Parmesan cheese and the chopped nettle.

Melt the butter in a 24 cm (9 1/2 in) saucepan, with a substantial rim. Pour in the eggs and cook for a few minutes on a medium heat. The sides will set and seem cooked almost immediately. Swirl the pan around to distribute the uncooked egg mixture, loosening the sides and bottom of the frittata to ensure it doesn't stick.

Transfer the pan to just under the hot grill (broiler) — to set the top of the frittata, which should still remain a little soft on the top. Slide the frittata out onto a serving plate, using a flexible spatula, and cut into wedges. Serve sprinkled with a few drops of lemon juice.

Penne ai carciofi

Penne with artichokes

If you like, you can add about 50 g (1³/₄ oz) of chopped unsmoked *pancetta* (belly bacon) to the pan with the artichokes for a stronger flavour.

Serves 6

juice of 1 lemon

6 medium-sized globe artichokes

3 tablespoons olive oil plus a little extra for serving

2 garlic cloves, peeled and finely chopped

a handful of chopped parsley

2 sprigs of thyme, leaves stripped off stalk

500 g (1 lb 2 oz) short pasta such as penne

about 120 g (1¹/₄ cups) freshly grated Parmesan cheese, to serve

extra virgin olive oil, to serve

Prepare a bowl of cold water with the lemon juice. Trim the artichokes of their tough outer leaves. Those you leave are the ones you will eat, so make sure there are no tough leaves. Chop off a third of the top spear. Cut off the stem, leaving about 3 cm (1¹/₄ in) and trim down towards the end into a pyramid point, trimming away the dark outer green stem. Cut them in half vertically and scrape out the choke. Slice each half, still vertically, into about six pieces, depending on the size of the artichoke. Drop the pieces into the lemon water to prevent them from discolouring while you prepare the rest.

Heat the olive oil in a saucepan. Drain the artichokes and pat them dry. Add them to the saucepan with the garlic and half of the parsley. Add the thyme leaves and season with salt and pepper. Sauté for a few minutes until they are lightly golden. Add about 750 ml (3 cups) of water, or meat or chicken stock if you have any, lower the heat and simmer for 30–40 minutes until the artichokes are very soft. Break up the artichokes a little with a wooden spoon. Add more liquid if it seems dry — it should have the consistency of a chunky sauce with about a cup of liquid to coat the pasta.

Cook the pasta in boiling salted water following the packet instructions. Drain and add to the artichoke sauce with the remaining parsley, tossing to coat all the pasta. Serve sprinkled with Parmesan cheese and drizzled with extra virgin olive oil.

Risotto alla fragola

Strawberry risotto

The first of the year's strawberries become available in late April. This is a stunningly unusual and exciting dish which always seems to raise an eyebrow when the menu is mentioned. You can make the risotto using either water, meat or chicken stock as your liquid.

Serves 6

1.5 litres (6 cups) of meat*
or chicken stock* (see
pages 388 or 387) or water

60 g (2¼ oz) butter

1 medium French shallot
(eschalot), peeled and very
finely chopped

250 g (9 oz) ripe
strawberries, washed,
hulled and halved

3 tablespoons good-quality
brandy

500 g (1 lb 2 oz) risotto rice

50 g (½ cup) freshly grated
Parmesan cheese plus
extra for serving

Heat the stock in a large saucepan and keep it on a gentle simmer.

Heat half of the butter in a heavy-bottomed saucepan.
Sauté the French shallot on a low heat until it has softened and
add half of the strawberries. Cook gently for a couple of minutes,
then add the brandy. When it has evaporated, add the rice and stir
with a wooden spoon to coat all the rice. Season with salt and
pepper and add a ladleful of hot stock, stirring almost continuously
to prevent the rice from sticking.

When the rice has absorbed the liquid, add another ladleful
and continue stirring, making sure you move all the rice at the
bottom of the pan with the spoon. After about 20 minutes taste the
rice. It should be soft yet firm, and the texture should be creamy
and slightly liquid. You may have to continue cooking it for a few
more minutes.

Add the remaining strawberry halves, the butter and the
50 g (1¾ oz) of Parmesan cheese and stir in. Serve immediately
with a grinding of black pepper and extra Parmesan cheese.

Risotto con calamari e pomodoro

Risotto with calamari and tomato

In this recipe, the calamari is cooked separately in the tomato
and herbs and added to the rice in its final cooking stages so
that the calamari remains soft. Parmesan cheese is not
generally served with fish and seafood risottos, yet many
people insist that this dish cannot be served without it.

Serves 6

1 kg (2 lb 4 oz) calamari

3 garlic cloves, peeled

1 stalk of celery, trimmed

1 large carrot, peeled

1 large white onion, peeled

5 tablespoons olive oil

a handful of chopped
parsley

250 ml (1 cup) white wine

400 g (14 oz) tin of peeled
tomatoes with their juice,
cut into chunks

1 small dried red chilli,
crumbled

1.5 litres (6 cups) water
(or fish or vegetable stock,
if available, see pages 386
or 389)

500 g (1 lb 2 oz) risotto rice

extra virgin olive oil, to
serve

To clean the calamari, pull the tentacle part out of the body and from the inside pull out the transparent bone and discard. Rinse out well under cold running water. Hold the tentacles firmly with one hand squeezing out the little beak bone and cut it away, leaving the tentacles whole. They should resemble a neat crown. Rinse. Cut the body part into thin rings and the tentacle part into halves or quarters, depending on their size.

Put the garlic, celery, carrot and onion into a blender and pulse-chop until they are minced, or chop very finely by hand. Heat 3 tablespoons of the olive oil in a saucepan and add the vegetables. Don't worry if it seems too dry. Sauté to soften, then add the calamari and half of the parsley. Cook on a high heat for a couple of minutes before adding the wine. When some of the wine has evaporated, add the tomato and chilli, and season with salt and a little pepper.

Continue to cook on a medium heat for about 10 minutes or until the tomato has melted and is cooked. Remove from the heat. The calamari should be soft with quite a bit of sauce.

Heat the water or cooking liquid. In a separate saucepan suitable for making risotto, heat the remaining 2 tablespoons of olive oil. Add the rice and stir to coat. Add 1 ladleful of hot water or stock, and stir with a wooden spoon. When the liquid has been absorbed by the rice, add another ladleful and continue stirring to prevent the rice from sticking, making sure to move all the rice at the bottom of the pan with the wooden spoon.

Check the seasoning, and add salt and pepper if necessary. After about 20 minutes, taste the rice. It should be soft yet firm and the texture should be creamy and slightly liquid. If not, carry on cooking for a while longer. Add the calamari, stir in and cook for a few minutes more to fuse the flavours.

Stir in the remaining parsley, drizzle with extra virgin olive oil and serve immediately.

Gnocchi verdi con panna ed erbette

Green nettle gnocchi with cream and fresh herbs

Nettle grows wild amongst the grasses in spring time, and is appreciated for its vitamin-rich healing properties. Nettle needs to be handled with gloves, until its sting is removed in the washing water. As it is not readily available, you may substitute spinach in this recipe.

Wash the potatoes and boil them in their skins in lightly salted water for 15–20 minutes, being careful not to overcook them. Drain and when cool enough to handle, peel them. Pass the potatoes through a food mill — or grate them through the large holes of a grater, into a wide bowl.

Wearing gloves, rinse the nettle in a couple of changes of cold water, then boil for a couple of minutes in lightly salted water. Drain well and when cool enough to handle squeeze out the excess water with your hands. Chop finely on a wooden board and mix into the potatoes. Add the egg and the Parmesan cheese, then season with salt and pepper. Add enough flour to make a soft and elastic dough, mixing with your hands.

Bring a large saucepan of salted water to the boil. Lightly flour your work surface. Working quickly, break off pieces of the dough and roll out into long cylindrical strands of about 1 cm ($^1/_2$ in) in diameter. Cut these strands into pieces at about 2 cm ($^3/_4$ in) intervals with a sharp knife. Put them onto a lightly floured tray or large plate until you are ready to cook them.

Cook the prepared gnocchi in batches in the boiling water for about 2–3 minutes. When they float to the surface they are ready. Keep the gnocchi in a buttered oven dish if you will not be mixing them immediately into the sauce.

Melt the butter in a large saucepan. Add the herbs and sauté for a minute or so to flavour the butter. Add the brandy, cook for another minute, then add the cream. Heat through until it bubbles up.

Remove the gnocchi with a slotted spoon or wire strainer, allowing the water to drain off and add them to the saucepan. Toss to coat evenly. You can add a little hot milk, or some of the cooking water to thin it out if necessary, though it should not be too liquid. Sprinkle with Parmesan cheese and serve immediately.

Serves 6

800 g (1 lb 12 oz) waxy potatoes

800 g (1 lb 12 oz) young green nettle leaves

2 eggs, lightly beaten

50 g ($^1/_2$ cup) freshly grated Parmesan cheese

about 200 g (7 oz) plain (all-purpose) flour

50 g (1$^3/_4$ oz) butter

1 tablespoon each of these fresh chopped herbs: tarragon, sage, mint, basil, thyme, and parsley

a splash of good-quality brandy

250 ml (1 cup) thick (single) cream

about 120 g (1$^1/_4$ cups) freshly grated Parmesan cheese, to serve

Agnello arrosto con erbe e patate

Agnello arrosto con erbe e patate

Roast lamb with potatoes and herbs

This is a traditional Easter dish and on the Sunday in question, there is hardly a table in Tuscany not graced by a delicious sage-and-rosemary-scented roast.

Serves 6

about 185 ml (3/4 cup) herbed olive oil* (about 1/4 recipe, see page 377)

1 or 2 legs of deboned spring lamb, about 1.5 kg (3 lb 5 oz) in total

1. 2 kg (2 lb 10 oz) small new potatoes, washed and scrubbed well

250 ml (1 cup) white wine

Make some herbed oil if you don't have any. Preheat the oven to 200°C (400°F/Gas 6).

Trim the lamb of any fat and lay it open onto your work surface. Season with salt and pepper on both the inside and outside. Put about 4 abundant tablespoons of herbed oil on the inside. Roll up the lamb and tie with kitchen string to secure.

Rub the outside with about 4 tablespoons of herbed oil. Put into a large roasting dish and into the oven. Turn the lamb to brown on all sides. It should take about 10–15 minutes on each side.

If the potatoes are small, leave them whole — if not cut them into chunks leaving the skins on. Add the wine and potatoes to the lamb, and continue cooking for another 1–1 1/4 hours or until the lamb is nicely browned, yet tender, and the potatoes golden, crisp and soft inside. Turn the lamb and potatoes over once or twice. It may be necessary to remove the lamb before the potatoes, to avoid overcooking it. In this case, keep the lamb on a plate, covered with aluminium foil and continue roasting the potatoes until they are done.

Transfer the lamb to a wooden board. Remove the string and cut the lamb into thick slices. Put them onto a serving dish and splash with the pan-juices. Remove the potatoes from the oven and season with salt to taste. Pile them up around the lamb, or on a separate platter, and serve immediately.

Carciofi ripieni

Stuffed artichokes

These artichokes accompany a roast lamb beautifully. You may use meat or chicken stock in place of the vegetable stock here, depending on what you will be serving with the artichokes.

Serves 6

12 medium globe artichokes

1 medium bunch of parsley, chopped

4 garlic cloves, peeled and finely chopped

3 tablespoons olive oil

about 30 g (1 oz) butter

500 ml (2 cups) vegetable stock* (see page 389)

Rinse the artichokes. Trim away the tough outer leaves. Those you leave will be the ones you will eat, so make sure they are not tough.

Cut away about a third of the top spear of each artichoke. Cut away the stem completely so that it is in line with the artichoke bottom.

Put each artichoke bottom-side-up onto a wooden board, and push gently against the artichoke with your hand to widen the central cavity of the artichoke. Or you can gently open up the artichoke leaves to widen them out. Using kitchen scissors, snip away any top spikes of the internal small leaves.

Mix the chopped parsley and garlic together and divide the mixture between the artichoke cavities and the leaves. Use a teaspoon or your fingers.

Choose a high-rimmed saucepan, where the artichokes will fit fairly precisely in a single layer, and put them in upright. Drizzle with the olive oil, season with salt and pepper, and add the stock. Put a nob of butter into each artichoke and bring the stock to the boil. Spoon a little of the stock over the artichokes, lower the heat, cover and simmer for 30–40 minutes or until the artichokes are tender. Remove the lid and continue cooking to reduce the liquid to only a little in the pan. Serve warm or at room temperature.

Carciofi ripieni

Rombo alle erbette

Rombo alle erbette

Baked fish with herbs

You can use any fish fillets such as cod, halibut, salmon or trout, in this delicate dish, which is very quick and easy to prepare. Substitute any herbs you like — in a combination or on their own.

Serves 6

6 fillets or slices flounder (turbot), 150–200 g (5^1/$_2$–7 oz) per piece

about 30 g (^{1}/$_4$ cup) plain (all-purpose) flour for dusting the fish

3 tablespoons olive oil

125 ml (^{1}/$_2$ cup) white wine

60 ml (^{1}/$_4$ cup) water

2 garlic cloves, peeled and finely chopped

1 tablespoon each of these finely chopped fresh herbs: parsley, rosemary, sage, mint and thyme

30 g (1 oz) butter

Preheat the oven to 220°C (425°F/Gas 7).

Cut the fish fillets into two pieces if necessary to make cooking them easier. Season with salt and pepper. Lightly dust both sides with flour.

Put the olive oil into an oven dish and add the fish, the wine and water. Scatter on the garlic and the mixed herbs, and spoon some of the liquid over the fish. Dot with the butter.

Put into the hot oven and cook for about 20 minutes. The fish should be opaque white and soft, with a little sauce bubbling up. Cook longer if necessary. Serve hot.

Tagliata con rucola ed aceto balsamico

Seared sirloin with rocket and balsamic vinegar

The meat here should be about 2.5 cm (1 in) thick and seared on a very hot grilling (griddle) pan or on a barbecue. The inside usually remains fairly medium-rare, but naturally you can cook it to your liking. Leave a little of the fat on for the flavour, if you like, and add some extra olive oil or balsamic vinegar to each plate to taste.

Serves 2

500–600 g (1 lb 2 oz–1 lb 5 oz) sirloin steak

About 120 g (4½ oz) rocket (arugula), rinsed, dried and trimmed of any tough stalk ends

2 tablespoons extra virgin olive oil

2 tablespoons balsamic vinegar

Heat a cast iron grill (griddle) on the stovetop. When it is very hot, add the plain piece of meat. Keep the heat on medium to avoid burning the outside and leaving the inside raw.

Cook for 6–8 minutes on each side until dark or grill marks appear, then turn over the meat. The thickness of the meat should allow it to remain juicy inside while nicely seared on the outside.

Transfer the meat to a cutting board and sprinkle with salt. Cut the meat into slices of about 2 cm (¾ in), slightly on the diagonal.

Divide the rocket and put a mound onto each plate. Add the strips of meat over the rocket. Drizzle each serving with a little olive oil and balsamic vinegar, or to taste. Add a little salt to the rocket. Grind over pepper and serve immediately.

Tagliata con rucola
ed aceto balsamico

Scaloppine con carciofi e prosciutto

Veal escalopes with artichokes and prosciutto

In Italy, veal can be bought ready for *scaloppini*. Generally,
they are sliced from the tenderloin of milk-fed veal. Ask your
butcher to cut it into thin 60 g (2¹/4 oz) slices, or they can
be cut thicker and pounded gently to flatten. Have your
ingredients ready before you start, as this takes only a
couple of minutes to cook.

The recipe quantities here serve three. To serve more, you can cook the meat in batches and transfer to a plate to keep warm while cooking the rest. Wipe the pan clean and add fresh olive oil for the next batch.

Serves 3

6 slices of veal tenderloin, trimmed of fat

3 medium-sized globe artichokes

6 tablespoons olive oil

2 garlic cloves, peeled and finely chopped

about 60 g (1/2 cup) plain (all-purpose) flour for dusting the veal

125 ml (1/2 cup) white wine

6 thin slices *prosciutto crudo*

1 sprig fresh tarragon, leaves roughly chopped

Squeeze the juice of half a lemon into a bowl of cold water. Trim the artichokes of their tough outer leaves. Those you leave will be the ones you will eat, so be sure that the remaining leaves are soft. Chop off about a third of the top spear. Cut the stem, leaving about 3 cm (1 1/4 in), and trim down towards the end in a pyramid-shaped point, removing the dark outer green stem. Cut them in half vertically, and scrape out the choke. Slice each half, still vertically, into about six pieces and drop into the lemon water to prevent them from discolouring while you prepare the rest. Drain and pat dry with paper towels.

Heat 2 tablespoons of the olive oil in a saucepan. Add the artichokes and the garlic, and season with salt and pepper. Sauté for about 5 minutes or until lightly golden before adding 125 ml (1/2 cup) of water. Simmer, covered for about 10 minutes, until they are soft and there is only a little liquid left in the pan.

If necessary gently pound the veal slices, between two sheets of baking paper, to a thickness of 3 mm (1/8 in). Season with salt and pepper and dust lightly in flour.

Heat the remaining 4 tablespoons of olive oil in a large, wide frying pan. Add the veal slices and, on a medium heat, fry for a minute or so on each side to brown lightly. Add the wine and when it evaporates a little, add a piece of prosciutto and the tarragon to each piece of veal. Simmer for a couple of minutes to just wilt the prosciutto, then add the artichokes with a few drops of water if it seems like it needs a little more liquid. Let it bubble up for 30 seconds and serve immediately.

Carciofi saltati in padella

Sliced, sautéed artichokes

The artichoke slices are cooked together with a whole *pancetta* slice, which is then divided into a few chunks and served with the artichokes. You can leave out the *pancetta* if you like, and add any other fresh herbs.

Serves 6

9 medium-sized globe artichokes

4 tablespoons olive oil

4 garlic cloves, peeled and finely chopped

1 slice of unsmoked *pancetta* (belly bacon), about 1 cm (^{1}/2 in) thick

250 ml (1 cup) vegetable stock* (see page 389) or water

3 tablespoons chopped fresh parsley

Prepare a bowl of cold water with the juice of half a lemon. Trim the artichokes of their tough outer leaves. Those you leave are the ones you will eat so make sure that they are not tough. Chop off about a third of the top spear. Cut off the stem, leaving about 3 cm (1^1/4 in) and trim down towards the end into a pyramid point, trimming away the dark outer green stem. Cut them in half vertically and scrape out the choke. Slice each half, still vertically, into about six pieces, depending on the size of the artichoke. Drop into the lemon water to prevent them from discolouring while you prepare the rest. Drain and pat dry with paper towels.

Heat the olive oil in a large saucepan. Add the artichokes, garlic and the piece of *pancetta*. Sauté for about 5 minutes until lightly golden and season with salt and pepper. Add about 250 ml (1 cup) of vegetable stock if you have any, or water. Cover and simmer for 10 minutes more until the artichokes have softened. Add a few more drops of liquid if necessary to keep them just moist. Stir in the parsley.

Serve hot or at room temperature.

Carciofi sott'olio

Artichokes preserved in olive oil

These are fantastic to have on hand in your cupboard to add to salads, serve as an antipasto, or as part of panini fillings. The amounts given here will be enough to make two 1 litre (4 cups) preserving jars. See note on preserving (page 400).

2.5 kg (5 lb 8 oz) baby artichokes (about 35 or 40)

500 ml (2 cups) white wine vinegar

250 ml (1 cup) white wine

a few sage leaves

a small sprig of rosemary

salt

a few small dried red chillies

garlic cloves, peeled and left whole

a few black peppercorns

a few bay leaves

olive oil to cover the artichokes in the jars, about 1 litre (4 cups)

Squeeze the juice of a lemon into a large bowl of cold water. Clean the artichokes, trimming away the tough outer leaves and leaving the ones that you will eventually eat. Cut away the top third of the artichoke and scrape out the choke, if there is one, with a teaspoon.

Leave about 2 cm (3/4 in) of the stem, trimming the hard outer dark green part away down to a fine point. Leave the artichokes whole if they are small or divide them in half or quarters if they are larger. Put them into the lemon water to prevent them from discolouring while you prepare the rest.

Put the vinegar, white wine, sage and rosemary into a saucepan. Season with salt and bring to the boil. Add the drained artichokes — in two batches if necessary.

When the liquid comes back to the boil, cook for 4 minutes, then transfer the artichokes to a clean dry cloth with a slotted spoon. Pat dry. Discard the cooking liquid. Divide the artichokes among clean, sterilised glass jars and pack each jar with a chilli, a couple of garlic cloves, a few whole peppercorns and a couple of bay leaves. Cover completely with oil. Push the artichokes down with a fork and make sure there are no air bubbles before closing the jars tightly. They will be ready in about three weeks, but will last many months provided they remain completely covered in oil.

Store in a cool dark place. Once opened, keep in the refrigerator and consume fairly quickly.

Fragole con aceto balsamico

Strawberries with balsamic vinegar

You may use a strawberry or raspberry vinegar instead of the balsamic. This is a simple, light dessert often eaten with a slice of white bread in Tuscany. Try this served with vanilla biscuits* (see page 116) or vanilla ice cream* (see page 139).

Serves 6

250 ml (1 cup) red wine

250 ml (1 cup) water

1 kg (2 lb 4 oz) ripe strawberries

150 g (5 1/2 oz) caster (superfine) sugar

1 1/2 tablespoons balsamic vinegar

Put the wine and water into a bowl. Gently rinse the strawberries and drain them well. Carefully remove their green tops. If they are small, leave them whole, otherwise divide them into halves or quarters. Put them into a non-corrosive (such as stainless steel) bowl, and sprinkle with the sugar and the balsamic vinegar. Mix through and refrigerate for at least 30 minutes before serving.

Biscottini di vaniglia

Vanilla biscuits

This dough is very soft, resulting in particularly buttery and delicate biscuits.

Makes 35 biscuits

120 g (4½ oz) butter, softened

150 g (5½ oz) caster (superfine) sugar

1 teaspoon vanilla essence

2 eggs

250 g (2 cups) plain (all-purpose) flour

Whip the butter in a bowl with the sugar and vanilla until it is light and fluffy. Add the eggs and beat in well. Work in the sifted flour and a pinch of salt, using a wooden spoon to make a soft, sticky dough.

Wrap it up in plastic wrap, pressing it down to form a disc, and refrigerate for at least an hour before rolling out and cutting the dough.

Preheat the oven to 180°C (375°F/Gas 5). Line a large baking tray with baking paper.

Dust your work surface and lightly pat your hands with flour. Roll out the dough, flattening it with your hands to a thickness of about 5 mm (¼ in). Add a little extra flour if you think it needs it — but as little as possible as this will make the biscuits hard.

Cut rounds or shapes with a 5 cm (2 in) biscuit cutter or the top of a glass. Set out the biscuits on the baking tray leaving a little space between each.

Bake in the preheated oven for about 10–15 minutes, or until they are lightly golden. Remove from the oven and cool on a rack before storing in an air-tight container.

Zuccotto

Chocolate and vanilla sponge pudding

Serves 10–12

1 quantity sponge cake*
(see page 397)

1 quantity pastry cream*
(see page 394)

60 g (1/2 cup) unsweetened
cocoa powder

1 double espresso, filled to
a cup measure with extra
water if necessary (or
1 strong cup of coffee)

125 ml (1/2 cup) Marsala or
Vin Santo

This is a striking dessert made up of vanilla sponge layered
with vanilla cream and chocolate cream.

Make the sponge in a 30 x 40 cm (12 x 16 in) baking tray, lined
with baking paper. Leave the sponge to cool completely.

Make the pastry cream and divide equally between two
bowls. Sift the cocoa powder into one and whisk in well. Combine
the coffee and the liqueur in a separate bowl.

Transfer the sponge from the tray to your work surface. Cut
into 8 mm (1/3 in) strips along its width. Use some of the strips to
line the base and sides of a deep round bowl about 2 litres
(8 cups) in capacity. Cut to fit where necessary. Using a pastry
brush, brush the sponge layer with the coffee and Marsala mixture.

Spread just less than half of the vanilla cream onto the
sponge layer. Completely cover with a layer of sponge strips. Brush
with the coffee mixture and spread over slightly less than half of the
chocolate cream. Cover with sponge and brush with the coffee.
Repeat with the remaining vanilla, another layer of sponge brushed
with coffee, then the remaining chocolate cream. Finish with a layer
of sponge brushed with the coffee mixture. Neatly trim away any
protruding strips. You should have a perfect bowler hat-shaped
zuccotto encased in sponge strips. Tightly, but firmly press down
with your palms to gently compact the zuccotto in the bowl and
cover with plastic wrap.

Refrigerate for at least 3–4 hours before serving — or even
overnight. To serve, remove plastic wrap, invert onto a round tray
or platter and cut into wedges.

MAY

There are two surprises this month. The first is to wake up one morning some time towards the very beginning of May and to see the first poppies — magnificently minimalistic and bright tomato-red, standing against their background of luminous-green hills.

Then there are the lucciole — the very elegant fireflies. One clear night, driving through the unlit countryside, I found myself without warning in the middle of the ultimate, private, silent Peter Pan theatre of lights. They had lit up the dark night and certainly my life with their very short, sparkler-like existence.

There are the rows of roses too, forcing you to stop and acknowledge them. There are artichokes in full bloom now, and gorgeous lemons, broad beans, lovely bright green peas, the beginnings of zucchini, cherries and capers to be collected and preserved, and the beginning beckonings of gelati and sorbetti.

Tortino di carciofi

Artichoke omelette

Omelettes are excellent when made with some vegetables. Use a few mushrooms, some sautéed red onions, zucchini, or anything else you can come up with in place of the artichokes.

Serves 1

1 medium-sized globe artichoke

flour for dusting the artichokes

3 tablespoons olive oil

2 eggs

$1/2$ tablespoon chopped parsley

a little lemon juice

Prepare a bowl of cold water with a little lemon juice.

Clean the artichoke, trimming away the tough outer leaves; leave the ones you will eventually eat. Chop off about a third of the top spear. Cut the artichoke in half vertically and scrape out the choke. Leave about 3 cm ($1^1/4$ in) of the stem, trimming the dark outer green stem away down to a fine point.

Divide the artichoke into quarters lengthways and drop the pieces into the bowl of water to prevent them from discolouring until you are ready to use them. Pat the artichoke pieces dry with paper towels and dust them with flour.

Heat 2 tablespoons of the olive oil in a 15 cm (6 in) saucepan and add the artichoke pieces. Fry until golden on all sides and transfer them to a plate.

Remove the pan from the heat and wipe out the artichokes with paper towels. Drizzle in the remaining tablespoon of olive oil and return to the heat. Lightly whip the eggs in a bowl, season with salt and pepper and pour into the saucepan. Add the pieces of the artichokes to the centre of the pan. Cook the omelette for a couple of minutes on a low heat, loosening the sides and swirling the pan around to distribute the uncooked egg. When the omelette is slightly golden on the underside, and the top centre is only slightly runny, remove from the heat and transfer to a serving plate.

Sprinkle with the chopped parsley and a few drops of lemon juice, and serve immediately.

Baccelli e pecorino

Baccelli e pecorino

Broad bean and pecorino salad

This is a very traditional meal in May — beans, bread, cheese and olive oil.

Apart from the bean shell, each individual broad bean has two coats — the outer one is often removed to expose another, brighter green coat underneath.

Serves 6

500 g (1 lb 2 oz) fresh pecorino cheese

800 g (1 lb 12 oz) shelled broad (fava) beans

4 tablespoons extra virgin olive oil

1 tablespoon white wine vinegar

Cut the cheese into slivers or cubes. Put the broad beans into a bowl and splash with the olive oil and vinegar. Season with salt and pepper, and mix through. Put a pile of broad beans onto each plate, scatter with the pecorino cheese and serve.

Minestrone

Mixed vegetable soup

Serves 10

2 medium red onions, peeled and chopped

3 large tomatoes, skinned and chopped

3 medium zucchini (courgettes), cut into small chunks

1 large celery stalk with leaves, trimmed and thinly sliced

3 large carrots, peeled and cut into small chunks

3 medium potatoes, peeled and cut into small chunks

500 g (1 lb 2 oz) silverbeet, (Swiss chard) or spinach, washed, tough stalks removed and thinly sliced

freshly grated Parmesan cheese, to serve

extra virgin olive oil, to serve

This is the simplest of soups, which you can serve hot, or even at room temperature. You can vary the vegetables according to the season. This recipe uses no olive oil in its initial cooking stage, but is served with a good drizzle. Many Italians scrub their end crust of Parmesan cheese well before dropping it into the soup to cook . . . and then argue over who will get it at the table.

Put the vegetables into a stockpot, cover with about 3 litres (12 cups) of cold water and bring to the boil. If your pot cannot hold all the water now, add more when the volume has reduced. Skim the surface with a slotted spoon to remove any scum.

Lower the heat to medium-low, season with salt and simmer uncovered for about 1 1/2 hours. Add more hot water as it reduces. Remove from the heat and cool slightly before serving. Sprinkle individual servings with Parmesan cheese and drizzle with olive oil. Add a little black pepper, if you like. The soup may be served hot or at room temperature.

Risotto con gamberi e rucola

Risotto with prawns and rocket

In this risotto the addition of the slightly sharp-tasting rocket combines beautifully with the delicate sweetness of the prawns.

You can use the prawn heads and shells to make the stock for cooking the risotto. Parmesan cheese is generally not served with fish and seafood pastas or risottos. Naturally, you can decide.

Serves 6

3 tablespoons olive oil

1 white onion, peeled and finely chopped

500g (1 lb 2 oz) risotto rice

250 ml (1 cup) white wine

1.5 litres (6 cups) fish stock* (see page 386)

200 g (7 oz) rocket (arugula), trimmed of any tough stalks and finely sliced

200 g (7 oz) peeled prawns (shrimp)

50 g (1³/4 oz) butter

1 tablespoon good-quality brandy

Heat the olive oil in a large saucepan. Add the onion and sauté for a few minutes to soften, but not to brown. Add the rice, stirring to coat with a wooden spoon. Lightly season with salt and pepper (the stock will probably be seasoned as well). Add the wine and let it evaporate. Add one or two ladlefuls of warm stock and lower the heat slightly. After about 10 minutes add half of the sliced rocket. Keep adding a little more stock as it is absorbed by the rice. Cut the prawns into convenient chunks, or leave them whole or in halves, depending on their size.

Heat a third of the butter in a saucepan and add the prawns. Lightly season with salt and pepper, and cook for a couple of minutes over a high heat until the prawns turn whitish-pink. Add the brandy and let most of it evaporate. Remove from the heat and set aside.

Taste the rice after it has been cooking for about 20 minutes. It should be soft yet firm and the texture should be creamy and slightly liquid. You may have to continue cooking it for a few more minutes. When your risotto has achieved this consistency, add the rest of the rocket and the cooked prawns. Stir in the remaining butter and serve immediately.

Tagliolini al limone

Tagliolini with lemon

Tagliolini are slightly larger and flatter than spaghetti, and smaller than tagliatelle. This is a very delicate sauce, well suited to this fresh egg noodle.

Serves 6

1 quantity fresh pasta*
(see page 372)

juice and zest of 1 large
lemon

30 g (1 oz) butter

4 tablespoons good-quality
brandy

250 ml (1 cup) thick (single)
cream

about 120 g (1 1/4 cups)
freshly grated Parmesan
cheese

Make the pasta dough following the instructions. Cover with a clean cloth and leave it to rest at room temperature for about 30 minutes before rolling it out.

Roll out the dough, following the instructions, to the second last setting (depending on the type of pasta machine you have). Dust the dough lightly with flour and pass the pasta through the tagliolini cutters. If your pasta machine does not have this cutter, roll up the strip of dough (along the longest part) and cut the pasta with a sharp knife at 3 mm (1/8 in) intervals. Toss the pasta through your fingers to separate the noodles and put them onto a tray, lightly dusted with flour or fine semolina.

Bring a stockpot of salted water to boil. Grate the lemon zest, then finely chop. Heat the butter in a saucepan and add the lemon zest. When it begins to sizzle, add the brandy. When it has evaporated, add the cream, and the lemon juice, and heat through for a minute until it bubbles up. Season with salt and pepper, and remove from the heat.

Put the pasta in the boiling water and cook for 3–4 minutes, testing one to see if it is done. Cook for longer if necessary. Drain, reserving about a cup of the pasta cooking water, and toss the pasta quickly into the warm sauce to coat evenly. Add a little of the reserved water if it seems like it needs more liquid. Sprinkle with Parmesan cheese and serve immediately.

Spaghetti alle vongole

Spaghetti with clams and cherry tomatoes

This is one of the light, fresh and yet full-flavoured pasta dishes so frequently served along the coast. Small clams are usually used for this dish. The spaghetti remains *in bianco* (without a tomato sauce), and the cherry tomato halves are tossed into the pan at the last minute to heat them through.

Serves 6

1 kg (2 lb 4 oz) small, fresh clams (vongole)

4 tablespoons olive oil plus a little extra

3 garlic cloves, peeled and finely chopped

1 small dried red chilli, crumbled

1 medium bunch of parsley, chopped

125 ml (1/2 cup) white wine

500 g (1 lb 2 oz) spaghetti

200 g (7 oz) ripe cherry tomatoes, halved

Soak the clams in lightly salted water for a few hours. Change the water frequently and drain in a colander to get rid of any sand. Rinse and drain well.

Heat the olive oil in a large wide stockpot. Add the garlic, chilli and half of the parsley. As soon as you begin to smell the garlic, add the clams and the white wine. Turn up the heat to high, put a lid on, and cook for 5 minutes or until the shells have opened.

Remove from the heat. Discard any clams that have remained tightly shut. Remove about half of the clams from their shells, discard these shells and return the clam meat back to the pot, leaving the rest of the clams in their shells.

Cook the spaghetti in boiling, salted water. While the spaghetti is cooking, add the cherry tomatoes to the clam pot and season with salt and pepper. Return to the heat for a few minutes to heat through. Drain the spaghetti when it is ready and add it to the clam pot, tossing with a pair of tongs.

There should be a fair amount of liquid from the clams to coat the pasta. Put into individual pasta bowls, sprinkle with the remaining parsley and serve immediately, with an extra drizzle of olive oil.

Cotolette di agnello fritte

Fried, crumbed lamb cutlets

These may form part of the *fritto misto** (see page 133), served alone or together with fried artichokes.

Serves 6–8

5 eggs

240 g (3 cups) breadcrumbs

18 medium-sized lamb chops, trimmed of fat

light olive oil for shallow frying

lemon wedges, to serve

Whip the eggs in a wide bowl and season with salt and pepper. Put the breadcrumbs on a large flat plate. Flatten the chops with a meat mallet and dip them into the egg to cover completely. Shake off the excess and pat them into the breadcrumbs on both sides, pressing down with your palm to ensure they stick. Transfer them to a large clean plate until you are ready to fry them.

Pour enough oil in a 2 cm (^{3}/4 in) deep saucepan to ensure the chops can be shallow-fried without sticking to the bottom. Heat the oil on a medium–low heat, and when it is hot, begin frying the cutlets in batches. Fry on both sides until they are golden brown, crispy and cooked through.

Transfer the cooked cutlets to a plate lined with paper towels to absorb the excess oil while you finish frying the rest. Pile them up onto a clean platter, sprinkle with salt and serve the cutlets with lemon wedges.

Pollo al limone

Chicken in lemon

This can be prepared ahead of time and just heated through to serve — together with some boiled potatoes and vegetables or simply with lots of bread to soak up the sauce.

Serves 4

1 chicken, about 1.5 kg (3 lb 5 oz), cleaned, insides removed, skinned and cut into 8 portions

5 tablespoons olive oil

1 large white onion, peeled and roughly chopped

2 celery stalks, trimmed and roughly chopped

2 large carrots, peeled and roughly chopped

250 ml (1 cup) white wine

2 bay leaves

500 ml (2 cups) hot water

the juice of 2 lemons

about 3 tablespoons chopped parsley

Rinse the chicken pieces in cold water and pat them dry with paper towels.

Heat half of the olive oil in a large saucepan. Add the chicken pieces and sauté until the chicken is lightly browned on both sides. Season with salt and pepper. Meanwhile, heat the remaining olive oil in a large stockpot. Add the vegetables and sauté for a few minutes until they have softened. Add the browned chicken pieces to the vegetable pot. Add the wine and the bay leaves and cook until most of the wine has evaporated. Lower the heat to a minimum and add the water, then half of the lemon juice.

Cover and simmer for about 1 1/2 hours or until the chicken is very tender. Check that the sauce level is at about 2 cups — if not, add a little more water. Remove the pot from the heat.

Put the vegetables with some of the sauce into a blender or food processor and blend to a smooth consistency. (Or remove the chicken to a plate, purée the remaining contents and return the chicken to the pot.)

Add the remaining lemon juice and stir in the parsley. Check the seasoning and add more salt and pepper if necessary. Serve the chicken pieces warm, with the sauce spooned over them.

Scaloppine al limone

Veal escalopes with lemon

In this very versatile dish you can replace the lemon juice and water with white wine, Marsala, cream, or a few mushrooms, herbs and so on.

In Italy, veal can be bought ready for *scaloppini*. They are generally sliced from the tenderloin of milk-fed veal. Ask your butcher to cut thin, 60 g (2¼ oz), slices — or they can be cut thicker and pounded gently to flatten. Have your ingredients ready before you start, as this takes only a couple of minutes to cook. The recipe quantities here serve three. To serve more, you can cook the meat in batches and transfer to a plate to keep warm while cooking the rest. Wipe the pan clean and add fresh olive oil for the next batch.

Serves 3

6 slices, 60–70 g (2¼–2½ oz), veal tenderloin, trimmed of fat

about 60 g (½ cup) flour for dusting the veal

4 tablespoons olive oil

about ½ tablespoon butter

juice of 1 lemon

Gently pound the veal slices to a 3 mm (⅛ in) thickness between two sheets of baking paper. Season with salt and pepper, and dust lightly with flour.

Heat the olive oil and butter in a large, wide frying pan. (If you don't have a big enough pan, cook half of the veal slices in half of the oil and butter. Transfer those to a plate while you fry the other half, and return all the slices to the pan for a minute or so to ensure they get coated in a bit of sauce.) Add the veal slices and, on a medium-high heat, fry for a minute or so on each side to brown lightly. Take care not to overcook as the meat may toughen.

Add a splash of water or vegetable stock if you have any (not more than 60 ml or ¼ cup), and the lemon juice. Let it boil for a minute or so; adjust the seasoning if necessary and serve.

Fritto misto di pesce e verdure

Mixed fried fish and vegetables

Serves 6–8

24 thin-stemmed asparagus, trimmed of woody stalk end

6 medium-sized globe artichokes

2 medium-sized zucchini (courgettes)

2 medium-sized, slightly unripe tomatoes

12 baby calamari, about 800 g (1 lb 12 oz) in total

light olive oil or vegetable oil for frying

20 medium-large fresh prawns (shrimp), peeled and deveined

12 fillets small red mullet, about 30 g (1 1/4 oz) each

lemon wedges and salt, to serve

Batter

4 eggs

310 g (2 1/2 cups) plain (all-purpose) flour

375 ml (1 1/2 cups) cold, sparkling water

125 ml (1/2 a cup) cold white wine

This is a combination of various fish and vegetables which you may vary according to the season or to your taste. The pieces must be dried with paper towel before being either dusted in flour, egg and breadcrumbs, or dipped into a batter. They are then fried in batches, in hot olive oil.

The oils used for frying the fish and the vegetables are usually kept separate. If not, the vegetables are fried before the fish. If you can manage two pans on the stovetop simultaneously, you will cook up this dish quite quickly. The sooner you eat the fish and vegetables after they are fried, the better they will be.

Rinse the asparagus to get rid of all sand and pat dry. Trim the artichokes of their tough outer leaves. The ones you don't trim off are the ones you will eat, so make sure they are not hard. Trim the stem down to a pyramid point of about 1 cm (1/2 in), removing the dark outer green stem. Cut off about a third of the spear. Divide the artichokes in half lengthways. Scrape away the choke and divide each half into three vertically. Drop them into a bowl of water mixed with the juice of a lemon to prevent them from discolouring in the meantime.

Wash and dry the zucchini. Cut them into half lengthways or quarters if they are large. Divide the sticks horizontally into half or three, depending on the length of the zucchini. Divide the tomatoes vertically into about eight slices.

Clean the calamari — pull the tentacle part out from the body, then pull out the transparent bone from the inside and discard. Rinse well under cold running water. Hold the tentacles firmly with one hand, squeezing out the little beak bone and cut it away, leaving the tentacles whole. They should resemble a neat crown. Rinse. Cut the body part into thick rings and pat dry.

To make the batter, lightly whip the eggs with the flour and add the cold water and wine for a smooth consistency. Season with salt and pepper.

Pour enough oil to come about 3 cm (1 1/4 in) up the side of a deep frying pan. Heat the oil on a medium heat. Begin dipping your vegetables into the batter, shaking off the excess and frying them in batches. Do not overcrowd the pan. Turn them over with a pair of tongs when they are golden and crispy, and fry the other side. If they are browning too quickly and not cooking through, lower the heat.

Transfer to a large plate or tray lined with paper towels to absorb the excess oil. Remove any bits and crumbs of batter left in the oil with a slotted spoon to prevent them from burning. Top up with oil if necessary and heat through before adding more batter-coated ingredients.

Begin dipping the fish into the batter, shaking off the excess and frying in batches on both sides until cooked through, crispy and golden. Transfer to a plate lined with paper towels.

Pile up the fish and vegetables onto a large serving platter and sprinkle with salt. Add lemon wedges and serve immediately.

Fritto misto
di pesce e verdure

Piselli alla fiorentina

Green peas cooked with prosciutto

Peas and ham seems to be a universally popular match. Naturally, this recipe uses *pancetta* (belly bacon) with the freshest of new spring peas. This side dish can be served with any main course.

Serves 6–8

3 tablespoons olive oil

1 small white onion, peeled

1 garlic clove, peeled

100 g (3 1/2 oz) unsmoked *pancetta* (belly bacon), diced

1 kg (2 lb 4 oz) fresh green peas, shelled

1/2 tablespoon tomato paste (purée)

Heat the olive oil in a saucepan on a medium heat. Add the whole onion, the garlic clove and the *pancetta*. Sauté for a couple of minutes, then add the peas. After about 10 minutes, add 500 ml (2 cups) of water and the tomato paste and continue cooking for another 15–20 minutes or until the peas are tender. If necessary, add a little more water, although the finished peas should have only a little liquid. Taste the peas before adding salt and pepper, as the *pancetta* will flavour the peas.

Serve hot or at room temperature.

Torta di limone e mandorle

Lemon and almond cake

This is a delicious and simple-to-make cake, and lovely in this size. Serve it on its own or with a little homemade jam* (see jam recipes listed in the index) or a small pile of fresh fruit, such as raspberries or cherries, and a dollop of mascarpone cream* (see page 398). You can buy the almonds ready ground, or grind them in a food processor but not too fine, as the coarse bits give the cake a great texture.

Makes one 20 cm (8 in) cake

125 g (4¹/2 oz) butter, slightly softened

125 g (4¹/2 oz) caster (superfine) sugar

3 eggs, separated

125 g (4¹/2 oz) almonds, finely ground

60 g (2¹/4 oz) plain (all-purpose) flour

1 teaspoon baking powder

juice of 2 small lemons

grated (yellow) zest of 2 small lemons

icing (confectioners') sugar, to serve

Preheat the oven to 180°C (350°F/Gas 4). Whip the butter in a bowl with the sugar until it is creamy. Add the egg yolks, one by one, and mix well between each addition. Whisk in the almonds, the sifted flour and the baking powder. Add the lemon juice, the grated zest and whisk together. In a separate bowl whip the egg whites to soft peaks and fold them into the batter.

Butter and flour a 20 cm (8 in) springform cake tin. Scrape the batter into the cake tin. Bake in the preheated oven for 30–40 minutes, until the top is lightly golden, and a skewer inserted comes out clean. Let it cool slightly before opening the side of the cake tin.

Serve warm or at room temperature, dusted with icing sugar.

Ciliege cotte

Cooked cherries

You can add a vanilla bean or any other spices you like to the syrup.

Serves 6

400 g (14 oz) caster (superfine) sugar

500 ml (2 cups) water

1 kg (2 lb 4 oz) cherries, washed, pitted and stalks removed

5 fresh mint leaves, chopped

Put the sugar and water into a saucepan. Bring to the boil and boil for 5 minutes. Lower the heat and add the cherries. Simmer for 10 minutes in the syrup. Remove from the heat and let the cherries cool in the syrup. Serve warm or cold with the mint stirred and accompanied by vanilla ice cream* (see opposite page) or deep-fried pastry ribbons* (see page 66).

Although they are ready to be eaten immediately, they will keep, stored for up to a year. Once opened, refrigerate and consume fairly quickly.

Ciliege in sciroppo

Cherries preserved in syrup

Makes 1.5 litres (6 cups)

400 g (14 oz) caster (superfine) sugar

500 ml (2 cups) water

1 kg (2 lb 4 oz) unblemished ripe cherries, washed, pitted and stalks removed

When there are cherries in abundance, they are preserved in syrup to keep for the months ahead when they are unavailable, and to serve as a quick, delicious dessert on their own, or with vanilla ice cream* (see opposite page). Drained of their juice, they can be used to fill a baked tart case together with pastry cream or whipped cream. See note on preserving (page 400).

Put the sugar and the water into a large saucepan. Bring to the boil and boil for 5 minutes. Add the cherries, lower the heat slightly and simmer for 5 minutes. Remove from the heat. Put the cherries into clean, sterilised jars and cover with the syrup. Cool very slightly and tightly seal the lids. Put the jars into a large saucepan and cover with water. Bring to the boil, then boil for 20 minutes. Turn off the heat and leave the jars to cool completely in the water. Check that a vacuum has been created on the lid. Store in a cool dark place.

Gelato alla vaniglia

Vanilla ice cream

It is possible to make ice cream without an ice-cream machine. Achieving the light and creamy texture, however, requires whisking by hand to break down the ice particles. You can use a vanilla bean here in place of the essence — just heat up the milk, cream and sugar in a saucepan with the split vanilla bean to extract its seeds. Cool and strain before freezing. Remove the ice cream from the freezer before serving to soften it slightly.

Makes over 1 litre (4 cups)

500 ml (2 cups) thick (single) cream

250 g (9 oz) sugar

500 ml (2 cups) milk

2 teaspoons vanilla essence

1 tablespoon good-quality brandy

Whisk the cream and sugar together in a bowl suitable for the freezer, until the cream begins to thicken slightly and the sugar has completely dissolved. Whisk in the milk. Add the vanilla and the brandy. Cover, and put the bowl into the freezer.

After an hour, remove the bowl from the freezer, give an energetic whisk with a hand whisk or electric mixer, and return the bowl to the freezer. Whisk again after another couple of hours. When it is nearly solid, give one last whisk, transfer to a suitable freezing container with a lid and let it set until it is solid.

Alternatively, pour the mixture into your ice-cream machine and freeze — following the manufacturer's instructions.

Vanilla ice cream with egg

You can use less milk and more cream in this recipe if you prefer a richer ice cream.

Makes over 1 litre (4 cups)

1 vanilla bean

700 ml (24 fl oz) milk

250 ml (1 cup) thick (single) cream

4 egg yolks

200 g (7 oz) caster (superfine) sugar

Split the vanilla bean in half lengthways and put into a saucepan with the milk and cream, and bring to the boil. Remove from the heat. Whip the yolks in a bowl with the sugar until creamy. Ladle a little hot cream mixture into the egg mixture, whisking immediately to acclimatise the eggs and prevent them from cooking. Add another ladleful, then add all of it to the cream pan. Return the pan to the lowest possible heat, stirring continuously with a wooden spoon for a few minutes.

Remove from the heat, strain into a suitable container for freezing. Leave it to cool completely, mixing every now and then, before following the freezing instructions from the previous recipe.

Sorbetto di limone

Lemon sorbet

This is ideal on a warm day, after a heavy meal or as a palate cleanser. It is difficult to make sorbet without an ice-cream machine, as it tends to freeze into a block of ice.

Makes 1.3 litres (45$\frac{1}{2}$ fl oz)

300 g (10$\frac{1}{2}$ oz) caster (superfine) sugar

1 litre (4 cups) water

4 medium-sized juicy lemons

Put the sugar into a saucepan with 250 ml (1 cup) of the water to boil. Boil for a couple of minutes to make a syrup and remove from the heat. Mix in the remaining water and the lemon juice. Cool completely before pouring the mixture into your ice-cream machine. Freeze, following the manufacturer's instructions. Transfer the sorbet to a suitable container and store in the freezer.

Torta di limone

Lemon tart

Makes one 26 cm (10¹/₂ in) tart

¹/₂ the quantity of sweet pastry* (see page 391)

Lemon cream

175 g (6 oz) caster (superfine) sugar

juice of 3 lemons

350 ml (12 fl oz) thick (single) cream

4 eggs

grated zest of 1 lemon

Make the pastry and leave it to rest in the refrigerator for about an hour before rolling it out. Preheat the oven to 180°C (350°F/Gas 4).

Use a 26 cm (10¹/₂ in) fluted loose-bottomed tart case, with sides about 3.5 cm high (1¹/₂ in). Follow the instructions (see page 391) for rolling out the pastry and baking it partially blind.

Put the sugar, lemon juice and cream into a bowl, and whisk to dissolve the sugar.

Add the eggs, one by one, whisking well after each addition. Stir in the lemon zest.

Pour the mixture into the prepared tart shell. You can mix an egg yolk with a couple of teaspoons of milk and brush onto the visible pastry for a glossier finish. Carefully return the tart to the oven. Bake for 20–30 minutes, or until it is no longer liquid when you gently move the tin. Remove from the oven and cool before removing the tart case.

Serve at room temperature or cold, in slices, plain or with a small pile of fruit such as a cherry salad.

Marmellata di ciliege

Cherry jam

If you don't have a special jam saucepan, use a large heavy-bottomed non-corrosive (stainless steel) pan. It is better to fill smaller jars with jam, as once opened, they must be kept in the refrigerator and consumed as soon as possible. See note on preserving (page 400).

Makes about 1.5 litres
(6 cups)

2 kg (4 lb 8 oz) ripe cherries

1.3 kg (3 lb) caster
(superfine) sugar

Wash, dry and pit the cherries. Put them into a large saucepan with 250 ml (1 cup) water. Bring to the boil, then lower the heat slightly and cook for about 15 minutes, mashing the cherries with a wooden spoon. Add the sugar and simmer for another hour or so, stirring from time to time to prevent the mixture from sticking. If you like a smooth jam, purée with a hand-held blender or processor. Spoon a little of the jam onto a plate and tilt it to the side slightly. It should slide down with a little resistance. If not, simmer for a little longer.

Put the hot jam into clean sterilised jars and tightly close the lids. Put the jars upright into a large saucepan, cover with cold water and bring to the boil. Boil for 20 minutes, remove from the heat and leave the jars to cool in the water before removing them. Check the lid to ensure that a vacuum has been created. Alternatively, tightly close the lids and turn the jars upside down. Cover with a tea towel and leave to cool. Check that a vacuum has been created on the lid.

Store upright in a cool dark place. The jam is ready to be eaten immediately, but will store for months. Once opened, keep in the refrigerator.

JUNE

It seems like a bus-load of insects arrived here last night — just in case we hadn't realised that summer was here.

There is the hum of bees and those dratted mosquitoes, along with the beginnings of citronella-smelling creams in attempts to remain un-bitten. Everyone is suddenly outdoors and wearing only one layer. No more just-in-case socks stuffed into car cubby holes.

Time to start eating outside with quick antipasti and foods at room temperature. This is a time for picnics. Pine nuts are drying and can be heard dropping to the ground near basil-scented verandas. Things are beginning to look colourful. There are green beans, burnished purple eggplants, apricots, garlic, sweet red onions, capers, green radicchio, nectarines and zucchini with their beautiful yellow flowers. There are still the always-present carrots, parsley, silverbeet, sage and rosemary, and this is the beginning of the very useful tomato season.

Focaccia all'olio

Flat olive oil bread

This can be served in place of any other bread or is excellent with fillings when it is well risen. You can also scatter some fresh rosemary or other fresh herbs on top before baking.

Makes 1 oven tray of about 30 x 40 cm (12 x 16 in)

25 g (1 oz) fresh yeast

310 ml (1¼ cups) tepid water

a pinch of sugar

500 g (1 lb 2 oz) bread flour

2 tablespoons of olive oil plus extra for drizzling

Put the yeast into a bowl with the water and the pinch of sugar and leave it to activate.

Put the flour and 1 teaspoon of salt into a large, wide bowl or onto a work surface. Add the yeast to the flour and mix in with a fork to incorporate. Add the 2 tablespoons of olive oil and begin kneading with your hands for about 10 minutes until you have a compact, smooth dough. Add a little more flour or water if necessary. Alternatively, make the dough in a mixer using a dough hook.

Put the dough into a bowl, cover with a cloth, and leave to rise in a warm place for about 1½ hours or until it has doubled in size.

Spread the dough with your fingertips into a lightly oiled oven tray. Drizzle the surface with a little olive oil and sprinkle with salt and pepper. Cover with a cloth and leave in a warm place for another 30–60 minutes, or until it has risen.

Meanwhile, preheat the oven to 200°C (400°F/Gas 6). Bake the focaccia in the hot oven for 30–40 minutes or until the top is golden and crusty. Cut into serving pieces and serve warm.

A Tuscan picnic

Affettato misto

Mixed sliced cold meats

A meal in Tuscany is often made out of their wonderful cold meats, which are ideal for picnics and quick lunches — particularly when paired with bread, a few olives, a few chunks of cheese, and perhaps some preserved artichokes* (see page 112). These cold meats are available from Italian delicatessens. If not, you can substitute other varieties of sliced cold meats. Have them all cut into approximately 3 mm (^{1}/8 in) slices.

Serves 4

8 slices of *finocchiona* (fennel salami)

8 slices of Tuscan salami

8 slices of *capocollo*

8 slices of *prosciutto crudo*

Divide the slices into individual portions.

Serve with thick slices of white, country-style bread, or focaccia bread* (see opposite page) and if you like, with pieces of unsalted butter.

Picnic panini

Here are some fillings for *panini* (bread rolls).

prosciutto crudo
Parmesan cheese
rocket (arugula) and
olive oil

chilli pecorino cheese and
melon jam* (see page 221)

preserved artichokes*
(see page 112)
truffle oil and
pecorino cheese

mozzarella cheese and
grilled capsicum* (pepper),
(see page 204)

grilled eggplants* (aubergines),
(see page 201) and
pesto* (see page 162)

sliced long-boiled beef or veal
salsa verde* (see page 378) and
chilli oil* (see page 242)

Rotolini di melanzane

Eggplant rolls

These can be served as an antipasto or, if you prefer, as a side vegetable dish.

Serves 6

2 large eggplants
(aubergines)

olive oil for frying

120 g (4¹/₂ oz) thinly sliced
ham (about 5 slices), each
piece divided into quarters

200 g (7 oz) mozzarella or
provolone cheese, cut into
3 mm (¹/₈ in) thick slices
and halved

about 20 basil leaves

20 g (¹/₄ cup) freshly grated
Parmesan cheese

20 g (¹/₄ cup) grated mature
pecorino cheese

3 tablespoons breadcrumbs

Slice the eggplants lengthways into 3 mm (¹/₈ in) slices. Put them into a colander, sprinkle them with a little salt and leave for about 30 minutes to allow the bitter juices to drain away. Rinse and pat dry with paper towel.

Preheat the oven grill (broiler). Heat enough oil in a frying pan to shallow-fry the eggplants. Fry them in batches for about 3 minutes on each side until golden and cooked through. Transfer to a plate lined with paper towels to absorb the excess oil. Top each eggplant slice with a piece of ham, a mozzarella or provolone cheese slice, a basil leaf, and a sprinkling of parmesan and pecorino cheese. Roll up along the longest side of the eggplant and secure with a toothpick. Sprinkle with breadcrumbs and put into an oven dish. Put into the hot oven to heat through for a few minutes. Serve immediately.

Pinzimonio

Crudités

This is a delicious fresh antipasto dish, which relies on the freshness and quality of its ingredients. Raw vegetables are dipped into the finest extra virgin olive oil served on the side. Lemon wedges are served separately for everyone to make their own little mix to suit their tastes, and ingredients are varied according to season.

Serves 6

3 medium-sized fennel bulbs

6 small spring onions (scallions), trimmed

1 small head of celery with leaves (preferably the pale, inner stalks)

1 small bunch of radishes

6 medium-sized globe artichokes

1 lemon, cut into wedges to serve plus a little extra juice for cleaning artichokes

about 375 ml (1 1/2 cups) extra virgin olive oil

Wash the vegetables, drain well and pat dry. Prepare a bowl of cold water with some lemon juice.

Trim the artichokes of their tough outer leaves. Chop off about a third of the top spear. Cut off the stem, leaving about 3 cm (1 1/4 in) and trim down towards the end into a pyramid point, trimming away the dark outer green stem. Divide lengthways into quarters. Trim away the choke. Put them immediately into the water to prevent them from discolouring, until you are ready to serve them, then drain and pat dry.

Cut the fennel into half lengthways and cut away any tough or damaged outer leaves. Divide each half vertically into three.

Divide the spring onions and celery vertically into half or quarters if they are large. Trim the radishes and leave them whole with their leaves.

Divide the vegetables equally and pile them onto individual serving plates.

Put a small ramekin onto each plate. Divide the olive oil amongst the ramekins. Sprinkle with salt and pepper, and serve the lemon wedges on the side.

Insalata di polpo

Octopus salad

This antipasto dish can be prepared up to 24 hours ahead of time. If you've never made a dish with fresh octopus, this is an easy introduction.

Serves 6

1.5 kg (3 lb 5 oz) octopus

Cooking liquid

1 celery stalk, trimmed

1 carrot, peeled

1 onion, peeled

a few whole, black peppercorns

about 3.5 litres (14 cups) water

125 ml ($\frac{1}{2}$ cup) white wine vinegar

juice of 1 lemon

6 tablespoons of extra virgin olive oil

1 chopped fresh red chilli

2 garlic cloves

a handful of fresh parsley

If your fishmonger has not already cleaned the octopus, cut a slit through the head part. Open it out flat and remove the innards and eyes, and the beak part. Rinse.

Put the celery, carrot, onion and peppercorns into a large saucepan. Cover with the water and vinegar. Season with salt and bring to the boil. Add the whole, cleaned octopus. Skim the surface with a slotted spoon to remove any scum. Cook for 1–1$\frac{1}{2}$ hours on a medium heat, covered, or until you can insert a fork into the octopus with no resistance. It should not, however, be too soft. Remove from the heat and cool the octopus in its stock.

Remove from the liquid and cut the whole octopus into rounds of about 5 mm ($\frac{1}{4}$ in).

Squeeze over the lemon juice, add the olive oil, the chilli, garlic and parsley, and season with salt and pepper. Mix through. Serve immediately or refrigerate for a few hours before serving.

Panzanella

Bread, tomato and olive oil salad

This is a rustic, country-bread salad and an excellent way of using up any leftover bread. This is the basic delicately dressed recipe, which you can adjust to suit your taste.

If possible, leave the bread cut up in thick slices out of its bag to dry out for a day or so before making the salad.

Serves 6

500 g (1 lb 2 oz) ripe tomatoes

1 large red onion, halved and finely sliced

500 g (1 lb 2 oz) 2-day old white, country-style bread

2 or 3 stalks of celery, about 250 g (9 oz), using pale inner stalks, trimmed and finely sliced

4 tablespoons chopped fresh parsley

about 10 basil leaves, roughly torn

about 8 tablespoons extra virgin olive oil

5 tablespoons of red wine vinegar

Cut the tomatoes into small chunks and put them into a colander sprinkled with a little salt for about 10 minutes to drain away their juices. Put the onions into a small bowl of cold water sprinkled with a little salt and a splash of vinegar.

If your bread is not already in slices, break it up into chunks and put into a bowl with enough cold water to just cover the bread. Leave it for about 10 minutes to soften. Squeeze the bread thoroughly with your hands, and finely crumble it into a large serving bowl. If the bread is not squeezed well enough, the salad will be soggy.

Put the tomatoes, drained onions, celery, parsley and the basil into a separate smaller bowl and dress with the olive oil and the vinegar, then season with salt and pepper. Mix well and then add to the bread.

Mix through well, adjusting any seasoning to taste, and serve.

Risotto al radicchio rosso

Risotto with red radicchio

Radicchio has a very definite and almost bitter, yet pleasant taste. Mixed with the butter and Parmesan cheese in the risotto, it acquires a mildly sweeter taste. This makes a lovely pale burgundy risotto, and would beautifully precede roast pork, quail or any game.

Serves 6

1.5 litres (6 cups) vegetable stock* (see page 389)

400 g (14 oz) red radicchio (*Trevisano* or *Chioggia*)

4 tablespoons olive oil

1 medium red onion, peeled and finely chopped

500 g (1 lb 2 oz) risotto rice

250 ml (1 cup) red wine

50 g (1³/₄ oz) butter

50 g (¹/₂ cup) freshly grated Parmesan cheese plus extra for serving

Heat the stock in a saucepan on the stovetop. Trim the radicchio of its tough stalk and any tough or damaged outer leaves and discard. Wash the leaves and cut into thin strips.

Heat the olive oil in a separate heavy-bottomed saucepan suitable for making the risotto. Add the onion and sauté on a medium heat until it has softened. Add most of the radicchio, leaving a small handful aside to add later. Lower the heat and simmer for about 5 minutes. Add the rice, stir to coat and cook for another minute.

Add the wine and when it has evaporated, season with salt and pepper, and add 1 or 2 ladlefuls of the hot stock. Stir with a wooden spoon and when the rice has absorbed the liquid, add more liquid and stir almost continuously to prevent it from sticking. Continue in this way for about 20 minutes, then taste the rice. Adjust the seasoning if necessary. The rice should be soft, yet slightly firm and creamy, and quite liquid. When it has achieved this consistency, stir in the remainder of the radicchio with the butter and Parmesan cheese.

Serve immediately, sprinkled with extra Parmesan cheese.

Penne con melanzane

Penne with eggplant

In the summer months eggplants are very popular prepared in a variety of ways — baked, roasted, marinated in olive oil, grilled, fried — and especially in a sauce for pasta.

You could also add a few cubes of mozzarella cheese and some baby capers to this dish at the last moment.

Serves 6

2 medium-sized eggplants (aubergines)

3 tablespoons olive oil

3 garlic cloves, peeled and finely chopped

a small handful of chopped parsley

1 kg (2 lb 4 oz) fresh, ripe tomatoes, skinned and roughly chopped

light olive oil for frying

500 g (1 lb 2 oz) penne pasta

a few basil leaves, roughly torn

about 120 g (1 1/4 cups) freshly grated Parmesan cheese, to serve

Slice the eggplants into thin rounds. Sprinkle with salt and leave in a colander, in the sink, for about 30 minutes to let the bitter juices drain away.

Heat the 3 tablespoons of olive oil in a saucepan and add the garlic and a little of the chopped parsley. When you begin to smell the garlic, add the tomatoes with half a cup of water. Season with salt and pepper, and simmer for about 20 minutes, breaking up the tomatoes with a wooden spoon until they have melted into a sauce.

Rinse the eggplant slices and pat dry with paper towels. Heat a little light olive oil in a large frying pan and fry the eggplants in batches on both sides so they are golden brown. Transfer them to a plate lined with paper towels to absorb the excess oil.

Cut the eggplant slices into strips and add them to the simmering tomato sauce, and simmer for a few more minutes. Add a little more water if it seems necessary.

Meanwhile, cook the penne in boiling salted water following the packet instructions. Drain and add to the saucepan, or if the saucepan isn't big enough, to a large wide bowl. Add the sauce, the basil and the remaining parsley, and toss quickly to coat all the pasta. Serve immediately with freshly grated Parmesan cheese.

Spaghetti con zucchini

Spaghetti with zucchini

This is so quick to make and while you could always add a few other ingredients, sometimes it's delicious to use just one. You might add a mature grated ricotta cheese instead of the Parmesan cheese, but you should definitely serve this pasta with a drizzle of chilli oil* (see page 242).

Serves 6

6 tablespoons olive oil plus extra for drizzling

3 garlic cloves, peeled and lightly crushed with the flat side of a knife blade

600 g (1 lb 5 oz) of small zucchini (courgettes), about 10, trimmed and thinly sliced

500 g (1 lb 2 oz) spaghetti

10 basil leaves, roughly torn

about 120 g (1¼ cups) freshly grated Parmesan cheese

Bring a large saucepan of salted water to boil.

Heat the olive oil in a saucepan with the garlic. When you begin to smell the garlic, add the zucchini and season with salt and pepper. Sauté for 10–15 minutes on a medium-low heat, tossing the zucchini until they are quite golden in parts.

Cook the pasta in the boiling water following the packet instructions. Drain, reserving about 250 ml (1 cup) of the cooking water.

Put the pasta into the zucchini saucepan if it fits. Add the basil and quickly mix through, adding enough of the reserved water to keep the pasta moist.

Serve immediately, with a good drizzle of olive oil or chilli oil, and sprinkled with Parmesan cheese.

Risotto con zucchini

Risotto with zucchini

Most risottos use stock as the cooking liquid, resulting in a more full-flavoured risotto. You could also add some sliced courgette flowers and any other fresh herbs or ingredients to this simple risotto.

Serves 6

1.5 litres (6 cups) vegetable stock* (see page 389)

4 tablespoons olive oil

1 medium white onion, peeled and finely chopped

2 garlic cloves, peeled and finely chopped

600 g (1 lb 5 oz) small zucchini (courgettes), trimmed and finely sliced

a handful of chopped fresh parsley

about 6 basil leaves, roughly torn

500 g (1 lb 2 oz) risotto rice

250 ml (1 cup) white wine

50 g (1¾ oz) butter

50 g (½ cup) Parmesan cheese plus extra for serving

Heat the stock in a saucepan on the stovetop.

Heat the olive oil in a large heavy-bottomed separate saucepan suitable for risotto, and add the onion. Sauté until it has softened slightly, then add the garlic.

Sauté for another minute. Add the zucchini slices, season with salt and pepper, and cook on a gentle heat for a few minutes. Toss in half of the chopped parsley and basil. Add the rice to the pan and stir to coat with a wooden spoon, cooking for a minute or two.

Add the wine and when it has evaporated, add a ladleful or two of hot stock. Stir, taking care to move all the rice at the bottom of the pan to avoid sticking. When the rice has absorbed the liquid, add more stock and stir.

Continue in this way until the rice has achieved the right consistency, which should be creamy, yet slightly firm and a little liquid. If you run out of broth, continue with hot water. Taste the risotto after 20 minutes — it may need another 5 minutes or so.

Stir in the butter, Parmesan cheese, the remaining parsley and basil leaves. Serve immediately with extra grated Parmesan cheese.

Linguine al pesto

Linguine with pesto

Serves 6

Pesto

40 g (¹/₄ cup) shelled and skinned pine nuts

10 g (¹/₄ oz) shelled walnuts

3 garlic cloves, peeled

about 250 ml (1 cup) olive oil

a bunch of basil, roughly torn

30 g (¹/₃ cup) freshly grated Parmesan cheese plus extra for serving

30 g (¹/₃ cup) freshly grated mature pecorino cheese

1 potato (about 150 g or 5¹/₂ oz), peeled, halved lengthways and cut into 3 mm (¹/₈ in) slices

500 g (1 lb 2 oz) linguine

Traditionally, this sauce is made by hand using a mortar and pestle. If you are making it in a blender, pulse-blend the ingredients to maintain a fairly rough texture. This recipe makes 375 ml (1¹/₂ cups).

If you will not be using the pesto immediately, store in the refrigerator in a tightly closed jar, covered with a thin layer of olive oil, where it will keep for up to a week.

A potato is not always added to this dish, but it is said that its starch helps the pesto to hold onto the pasta, apart from also tasting good.

To make the pesto, lightly toast the nuts in the oven or in a saucepan on the stovetop. Pound the garlic in a mortar with a few drops of the olive oil and a few of the basil leaves and some of the nuts. Keep adding more leaves and nuts until you have a rough-textured paste. Put the paste into a bowl and add the Parmesan and pecorino cheeses, a little salt and a grinding of black pepper. Gently stir in the olive oil, mixing to amalgamate the ingredients. Bring a large saucepan of salted water to the boil. Add the potato slices and cook for about 4 minutes, then add the linguine and follow the package instructions. Drain, reserving a little of the cooking water.

Put the linguine (with the potato) into a large bowl, and stir in the pesto, adding more or less to taste. Toss quickly to coat evenly, adding a few drops of the pasta cooking water if the pasta seems dry. Serve immediately with extra Parmesan cheese.

Zucchini ripieni

Stuffed zucchini

This can be served as part of an antipasto or as a side dish. Although there is no significant taste difference, you might find that round zucchini are easier to fill than the long variety.

Serves 6–8

10 medium-sized round or long zucchini (courgettes), about 120 g (4^1/2 oz) each

7 tablespoons olive oil

2 garlic cloves, peeled and finely chopped

1 small onion, peeled and chopped

300 g (10^1/2 oz) minced (ground) beef

1 Italian sausage, about 80 g (3 oz), skinned and crumbled

250 ml (1 cup) single cream

4 tablespoons freshly grated Parmesan cheese

nutmeg

Preheat the oven to 200°C (400°F/Gas 6). Rinse the zucchini. Cut away a very thin slice from the bottom, to ensure they sit flat. If using long zucchini, cut a boat shape along the top of the zucchini with a small, sharp knife. If using round zucchini, cut off about 2 cm (^{3}/4 in) from the top and reserve these as lids. Scoop out most of the flesh, taking care not to cut through the zucchini. Arrange the zucchini shells into an oven dish in a single layer.

Finely chop the removed zucchini flesh. Sauté the garlic and zucchini flesh in 3 tablespoons of the oil, until the water from the zucchini has evaporated and the zucchini has softened.

Meanwhile, in a separate frying pan sauté the onion in 2 tablespoons of oil. Add the minced meat and the sausage meat. Season with salt and pepper. Sauté until the liquid has evaporated and the meat is golden. Add the sautéed zucchini and sauté for a few more minutes. Remove from the heat and cool slightly. Stir in the cream, Parmesan cheese and a little grated nutmeg.

Fill the zucchini cavities with the mixture and put on the lids. Add enough water to come about 1 cm (^{1}/2 in) up the bottom of the zucchini. Sprinkle with salt and pepper and drizzle over 2 tablespoons of oil. Cover the dish with aluminium foil and bake into the oven for 45–60 minutes or until the zucchini are cooked. Remove the foil and return the dish to the oven for another 15 minutes or so to brown lightly. Serve warm.

Zucchini sott'olio

Zucchini preserved in olive oil

Having such wonderful olive oil at hand, Italians are very good at preserving a variety of vegetables *sott'olio*. These are delicious as part of a mixed antipasto. Use small baby zucchini if possible, as they tend to be firmer.

Makes over 1 litre (4 cups)

1 kg (2 lb 4 oz) small zucchini (courgettes), cut into thin rounds

500 ml (2 cups) white wine vinegar

500 ml (2 cups) water

about 3 garlic cloves, peeled

1 tablespoon fresh oregano

olive oil to cover the zucchini (courgettes) in the jars, about 750 ml (3 cups)

If the zucchini are not small, cut them in half lengthways and scoop away some of the seeds with a teaspoon before slicing into rounds. Put the rounds into a colander, sprinkle with the salt and leave them for 30 minutes.

Put the vinegar and water in a saucepan to boil. When it comes to the boil, add the zucchini. Bring back to the boil and boil for 3 minutes. Drain and put the zucchini onto a clean, dry cloth to cool. Pat dry and pack them into clean, sterilised jars with the garlic cloves and oregano between them. Cover completely with olive oil.

They will be ready in about 3 weeks, but will last for months if they remain completely covered in oil. See note on preserving (page 400).

Pizza

You can vary the toppings and use anything from only tomatoes, basil and mozzarella cheese, to any of the following ingredients — olives, rocket, gorgonzola, grilled capsicum, zucchini, mushrooms, artichokes, red onions, anchovies, capers, salami, ham, spicy sausage, or other favourites.

Makes 3 large pizzas

25 g (1 oz) fresh yeast

310 ml (1¼ cups) warm water

a pinch of sugar

500g (1 lb 2 oz) white bread flour

1 tablespoon olive oil plus a little extra for greasing

about 500 ml (2 cups) simple tomato sauce* (see page 382)

1 teaspoon dried oregano

about 300 g (10½ oz) mozzarella cheese

In a bowl, combine the yeast with the tepid water and the pinch of sugar and leave it to activate. Put the flour and half a teaspoon of salt in a separate large, wide bowl or onto a work surface, and make a well in the centre. Add the yeast and the olive oil to the centre, and mix in with a fork to incorporate. Knead with your hands for about 10 minutes to get a smooth, compact dough. Add a little more flour or a little more water, as required. Put the dough into a lightly oiled bowl, cover with a cloth and leave to rise in a warm place for about 1½ hours or until it has doubled in size.

Prepare the tomato sauce following the instructions, making sure it is smooth by breaking up the tomatoes with a spoon or roughly puréeing it. Stir in the oregano and remove from the heat.

Preheat the oven to 200°C (400°F/Gas 6). Cut the mozzarella cheese into small cubes or grate it and set aside.

Punch the dough and divide into three balls. Put them onto a tray, cover with a cloth and leave them to rise for about 30 minutes.

Lightly grease 3 pizza trays (or flat baking sheets) with olive oil. You may have to cook the pizzas in shifts. Dust your work surface with flour. Using a rolling pin, roll each ball of dough out into 3 mm-thick x 30 cm (⅛ in-thick x 12 in) discs.

Put the discs onto the baking trays. Divide the tomato sauce between each pizza (roughly 5 tablespoons on each), and spread around with the back of a spoon to cover the diameter within 1 cm (½ in) of the rim. Add any other topping that you are using, apart from the mozzarella cheese and any other cheeses. Bake in the hot oven until the dough and underside of the pizza is lightly golden and firm. This should take about 15 minutes. Add the mozzarella cheese and return the tray to the oven for a few more minutes to melt. Serve immediately.

Vitello tonnato

Veal with tuna, caper and anchovy mayonnaise

This dish is convenient in that it may also be prepared a day or two in advance. Even without the tuna sauce, it is a simple, delicious roast.

Serves 6–8

1.3 kg (3 lb) piece veal topside

5 tablespoons olive oil

2 sprigs of sage

4 garlic cloves, peeled

250 ml (1 cup) white wine

Sauce

4 salt-packed anchovies, rinsed and filleted, or 8 fillets in olive oil

60 g (2¼ oz) (drained weight) capers in vinegar

150 g (5½ oz) tin (drained weight) tuna in olive oil

1 quantity mayonnaise* (see page 381)

caperberries or extra capers, to serve

Preheat the oven to 200°C (400°F/Gas 6). Put the veal into a roasting dish, drizzle with the olive oil and season with salt and pepper. Add the sage sprigs and garlic cloves, and put into the oven. Brown on all sides — this should take about 10–15 minutes on each side. Lower the heat to 180°C (350°F/Gas 4). Add the wine and when it has evaporated a little, add a cup of water, and continue to roast for another 30–40 minutes, until the veal is cooked through, tender and golden brown. Remove from the oven and cool completely before cutting into thin slices of about 3 mm (⅛ in). If you are making the veal ahead of time, let it cool before refrigerating. Remove it from the refrigerator about 30 minutes before serving so that it is not too cold.

To make the sauce, very finely chop the anchovies and capers. Mash the tuna with a fork. Put them all into a bowl and whisk in the mayonnaise. Check the seasoning — depending on the anchovies you may need a little salt, pepper and lemon juice. The sauce should not be too stiff. Add a little of the veal's roasting juice to thin it out if necessary. If not using the sauce immediately, keep it covered in the refrigerator.

Lay the veal slices on serving platters, slightly overlapping. Spread the sauce over the veal slices. Scatter them with the caperberries and, if you like, decorate with extra anchovy fillets, olives and tomato cubes. Eat any leftover sauce with tomato halves, or boiled eggs.

Bistecca fiorentina alla griglia

Chargrilled T-bone steak

This must be one of the most impressive spectacles in Tuscan restaurants. Outside or inside, waiters are seen pushing small wooden trolleys to carve the meat at the table. The meat used here is from the Chianina breed of cattle. The steaks are put onto the hot grill completely plain and are normally served rare, not bleeding, with a good drizzle of olive oil. They may also be cooked under a very hot oven grill or in a hot griddle pan or, in winter, inside, in the open fireplace.

Ranging from 600 g to 1.2 kg (1 lb 5 oz to 2 lb 10 oz), it is unusual for even the most hearty of carnivores to confront one of these steaks alone. The meat is often served with a mixed wild salad picked from the fields.

Serves 2

one beef T-bone steak, about 3 cm (1¼ in) thick, about 800 g (1 lb 12 oz)

extra virgin olive oil

Bring the steak to room temperature while you prepare the coals. You may add some oak wood to the coals for its aroma. When the heat from the coals has died down a little, put the steak onto the grill rack placed about 10 cm (4 in) from the coals. Grill (broil) for 3 minutes on each side for rare and about 5 minutes on each side for medium. This will depend on the heat from the coals, the thickness of the meat and the distance from the coals. Check to see that it has been grilled to your taste.

Remove the steak from the heat and transfer to a cutting board. Remove the fillet from the bone and the sirloin from the bone. Divide each into two and serve, seasoned with salt and pepper, and a drizzle of olive oil.

Calamari alla griglia

Crumbed, grilled calamari

This is quite unusual, in that crumbed food is more often fried than grilled. The breadcrumbs, together with the garlic and parsley flavour, the calamari and also keep it soft. The tentacles are not as easy to cook on a barbecue as they are under an oven grill — unless you have a special rack to prevent them from falling into the coals. If you don't use the tentacles, you can save them for a risotto or quick pasta dish with lots of garlic, parsley and white wine.

Serves 4

1 kg (2 lb 4 oz) medium-sized calamari, about 150 g (5^1/$_2$ oz) each

5 tablespoons olive oil

a small handful of chopped parsley

4 garlic cloves, peeled and finely chopped

100 g (1 cup) good-quality breadcrumbs

lemon wedges, to serve

Heat the oven grill (broiler) or light the coals of an outside grill or barbecue.

To clean the calamari, pull the tentacles out of the body. Pull the transparent bone out of the body and discard. Rinse well under cold running water. Hold the tentacles firmly with one hand squeezing out the little beak bone and cut it away, leaving the tentacles whole. They should resemble a neat crown. Rinse, drain and pat dry. Leave the body parts and the tentacle parts whole, and put into a bowl. Drizzle over the olive oil, season with salt and pepper and mix through.

Make a mix with the parsley, the garlic and the breadcrumbs. Put onto a plate or shallow bowl and pat the calamari tubes and tentacles into the mixture, pushing down lightly with your palm to ensure that they stick.

Put the calamari onto a rack at a distance of about 20 cm (8 in) from the hot coals, or closer under the hot oven grill. Grill for about 10 minutes on each side until the outsides are crisp and golden brown, cooked through and still soft inside. Serve immediately with lemon wedges and sprinkled with a little salt.

Fiori di zucca fritti

Fried zucchini flowers

While the idea of throwing a delicate blossom into hot oil might seem outlandish, these are gorgeous to eat. They are delicious served alone as an antipasto, or to accompany a second course. You could also add a thin slice of mozzarella and half an anchovy fillet into each flower before dipping them into the batter — for a rich yet delicious variation. Choose firm, bright flowers, picked as recently as possible.

Serves 6–8

about 30 zucchini (courgette) flowers

2 eggs

185 g (1 1/2 cups) plain (all-purpose) flour

250 ml (1 cup) cold sparkling water, or 125 ml (1/2 cup) white wine plus 125 ml (1/2 cup) water

light olive oil for frying

lemon wedges, to serve

Remove the pistil from the inner cavity of the flowers and discard. Rinse the flowers gently in a bowl of cold water and drain. Lay them out to dry on a clean cloth.

To make the batter, whip the eggs lightly in a bowl. Add the flour and mix to incorporate. Season with salt and pepper, and whisk in the water for a smooth consistency.

Pour enough oil to come about 3 cm (1 1/4 in) up the side of the frying pan. Heat the oil.

Dip the dry flowers into the batter and fry in batches in the hot oil, taking care not to overcrowd the pan.

Fry until they are golden and crispy on both sides. Make sure the oil is not too hot, and that the flowers fry consistently on a medium heat.

Transfer the cooked flowers to a plate lined with paper towels to absorb the excess oil. Sprinkle with salt and serve immediately with lemon wedges.

Melanzane alla parmigiana

Baked eggplant with tomato, mozzarella and Parmesan cheese

Every Italian home cook has a slight variation of this classic dish.

Serves 6

3 medium eggplants (aubergines), cut into 3 mm (1/8 in) slices

2 tablespoons olive oil

2 garlic cloves, peeled and finely chopped

5 ripe tomatoes, skinned and chopped, or 400 g (14 oz) tin of peeled tomatoes, chopped

about 10 basil leaves, roughly torn

flour for dusting the eggplants

olive oil for frying

300 g (10 1/2 oz) mozzarella cheese, cut into 5 mm (1/4 in) slices

50 g (1/2 cup) freshly grated Parmesan cheese

Cut the eggplant slices and put them in a colander. Sprinkle with salt and leave for about 30 minutes to allow the bitter juices to drain away.

Preheat the oven to 180°C (350°F/Gas 4).

To make the tomato sauce, heat the 2 tablespoons of olive oil in a saucepan. Add the garlic and as soon as you begin to smell the garlic, add the tomatoes and half of the basil. Season with salt and pepper, and simmer for 15–20 minutes, or until the tomatoes have melted into a sauce.

Rinse the eggplant slices and pat dry with paper towels. Lightly dust both sides with flour. Heat enough olive oil to come 1 cm (1/2 in) up the side of a saucepan. Heat the oil and fry the eggplants in batches until golden brown on both sides, adding a little more oil if necessary. Transfer them to a plate lined with paper towels to absorb the oil.

Spoon a little of the tomato sauce into a square or round oven dish of roughly 30 cm (12 in). Cover with a layer of eggplant slices. Add a few spoonfuls of tomato sauce, then a layer of the mozzarella cheese slices. Add the remaining basil leaves. Sprinkle with Parmesan cheese. Repeat to use up the ingredients. Put into the hot oven and bake for 20–30 minutes or until the top is lightly golden and crusty. Cool slightly before cutting into servings. Serve hot or at room temperature.

Radicchio rosso al forno

Baked red radicchio

The bitter taste of radicchio can be pleasing and unusual. It goes well with all grilled and roasted meats. The radicchio can also be quartered as indicated here, then threaded onto skewers, brushed lightly with olive oil and cooked under an oven grill or on a barbecue. Additionally, it goes well with a mixed meat and vegetable grill* (see page 201).

Serves 6

3 heads of red radicchio (*Trevisano* or *Chioggia*), about 900 g (2 lb) total weight

butter to grease the oven dish

4 tablespoons olive oil

Preheat the oven to 190°C (375°F/Gas 5). Clean and rinse the radicchio heads, removing any tough or damaged outer leaves, leaving the stalk intact. Divide them lengthways into quarters, so that the leaves are still held together by a quarter of the stem.

Generously butter an oven dish and add the radicchio. Drizzle with olive oil and season with salt and pepper. Bake in the hot oven for about 10 minutes on each side, or until the radicchio has softened and browned lightly.

Fagiolini in umido

Green beans cooked in tomato

This is a fairly standard dish when green beans are in season — sometimes it is also stewed without tomato and served simply with lemon and olive oil. This can accompany any main course. Serve with a good chunk of bread.

Serves 6

3 tablespoons olive oil

1 red onion, peeled and finely chopped

3 garlic cloves, peeled and finely chopped

1.2 kg (2 lb 10 oz) fresh, ripe tomatoes, skinned and chopped, or 800 g (1 lb 12 oz) tin of peeled tomatoes, with their juice, chopped

600 g (1 lb 5 oz) green beans, washed and trimmed

a small handful of chopped parsley

about 10 basil leaves, roughly torn

Heat the olive oil in a large saucepan. Add the onion and sauté on a low heat until lightly golden. Add the garlic and the tomatoes. Simmer for a few more minutes. Add the beans, parsley, basil and about 500 ml (2 cups) of hot water. Season with salt and pepper.

Lower the heat to a minimum, cover and simmer for 1–1 1/2 hours or until the beans are very tender with a bit of thickened tomato sauce. Stir from time to time, to make sure the beans or sauce don't stick to the bottom. Add a little more water if necessary. Serve hot or at room temperature.

Crostata di marmellata di albicocche

Apricot jam tart

This gives Tuscan home cooks a chance to show off their home-made jams. It can be made with any jam, such as cherry, plum, melon or fig, but looks particularly good with a red jam.

Makes one 24 cm (9¹/₂ in) tart

¹/₂ the quantity of sweet pastry* (see page 391)

about 300 g (10¹/₂ oz) apricot jam* (see page 181)

1 egg yolk

1 teaspoon milk

You can use bought jam for this tart, and as much or as little as you like. You can also make the tart in smaller tart cases.

Make the pastry, cover with plastic wrap and put it in the refrigerator for about an hour.

Preheat the oven to 180°C (350°F/Gas 4). Roll out the pastry, following the instructions, into a 24 cm (9¹/₂ in), loose-bottomed tart case. Cut away the top sides, leaving a border rim of about 2 cm (³/₄ in) only. Set aside the remaining pastry.

Spread the jam onto the bottom of the uncooked pastry. It should be enough to sufficiently cover the bottom of the tart. Neatly fold down the 2 cm (³/₄ in) sides flat over the jam.

Divide the remaining pastry into 12 pieces. Roll out thin rope shapes using both hands on a work surface. Alternatively, roll out the pastry into a disc, and cut neat 2 cm (³/₄ in) strips. Lay the strips across the top of the jam in a criss-cross pattern, about six or seven one way and six or seven the other way. Cut away any pastry which extends over the tart. The jam will be exposed in places by small diamond- or square-shaped windows.

Mix the egg yolk with the milk and brush gently over the surface of the pastry.

Bake for about 30–35 minutes in the preheated oven or until the pastry is cooked and golden and the jam has darkened and is bubbling up.

Cool slightly before cutting. Serve slightly warm or at room temperature, on its own, or even with whipped cream.

Pinolata della nonna

Grandmother's pine-nut cake

This cake has an almost standard appearance in every trattoria. This version is the one that Nonna made which has a sweet pastry base, filled with pastry cream, and sprinkled with pine nuts. You can also add about 30 g (1 oz) of sultanas to the prepared pastry cream.

Makes one 24 cm (9¹/₂ in) tart

¹/₂ the quantity of sweet pastry* (see page 391)

¹/₂ the quantity of pastry cream* (see page 394)

1 egg yolk

2 teaspoons milk

40 g (¹/₄ cup) pine nuts (or other nuts)

Make the pastry following the instructions. Cover with plastic wrap and refrigerate for an hour.

Make the pastry cream following the instructions and set aside to cool. Preheat the oven to 180°C (350°F/Gas 4).

Roll out two-thirds of the pastry, following the instructions, and line a 24 cm (9¹/₂ in) round tart case (even a springform cake tin). Cut away the rim, leaving a 4 cm (1¹/₂ in) border up the sides of the tin. Pour the pastry cream into the centre leaving a slight rim around the edge.

Roll out the remaining pastry to make a disc to cover the top of the tart. Roll it up in the rolling pin and unroll it over the pastry cream. Fold the edges of the bottom layer of pastry onto the top disc and seal lightly with the prongs of a fork or with your fingers to enclose the pastry cream in the pastry. Prick the top of the pastry with a fork in a few places to allow steam to escape. Lightly whip the egg with the milk and brush over the top of the pastry.

Sprinkle the pine nuts over and brush again with the egg to make sure that the pine nuts stick. Bake in the preheated oven for about 40 minutes until the pastry is cooked through and the top is golden.

Cool before cutting into serving portions. Serve slightly warm or at room temperature.

Albicocche in sciroppo

Preserved apricots in sugar syrup

This is good to make if you ever have a few extra apricots. It is handy for those moments when you need something sweet, or for drop-in visitors. Naturally, the apricots can be eaten unpreserved — just simmer for a couple more minutes in the sugar syrup and leave out the preserving process. You might also like to add other flavourings to the sugar syrup, such as a vanilla bean. See also preserved plums* (see page 218). See note on preserving (page 400).

Makes 1.5 litres (6 cups)

1 kg (2 lb 4 oz) ripe, unblemished apricots

500 ml (2 cups) water

350 g (12 oz) caster (superfine) sugar

strip of lemon zest

Wash the apricots. Put the water with the sugar and lemon zest into a saucepan. Bring to the boil and boil for about 5 minutes.

Add the whole apricots, lower the heat and simmer for 5 minutes.

Remove from the heat. Slip the skins off the apricots — they should come away very easily. Pack the apricots into clean, sterilised jars and divide the syrup amongst the jars. Cool slightly and tightly seal the lids.

Put the jars into a large saucepan, cover with water and bring to the boil. Boil for 20 minutes, then turn off the heat and leave the jars to cool completely in the water. Make sure that a vacuum has been created on the lid.

They are ready to be eaten immediately, but will keep, stored for up to a year, in a cool, dark place. Once opened, keep in the refrigerator and consume quickly.

These are good served with ice-cream or whipped cream.

Gelato di albicocche

Apricot ice cream

It is possible to make ice cream without an ice-cream machine. The result will be slightly less light and creamy, but still very good. The procedure requires whisking by hand to break down the ice particles that form. You can make this using other fruits, as well, such as plums, cherries, peaches, apples, pears or raspberries, although you may have to vary the amount of sugar you add, depending on the fruit.

Makes about 1 litre (4 cups)

400 g (14 oz) ripe apricots

250 ml (1 cup) thick (single) cream

250 ml (1 cup) milk

200 g (7 oz) caster (superfine) sugar

Pit the apricots. Purée the apricots in a blender until they are completely smooth.

Whisk together the cream, milk and sugar until the sugar has dissolved. Whisk in the apricot purée and put the mixture into a bowl suitable for the freezer. Cover and put into the freezer.

After about an hour, remove the bowl from the freezer and give an energetic whisk with a hand or electric mixer and return it to the freezer. Whisk again after another couple of hours.

When it is nearly solid, give one last whisk and return it to the freezer to let it set until solid.

Alternatively, pour the mixture into your ice-cream machine and freeze, following the manufacturer's instructions.

Remove the ice cream from the freezer 5–10 minutes before serving to soften it slightly.

Marmellata di albicocche

Apricot jam

If you don't have a special jam saucepan, use a large heavy-bottomed non-corrosive pan (such as stainless steel). It is better to fill smaller and more jars with jam as, once opened, they must be kept in the refrigerator and consumed as soon as possible. See note on preserving (page 400).

Makes about 1.2 litres (42 fl oz)

1. 2 kg (2 lb 10 oz) ripe apricots

grated zest of 1 small lemon

250 ml (1/2 cup) water

550 g (1 lb 4 oz) caster (superfine) sugar

Wash the apricots, cut them into pieces and discard the pips. Put them into a saucepan with the lemon zest and water, and bring to the boil. Cook for about 15 minutes on a medium heat to soften. Add the sugar and continue cooking on a low heat for another hour or so, stirring frequently to prevent it from sticking. Some time toward the end of this cooking time, use a hand-held processor to purée if you like your jam smooth.

Remove from the heat. Test that your jam is ready by dropping a teaspoonful onto a plate. Tilt the plate slightly. The jam should not run down, but should rather slide down with a little resistance. If it is not ready, return the pan and heat for longer.

Pour the hot jam into clean, sterilised jars and close the lids tightly. Put the jars upright into a large saucepan, cover with cold water and bring to the boil. Boil for 20 minutes, remove from the heat and leave the jars to cool in the water before removing them. Check the lid to ensure that a vacuum has been created.

Alternatively, close the lids tightly and turn the jars upside down. Cover with a tea towel and leave the jars to cool completely. Check the lid to ensure that a vacuum has been created.

Store upright in a cool, dark place. The jam is ready to be eaten immediately, but will keep, stored, for up to a year.

JULY

There are plums, nectarines, melons, peaches and tomatoes bursting out everywhere. And green, unripe walnuts — some of which will end up in the wonderful liqueur Nocino. There are chillies, onions and celery to form the beginning of many dishes. Not unnoticed are the bright, mixed summer berries and the unbearably tempting smells of other people's barbecues, mingling with July heat and checked tablecloths.

On the weekends the cities are empty and the beaches swollen with fair-weather friends. Absent are the small children who have already been in June and will not return again until September. New ice-cream shops seem to have flung open their freshly-painted doors everywhere to keep up with the demand.

There are new mauve outbursts of fresh delight on the rosemary and lavender bushes and Armani-beige bundles of corn stacked up everywhere in the fields. But the prize this month must go to the leaves-you-breathless rows of sunflowers, standing tirelessly in the heat and diligently, pupil-like, facing the front.

Bruschetta al pomodoro

Tomato bruschetta

The time for plain bruschetta in Tuscany is November when the new olive oil is to be sampled and bread is sliced, grilled and drizzled with the oil that will last for the year ahead. This well-known bruschetta uses wonderful ripe tomatoes, garlic, basil and the best extra virgin olive oil. It is surprising how good tomato on a slice of bread can taste. Serve as an antipasto.

Serves 6

6 medium-sized, juicy tomatoes

6 basil leaves, roughly torn

1 teaspoon dried oregano (optional)

extra virgin olive oil

6 thick large slices of white, country-style bread

1 large garlic clove, peeled

Dice the tomatoes and put them into a bowl. Add the basil and the oregano, and season with salt and pepper. Mix through about 2 tablespoons of extra virgin olive oil.

Grill (broil) the bread slices on both sides, and rub one side of each with the whole garlic clove. Drizzle with a little olive oil. Divide the tomatoes between the bread slices. Add another generous drizzle of olive oil over each bruschetta and serve.

Frittata in pomodoro

Egg omelette in tomato

Here, the tomato, rather than being an ingredient in the omelette, serves as a vehicle for it. You can serve this as part of an antipasto or as a quick, light meal with bread and a green salad.

Serves 4–6

500 ml (2 cups) simple tomato sauce*
(see page 382)

6 eggs

2 tablespoons olive oil

about 80 g (³/4 cup) freshly grated Parmesan cheese

a few basil leaves, roughly torn

First make the tomato sauce and when it is ready, remove it from the heat.

Whip the eggs lightly in a bowl, seasoning them lightly with salt and pepper.

Heat a tablespoon of the oil in a non-stick 24 cm (9¹/2 in) saucepan suitable for omelettes, and pour in half of the egg mixture. Cook on a low heat for a couple of minutes, loosening the sides of the omelette and swirling the pan around to distribute the uncooked egg. When it is lightly golden on the underside and still slightly runny, begin rolling the omelette up in the pan, using a large fork or straight-bottomed wooden spoon.

Slide the rolled omelette onto a plate while you repeat the process for the other omelette.

Cut the omelettes up into 5 mm (¹/4 in) strips. Put the strips into the tomato sauce and return the saucepan to the stovetop for a minute, just to heat through. Serve warm, sprinkled with the Parmesan cheese and basil.

Pomodori con riso

Tomatoes stuffed with rice

There are a variety of tomatoes used in Tuscany. The salad tomato, with a pinky-green tone, is sometimes enjoyed slightly underripe. Plum tomatoes, or any very ripe tomatoes, are most often used to make sauces. For stuffing, large ripe, yet firm, tomatoes are selected. Serve these as an antipasto or as a side dish.

Serves 6

6 medium-sized ripe, round tomatoes

5 tablespoons olive oil

3 garlic cloves, peeled and finely chopped

250 g (9 oz) long-grain rice

250 ml (1 cup) water

1 small stalk of celery, trimmed and finely chopped

4 tablespoons grated Parmesan cheese

10 basil leaves, roughly chopped

breadcrumbs

Preheat the oven to 180°C (350°F/Gas 4). Slice off the tops of the tomatoes and set aside. Gently scoop out the flesh with a spoon, taking care not to break the tomatoes.

Put the tomato shells into an oven dish in a single layer. Lightly season inside and out, with salt.

Purée the flesh in a blender, or pass through a food mill and put into a bowl. Heat 2 tablespoons of the olive oil in a small saucepan with the garlic. Add the rice and half a cup of water. Add the celery and the puréed tomato, and season with salt and pepper. Cook for 10 minutes on a medium heat. Remove from the heat and stir in the Parmesan cheese and the basil.

Fill the tomato shells with the prepared mixture. The rice will swell a little, so do not overstuff the tomatoes. Replace the tomato tops and splash with the remaining olive oil. Sprinkle the tops with breadcrumbs.

Add the remaining half cup of water to the oven dish. Cook in the preheated oven for about 40 minutes, until the rice is cooked and most of the liquid has been absorbed and the outsides of the tomatoes are lightly golden.

Pomodori gratinati

Gratinéed tomatoes

Serves 6

6 large ripe plum tomatoes

3 tablespoons chopped parsley

1 garlic clove, peeled and chopped

10 mint leaves, chopped

10 basil leaves, chopped

Preheat the oven to 180°C (350°F/Gas 4).

Wash and dry the tomatoes. Halve them lengthways and, with a teaspoon, gently scoop out the flesh and seeds. Finely chop and put into a bowl. Put the tomato halves in an oven dish, cut side up. Lightly season with salt.

1 teaspoon dried oregano

1 tablespoon freshly grated Parmesan cheese

1 tablespoon grated pecorino cheese

1$^{1}/_{2}$ tablespoons fine breadcrumbs

8 tablespoons olive oil

To the bowl of tomato flesh, add the parsley, garlic, mint, basil and oregano. Stir in the grated cheeses, the breadcrumbs and 4 tablespoons of the olive oil. Season with salt and pepper, and mix through. Spoon the mixture into the tomato halves.

Drizzle with the remaining olive oil and put into the hot oven for 20–30 minutes or until they are lightly golden and cooked. Serve warm or at room temperature.

Prosciutto e melone

Prosciutto with melon

Serves 4

1 medium-sized ripe sweet melon (canteloupe), cold from the refrigerator

about 24 thin slices *prosciutto crudo*

This well-known combination hardly needs a recipe, but forms an integral part of antipasto tradition when melons are at their peak. The salty *prosciutto* mingles wonderfully with the melon's natural sugar, and is deliciously refreshing and light.

Cut the melon into half and scoop out the seeds. Cut wedges, then cut the flesh part away from the skin.

Divide the wedges amongst the plates and drape with the *prosciutto* slices. Serve with chilled white wine.

Spaghettini al pomodoro

Spaghettini with tomato sauce

A general standard for measuring a superb home cook is often their *pasta al pomodoro*.

As the diminuitive implies, spaghettini are thinner than spaghetti, and seem to be the favourite choice for a tomato sauce in many households.

Add a good tablespoon of butter to the pasta when mixing in the sauce — it makes a slight and delicious difference. If you prefer, drizzle a little olive oil over each portion to serve.

For an *arrabiata* (hot tomato sauce), add a little chilli to the tomato sauce while it's cooking, or drizzle a little chilli oil over the pasta to serve.

Serves 6

½ quantity, about
400 ml (14 fl oz), tomato
sauce*, (page 382 or 383)

500 g (1 lb 2 oz) spaghettini

1 tablespoon butter

about 120 g (1¼ cups)
freshly grated Parmesan
cheese

Make the tomato sauce.

Bring a large saucepan of salted water to the boil. Cook the spaghettini following the package instructions. If your tomato saucepan is not big enough, transfer the sauce to a bowl large enough to contain all the pasta, and keep it warm. Drain the pasta, reserving a little of the cooking water. Add the pasta (and butter) to the sauce, and mix through quickly, adding a few drops of the cooking water if necessary. Serve immediately with the Parmesan cheese.

Conserva di pomodori

Preserved tomatoes

Fresh tomatoes are preserved to use in months when they are not readily available. If you have many fresh, perfect tomatoes — you can preserve them for future use.

This quantity can be stored in one large jar, or in many smaller jars. When preserving you will probably be making more tomatoes than indicated in this recipe.

Make sure that each jar gets a garlic clove and a few basil leaves. If you use salt, don't add extra until you cook the tomatoes. See note on preserving (page 400).

Makes 1 litre (4 cups)

1 kg (2 lb 4 oz) ripe, unblemished tomatoes, skinned and left whole

a few basil leaves

2 or 3 garlic cloves, peeled and left whole

Pack the whole skinned tomatoes into clean, sterilised glass jars each with a few basil leaves, and a garlic clove. Gently push down the tomatoes with your hands, to fit them in. Close the jars tightly. Put the jars upright into a large saucepan and cover with water.

Bring to the boil, then boil for 20 minutes. Remove from the heat and let the jars cool completely before removing them from the water. Check that a vacuum has been created on the lids and store in a cool, dark place. The juice from the tomatoes will just about cover them. They will keep for many months. Once opened, store in the refrigerator and consume fairly quickly.

Spaghetti alla pescatora

Seafood spaghetti

Serves 6–8

500 g (1 lb 2 oz) clams

500 g (1 lb 2 oz) mussels

500 g (1 lb 2 oz) large prawns (shrimp)

500 g (1 lb 2 oz) calamari

125 ml (1/2 cup) olive oil

5 garlic cloves, peeled and finely chopped

30 g (1/2 cup) chopped parsley

375 ml (11/2 cups) white wine

500 g (1 lb 2 oz) spaghetti

Summer menus definitely offer many more fish and seafood choices. Here, the seafood is all cooked separately and tossed together at the last minute. Although this may seem unnecessary, it serves to keep all the seafood perfectly cooked and makes it a rather special dish. Have all your prepared, cleaned seafood ready and everything chopped up and weighed before you start cooking.

Soak the clams in lightly salted water. Change the water a few times and drain in a colander to get rid of any sand. Rinse and drain well.

Carefully wash the mussels in cold water, discarding any that are open. Scrub the shells and remove the beards with an up and down motion to pry them loose. Keep the cleaned mussels in a damp cloth in the refrigerator if you are preparing them ahead of time.

Remove the heads of the prawns and the shell, leaving on the tail and about 1 cm ($1/2$ in) of the shell. Cut a slit down the back of each prawn and, with a small sharp knife, remove the dark line of intestinal tract.

To clean the calamari, pull the tentacle part out of the body and pull out the transparent bone from the inside and discard. Rinse well under cold, running water. Hold the tentacles firmly with one hand, squeezing out the little beak bone and cut it away, leaving the tentacles whole or in halves. They should resemble a neat crown. Cut the body into rings.

Put 2 tablespoons of the olive oil into a saucepan, heat on the stovetop and add a quarter of the garlic and parsley. Tip in the cleaned mussels with 125 ml ($1/2$ cup) of wine and season lightly with salt and pepper.

Cook the mussels over a high heat with the lid on until all the shells open. Remove the saucepan from the heat. Discard any mussels which have remained tightly shut. Put another saucepan onto the stovetop and heat 2 tablespoons of olive oil. Add about a third of the remaining garlic and parsley, and repeat the same cooking process for the clams. When they are ready, remove the pan from the heat. When they have cooled slightly, remove about half of the clams and mussels from their shells, discarding the shells. Toss the molluscs back into the pans.

Combine the mussels and clams. Be sure to keep all the juice and stock (from all the cookings). Wipe out the free pan and heat another 2 tablespoons of olive oil with some garlic and parsley on the stovetop. Add the calamari and sauté for a few minutes before adding 125 ml ($1/2$ cup) of wine.

Cook for a few minutes more so that the calamari are cooked through and soft, and the wine reduces. Empty this into the clam and mussel pan.

Meanwhile, bring a large saucepan of salted water to boil and cook the spaghetti following the packet instructions.

Wipe out the calamari pan and add the remaining oil, parsley and garlic, and heat it up on the stovetop. Add the prawns and cook until they brighten and seem opaque. Add a splash of wine, season lightly with salt and pepper, and cook on a high heat until the wine evaporates. Unite the prawns with their fellow sea-mates and return the pan to the heat for a few minutes. Toss through.

Drain the spaghetti and toss into the pan, mix through and serve immediately with a splash of extra virgin olive oil or a light scattering of ground chilli.

Pappa con il pomodoro

Thick tomato and bread soup

Many Tuscans are satisfied with the simplicity of their wonderful ripe tomatoes — mixed with a little garlic, superb olive oil and their unsalted bread. The few ingredients in this recipe form the basis of many dishes in Tuscany. It is worth mentioning that the quality of your ingredients makes your finished dish, particularly in a recipe like this one.

You can cut the bread into squares the night before and leave out to dry on a tray, uncovered. Some people add a few whole cloves to the tomatoes in this recipe, which gives a rather interesting taste.

Serves 6–8

500 g (1 lb 2 oz) of 2-day old white country-style bread

5 tablespoons olive oil

4 garlic cloves, peeled and crushed

1 kg (2 lb 4 oz) fresh, very ripe tomatoes, skinned and cut into chunks or 800 g (1 lb 12 oz) tin of peeled tomatoes with juice, cut into chunks

1 small dried red chilli

about 1.5 litres (6 cups) hot water

about 12 large basil leaves, torn in half

extra virgin olive oil, to serve (about 2 tablespoons per serving)

Slice the bread and cut the slices into small squares if you haven't already done so.

Heat the olive oil in a saucepan large enough to eventually contain all the ingredients. Add the garlic and when it begins to sizzle and flavour the oil, add the tomatoes and the chilli. Season with salt and pepper.

Cook on a medium heat for 10–15 minutes, breaking up the tomatoes with a wooden spoon, until the tomatoes have thickened and melted into a sauce. Add the bread and stir with a wooden spoon to mix the flavours. Lower the heat and add the water.

Simmer for another 10–15 minutes, until the consistency is that of a thick, soupy stew. Adjust the consistency, if necessary, by adding more hot water.

Check the seasoning (your bread may be salted), and add more salt and pepper if necessary. Stir in the basil leaves and serve in large individual soup bowls, splashed with extra virgin olive oil.

Pollo alla diavola

Chargrilled chicken

You can cook this under the oven grill or on a barbecue. Make sure that the grill is very hot before putting the chicken into the oven. You can use any other herbs that you like in the marinade.

Serves 4

1 chicken, about 1.5 kg (3 lb 5 oz), insides removed

1 sprig of sage, leaves stripped off stalk

1 sprig of thyme, leaves stripped off stalk

125 ml (1/2 cup) olive oil

1 garlic clove, peeled and chopped

juice of 1 lemon

lemon wedges, to serve

Cut the chicken along the backbone. Open out the chicken to flatten it completely. Make slashes with a sharp knife across the thickest parts of the breast and thigh meat to ensure they cook through. Chop up the sage and thyme leaves. Make a marinade with the olive oil, garlic, lemon juice and the chopped herbs. Splash over the chicken. Season with salt and pepper and leave to marinate for about an hour.

Heat the coals. Shake off any excess marinade from the chicken and put it onto the grill. Turn over the chicken after 10–15 minutes and brush with a little marinade. The total cooking time should be about 30–40 minutes.

Brush or drizzle on more marinade throughout the cooking time. Test that it is done by inserting a skewer or a sharp knife into the thickest part of the meat. The juices should run clear, not pink. The outside should be dark golden and crispy. If necessary, grill for longer. Serve with extra lemon wedges.

Baccalà alla livornese

Salt cod with tomato

Baccalà is widely available and very appreciated in Mediterranean countries. Because this unsmoked cod has been preserved with salt, it needs to be thoroughly soaked and rinsed repeatedly to eliminate the salt (normally for about two days) before cooking. You may even find it pre-soaked.

Serves 4

2 tablespoons olive oil

1 white onion, peeled and finely chopped

2 garlic cloves, peeled and finely chopped

600 g (1 lb 5 oz) fresh tomatoes, skinned, or 500 g (1 lb 2 oz) tin of peeled tomatoes with juice, chopped

800 g (1 lb 12 oz) salt cod (baccalà), soaked for at least 24 hours in regularly changed cold water

flour for dusting the fish

250 ml (1 cup) light olive oil for shallow frying the fish

small handful of freshly chopped parsley

Heat the 2 tablespoons of olive oil in a saucepan and add the onion and the garlic and cook until they have softened. Add the tomatoes, season lightly with salt and pepper, and simmer for 20 minutes or until the tomatoes have melted into a sauce. Add about 375 ml (1 1/2 cups) of water to obtain a fairly liquid sauce.

Rinse the soaked salt cod and pat dry with paper towels. Cut into pieces of about 6 cm (2 1/2 in). Pat the fish pieces lightly in flour on all sides.

Heat the light olive oil in a saucepan and when it is hot, add the fish. Fry on both sides until golden and crispy. Remove to a plate lined with paper towels to absorb the excess oil.

Add the fish to the tomato pan and simmer for another 5 minutes. Scatter with the parsley and serve hot or at room temperature with a grinding of black pepper.

Scaloppine alla pizzaiola

Veal escalopes with tomato and mozzarella

A pizzaiola is a pizza maker, so any dishes that go by this name feature the basic pizza ingredients — mozzarella cheese, tomato and oregano.

In Italy, veal can be bought ready for *scaloppine*. They generally come from the tenderloin of milk-fed veal. Ask your butcher to cut thin 60 g (2¹/₄ oz) slices, or they can be cut thicker and gently pounded to flatten. Have your ingredients ready before you start, as this takes only a couple of minutes to cook. The recipe quantities here serve three. To serve more, you can cook the meat in batches and transfer to a plate to keep warm while cooking the rest. Wipe the pan clean and add fresh olive oil for the next batch.

Serves 3

250 ml (1 cup) fresh tomato sauce* (¹/₂ the quantity, see page 382)

1 teaspoon dried oregano

six 60–70 g (2¹/₄–2¹/₂ oz) slices of veal tenderloin, trimmed of fat

60 g (¹/₂ cup) flour for dusting the veal

4 tablespoons olive oil

125 g (4¹/₂ oz) mozzarella cheese, cut into 3 mm (¹/₈ in) slices

Prepare a smooth tomato sauce and stir in the oregano.

Gently pound the veal slices between two sheets of baking paper, if necessary, to a thickness of 3 mm (¹/₈ in). Season with salt and pepper and dust lightly in flour.

Heat the olive oil in a large, wide frying pan. Add the veal slices and on a medium-high heat, fry the slices for a minute or so on each side to brown lightly. Add the tomato sauce to the pan and top each piece of veal with one or two slices of mozzarella cheese. Turn the heat to low and cook through for a couple of minutes more until the mozzarella cheese softens and melts very slightly. Serve immediately.

Grigliata mista

Mixed chargrilled meats and vegetables

Serves 6–8

This is a very common sight and smell in the summer months. In winter, meat is often cooked in the open fireplaces inside country homes.

You may use any variety of meats for this dish. Cook the vegetables first and leave them to marinate in the olive oil and herbs while you grill the meat. The quantity of meat here should allow each person to taste each type of meat. Choose from the recipes that follow to make up your *grigliata mista*.

Melanzane alla griglia

Grilled eggplants

2 large eggplants (aubergines), sliced about 3 mm (1/8 in) thick horizontally

185 ml (3/4 cup) extra virgin olive oil

a small handful of chopped parsley

3 garlic cloves, peeled and lightly crushed with the flat of a knife blade

1 small dried, red chilli, crumbled

Put the eggplant slices in a colander. Sprinkle with salt and leave for about 30 minutes to allow the bitter juices to drain away. Rinse and pat dry.

When the coals are ready, put the eggplant slices onto a chargrill (griddle) about 20 cm (8 in) away from the coals. Grill for a few minutes on each side or until grill marks appear and the eggplant is cooked through. Transfer them to a plate with a slight rim. Splash with the olive oil and add the parsley, the garlic and the chilli. Season with salt and pepper. Mix through carefully. You can add even more olive oil, as any left over oil may be used afterwards for dipping bread into and dressing a salad or a pasta.

La carne

Zucchini alla griglia

Grilled zucchini

3 medium–large zucchini (courgettes)

125 ml (1/2 cup) extra virgin olive oil

2 garlic cloves, peeled and lightly crushed with the flat of a knife blade

about 6 basil leaves, roughly torn

Divide the zucchini into half horizontally, then cut into vertical slices about 3 mm (1/8 in) thick. Put them onto the chargrill (griddle) about 20 cm (8 in) away from the coals and grill for a couple of minutes on each side until they are cooked through and grill marks appear. Transfer them to a bowl. Add the olive oil, garlic, basil leaves and season with salt and pepper. Mix through. Add more olive oil if necessary.

The zucchini may be eaten immediately, or left to marinate for a few hours.

Peperoni alla griglia

Grilled capsicum

2 large yellow capsicums (peppers)

2 large red capsicums (peppers)

60 ml (1/4 cup) extra virgin olive oil

2 tablespoons baby capers in vinegar, drained

a small handful chopped fresh parsley

2 garlic cloves, peeled and lightly crushed with the flat of a knife blade

You can add one or two chopped anchovy fillets to the olive oil dressing, or a drop of balsamic vinegar.

Put the capsicum onto the chargrill (griddle) about 20 cm (8 in) away from the coals. Cook until the skins are blistering and quite charred in places. Transfer them to a bowl and cover the bowl with plastic wrap. Leave them for a few minutes. This will loosen their skins and make peeling easier. When they are cool enough to handle, remove their skins, inner fibres and seeds.

Cut them into long strips and put them into a bowl. Drizzle with the olive oil and add the capers, parsley and garlic cloves. Season with salt and pepper, and mix through. The capsicum may be eaten immediately or left to marinate for a couple of hours.

La carne

The meat

125 ml (1/2 cup) olive oil

juice of 1 lemon

2 garlic cloves, peeled and lightly crushed with the flat of a knife blade

a few sage leaves

1 sprig of rosemary

1.5 kg (3 lb 5 oz) pork ribs, halved (ask your butcher to halve them horizontally through the rack), and separated into individual ribs

300 g (10½ oz) fresh unsmoked *pancetta* (pork belly) in slices of about 3 mm (1/8 in)

6 Italian sausages, pricked with a fork

3 veal chops, about 220 g (8 oz) each

600 g (1 lb 5 oz) lamb chops

Make a marinade with the oil, lemon, garlic, sage leaves and rosemary sprig. Season with salt and pepper. When the coals are ready, begin adding the meats onto a chargrill (griddle) about 20 cm (8 in) away from the coals. Add as many as will fit comfortably, beginning with the sausages and the ribs, which will take the longest. Turn them over with a pair of tongs. The cooking time will vary, depending on the meat, its thickness and the heat and distance from the coals. Brush the marinade over the meats frequently and cook until the meats are browned on the outsides and done to your liking. Transfer the meats to a plate as they are ready.

Pile the mixed meats onto a serving platter and serve with extra lemon wedges.

Insalata mista

Mixed salad

Serves 8–10

1 sweet red onion, peeled and finely sliced

150 g (5¹/2 oz) red radicchio

150 g (5¹/2 oz) escarole

150 g (5¹/2 oz) rocket (arugula)

1 fennel bulb

2 stalks celery

150 g (5¹/2 oz) lamb's lettuce (mâche)

100 g (3¹/2 oz) curly endive (frisée)

150 g (5¹/2 oz) oakleaf lettuce

3 medium-sized tomatoes

about 125 ml (¹/2 cup) extra virgin olive oil

125 ml (¹/2 cup) balsamic vinegar

a small handful of chopped parsley

Salads are generally served to accompany a main course, particularly a main course that is considered quite heavy. In summer, they are always greatly appreciated, and consist of beautiful mixed leaves. This is just an example — you should use a mix of the various salad leaves that are available. You can use lemon juice instead of the vinegar, if you prefer.

Put the onion slices into a bowl, cover with cold water and sprinkle a little salt over.

Trim the radicchio and escarole of their stalk and any tough or damaged outer leaves. Break up into individual leaves and wash.

Trim the rocket of its extreme stalk end if it is hard, and wash. Trim the fennel of any damaged outer leaves and rinse. Rinse the celery and trim it. Spin the salad leaves dry or drain very well in a colander and pat dry.

Cut the tomatoes into chunks. Thinly slice the celery, and fennel and put into a large bowl. Break up the salad leaves into convenient pieces and add them to the bowl. If the rocket leaves are small, leave them whole. If not, break them up. Drain the onions, rinse, pat dry and add them too.

Add the olive oil, the vinegar, the parsley and season with salt and pepper.

Toss through and adjust any seasoning to taste. Serve immediately.

Patate al pomodoro

Potatoes cooked with tomato

The potatoes here are stewed on the stovetop in a little liquid with tomatoes and onions. They result in a deliciously soft and creamy texture.

Serves 6

6 tablespoons of olive oil

1 medium red onion, peeled and finely chopped

2 garlic cloves, peeled and lightly crushed with the flat of a large knife blade

7 medium-sized, ripe tomatoes, skinned and chopped

1/2 a small, dried red chilli, crumbled

about 6 basil leaves, roughly torn

1.5 kg (3 lb 5 oz) potatoes, peeled and cut into 3 cm (1 1/4 in) cubes

Heat the olive oil in a stockpot. Add the onion and garlic, and sauté until they soften and are just beginning to turn golden. Add the tomatoes, chilli and basil, and cook for about 15 minutes until the tomatoes have melted into a sauce. Mash them up with a wooden spoon if necessary.

Add the potatoes, season with salt and pepper and, with a wooden spoon, stir to coat them. Add about 4 cups of hot water and stir. Cover, and as soon as it comes to the boil, lower the heat and simmer for 20–30 minutes, stirring every now and then to prevent the potatoes from sticking. Take the lid off for the last 15 minutes or so of the cooking time. Add a little more water if necessary and adjust the seasoning. The potatoes should be soft, creamy, but still whole, and covered in a fairly thick sauce.

Serve hot or at room temperature.

Torta al burro con
pesca noce caramellate

Torta al burro con pesca noce caramellate

Butter cake with caramelised nectarines

This is a stunning, summer afternoon tea cake which goes equally well as a dessert. The combination of fruit, cream and sponge makes it an all-time favourite.

Makes one 24 cm (9¹/₂ in) cake

200 g (7 oz) butter, cut up into small pieces plus a little extra for greasing

220 g (8 oz) caster (superfine) sugar plus 8 tablespoons for the nectarines

grated zest of 1 small lemon

3 eggs

1 teaspoon vanilla essence

250 g (9 oz) of plain (all-purpose) flour plus a little extra for cake tin

1 teaspoon baking powder

170 ml (²/₃ cup) milk

4 medium-sized, firm, ripe nectarines

1 quantity mascarpone cream* (see page 398)

Preheat the oven to 180°C (350°F/Gas 4).

Put the butter into a bowl. Add the 220 g (8 oz) of caster sugar and the lemon zest, and whip until light and fluffy. Add the eggs one by one, whipping well after each addition and mix in the vanilla. Add the sifted flour and the baking powder, and mix. Add the milk and whisk to incorporate.

Butter and flour a 24 cm (9¹/₂ in) springform or 26 cm (10¹/₂ in) bundt (ring mould) cake tin. Pour in the mixture. Bake for 50–60 minutes, until the top is golden and crusty, and a skewer inserted comes out clean.

While the cake is baking, drop the nectarines into a saucepan of boiling water for a few seconds. Remove with a slotted spoon to a bowl of cold water. Slip off the skins and cut the nectarines into halves or quarters.

Heat a saucepan over a medium–high heat on the stovetop until it is hot. Add the nectarines and when they begin to colour, add the 8 tablespoons of sugar. Lower the heat slightly. Toss the nectarines with the sugar until they are golden and the sugar has caramelised. Remove from the heat.

Remove the cake from the oven. Gently loosen the sides of the cake. Leave to cool a little before removing the side of the cake tin. Serve warm or at room temperature, in slices with a nectarine or two, drizzled with caramel and a dollop of mascarpone cream.

Torta di susine

Plum cake

This is a lovely, very homemade looking cake, not too sweet, and bursting with plums. You can use another fruit if you prefer, perhaps apples, pears, cherries, bananas or peaches.

Makes one 24 cm (9¹/₂ in)
cake

10–12 medium-sized black
or red-skinned plums,
about 900 g (2 lb) total
weight

150 g (5¹/₂ oz) butter,
melted plus a little extra
for greasing

3 eggs

1 teaspoon vanilla essence

150 g (5¹/₂ oz) caster sugar
plus 2 tablespoons for
sprinkling on top of
the cake

250 g (9 oz) plain
(all-purpose) flour

1¹/₂ teaspoons baking
powder

125 ml (¹/₂ cup) milk

Preheat the oven to 180°C (350°F/Gas 4).

Wash the plums and cut them into halves or quarters —
removing and discarding the pips. Lightly grease a 24 cm (9¹/₂ in)
x 6 cm (2¹/₂ in) high springform cake tin with butter, then line with
baking paper, flattening it onto the bottom and sides of the tin as
closely as possible.

Put the eggs into a bowl with the vanilla and the 150 g
(5¹/₂ oz) of sugar, and whip until voluminous, pale and fluffy. Add
the sifted flour and baking powder, and mix to incorporate. Whisk
in the melted butter and the milk.

Put a few of the plums onto the bottom of the cake tin and
scrape out the batter over them. Tip the remaining plums over the
batter. Sprinkle the top with the remaining 2 tablespoons of sugar.

It may be a good idea to put a piece of foil or an oven tray
under your cake tin to collect any spillage. Bake in the hot oven for
about 1 hour or until the top is golden, a skewer inserted comes
out clean and some plum juice has begun to caramelise. Leave it
for a few minutes longer in the oven, if necessary. Remove from
the oven and cool before removing from the cake tin.

Serve plain, sprinkled with icing sugar or with a dollop of
fresh, lightly sweetened whipped cream or mascarpone cream*
(see page 398).

Sorbetto di melone

Melon sorbet

Although it is possible to freeze ice cream without an ice-cream machine, sorbets are not very successful done in this way. You can, however, put the mixture into the freezer and scrape down the frozen sides now and again. The result will be more of a granita than a smooth sorbet.

Makes about 1 litre (35 fl oz)

1 medium-sized, ripe, sweet melon, about 1.3 kg (3 lb)

125 g (4^1/$_2$ oz) caster (superfine) sugar

juice of 1 medium lemon

Halve the melon. Scoop out the seeds and discard. Cut the flesh away from the skins and put into a blender. Purée until completely smooth. Heat the sugar with the lemon juice to just dissolve it and remove from the heat. Mix into the melon purée.

Pour the mixture into your ice-cream machine and freeze, following the manufacturer's instructions. Store in a suitable, closed container in the deep freezer.

Remove from the freezer 5–10 minutes before serving to soften slightly.

pannacotta con
frutti di bosco

Pannacotta con frutti di bosco

Pannacotta with mixed berry salad

The pannacotta will set harder the longer it stays in the refrigerator. It can be served with caramel* (see page 396) or a little melted chocolate sauce instead of the berry salad. Substitute another liqueur for the Vin Santo in the berry salad, or leave it out altogether.

Makes 12 x 150 ml (5 fl oz) ramekins or 1 large mould

15 g (1/2 oz) gelatine (about 7 x 2 g leaves) or 1 tablespoon gelatine powder

500 ml (2 cups) milk

1 litre (4 cups) single cream

250 g (9 oz) caster (superfine) sugar

1 teaspoon vanilla essence

600 g (1 lb 5 oz) mixed berries (raspberries, blueberries, blackberries), wiped clean

2 tablespoons Vin Santo

Soak the gelatine leaves in a bowl with cold water until they soften. If you are using the powdered gelatine, soak it in a few tablespoons of cold water.

Heat the milk and cream in a saucepan with 150 g (5 1/2 oz) of the sugar and the vanilla until just at boiling point and remove from the heat.

Remove the softened gelatine leaves from the water with your hands and squeeze out the water. Add to the cream mixture, or add the powdered dissolved gelatine to the cream. Stir in to dissolve and leave it to cool for a while, stirring the mixture now and then. Ladle the mixture into individual moulds or ramekins, or into one large mould. Refrigerate for 3–4 hours before serving.

Put the berries into a non-corrosive (stainless steel) bowl. Splash with the Vin Santo and sprinkle with the remaining 100 g (3 1/2 oz) of sugar, (which you may have to adjust depending on the sweetness of the berries.) Refrigerate for at least an hour before serving.

To serve, dip the bottom of the moulds into hot water for a couple of seconds only. Gently loosen the sides of the pannacotta with a spoon, and invert into a dessert plate. Spoon over a few tablespoons of the berry salad and serve.

Pesche al vino bianco

Peaches in white wine

This is a very simple, refreshing dessert for those hot days when peaches are at the height of their season. You can also use nectarines, which needn't be peeled.

Serves 6–8

8 medium-sized, ripe, firm peaches, peeled

300 g (10½ oz) caster (superfine) sugar

500 ml (2 cups) chilled white wine

If you can halve the peaches and remove the stone without squashing the peaches before slicing them, then do so. If the peaches are a little soft, cut thick slices toward the stone, then cut those slices away from the stone. Put the slices into a bowl and sprinkle with the sugar. Cover and leave in the fridge to macerate for at least an hour or so.

Add the wine, gently toss the peaches and return to the fridge for another 15 minutes before eating the peaches and drinking the remaining wine.

Susine in sciroppo

Preserved plums in sugar syrup

When there are plums in abundance, preserves are made to keep for the months ahead when they are unavailable and to serve as a quick, delicious dessert on their own, or with vanilla ice cream* (see page 139). Of course, they can be eaten unpreserved as well — just simmer them for a couple more minutes in the syrup and omit the next step.

They can also be used to fill a baked tart case (pits removed), together with pastry cream. You can include flavourings, such as vanilla bean or lemon peel if you like. See note on preserving (page 400).

Makes about 1.5 litres
(6 cups)

1 kg (2 lb 4 oz)
unblemished, ripe plums

350 g (12 oz) caster
(superfine) sugar

500 ml (2 cups) water

Wash the plums. Put the sugar and the water into a large saucepan. Bring to the boil and boil for 5 minutes. Add the whole plums, lower the heat slightly and cook for 5 minutes.

Remove from the heat. Pack the plums into clean, sterilised jars and divide the syrup between the jars. Cool slightly and seal the lids tightly. Put the jars into a large pot and cover with water. Bring to the boil, then boil for 20 minutes.

Turn off the heat and leave the jars to cool completely in the water. Check that a vacuum has been created on the lid. Store in a cool, dark place.

Although they are ready to be eaten immediately, they will keep, stored, for up to a year. Once opened, keep them in the refrigerator. Serve warm or cold.

Marmellata di susine

Plum jam

If you don't have a special jam saucepan, use a large heavy-bottomed, non-corrosive (stainless steel) saucepan. It is better to fill smaller jars with jam, since once opened they must be kept in the refrigerator and consumed as soon as possible. If you like your jam very sweet, add a little more sugar to this recipe. See note on preserving (page 400).

Makes 1.2 litres (42 fl oz)

1.2 kg (2 lb 10 oz) plums

125 ml (1/2 cup) water

550 g (1 lb 4 oz) caster (superfine) sugar

grated zest of 1 lemon

Wash the plums, cut them into quarters and discard the pips.

Put them into a heavy-bottomed saucepan with the water and cook for about 15 minutes on a medium heat to soften. Stir with a wooden spoon to prevent the plums from sticking. Add the sugar and lemon zest then lower the heat and simmer for another hour, or until you have a thickened jam. Stir frequently to prevent sticking. If you like your jam smooth, use a hand-held blender to purée. Remove from the heat. You can check that the jam has reached the setting stage by dropping a teaspoonful onto a plate. Tilt the plate slightly — the jam should not run down, but should rather slide down with a little resistance. If it is not ready, return to the heat for a little longer.

Pour the jam into clean, sterilised jars and close the lids tightly. Put the jars upright into a large pot, cover with cold water and bring to the boil. Boil for 20 minutes, remove from the heat and leave the jars to cool in the water before removing them. Check the lid to ensure that a vacuum has been created.

Store upright in a cool, dark place. The jam is ready to be eaten immediately, but will keep, stored for up to a year.

Marmellata di melone

Melon jam

If you don't have a special jam saucepan, use a large
heavy-bottomed, non-corrosive (stainless steel) saucepan. It
is better to fill smaller jars with jam, since once opened they
must be kept in the refrigerator and consumed as soon as
possible. See note on preserving (page 400).

Makes about 1 litre
(4 cups)

1 kg (2 lb 4 oz) skinned
sweet melon (cantaloupe)

125 g (1/2 cup) water

700 g (1 lb 9 oz) caster
(superfine) sugar

juice of 2 lemons

grated zest of 2 lemons

1 tablespoon good-quality
brandy

Cut the melon into cubes and put them into a saucepan with the
water. Bring to the boil and cook for about 15 minutes to soften.

Add the sugar, lemon juice and zest. When it comes back
to the boil, lower the heat and simmer for another hour or so. Stir
frequently to prevent the jam from sticking. Some time towards the
end, purée with a hand-held blender for a smooth jam. You can
check that the jam has reached the setting stage by dropping a
teaspoonful onto a plate. Tilt the plate slightly — the jam should not
run down, but should rather slide down with a little resistance.
Cook for a little longer if necessary. Melon jam however, tends to
remain fairly thin. Add the brandy, simmer for another minute and
remove from the heat.

Pour the jam into clean, sterilised jars and close the lids
tightly. Put the jars upright into a large saucepan, cover with cold
water and bring to the boil. Boil for 20 minutes, remove from the
heat and leave the jars to cool in the water before removing them.
Check the lid to ensure that a vacuum has been created.
Alternatively, close the lids tightly and turn the jars upside down.
Cover with a tea towel and leave them to cool completely. Check
that a vacuum has been created on the lid.

Store upright in a cool, dark place. The jam is ready to be
eaten immediately, but will keep, stored, for up to a year.

AUGUST

Lying on the bed at night in underwear with the window shutter flung wide open, chancing that a bat should fly through. Children are sleeping around the house in mosquito nets. Looking forward to some cooler days.

We are carried to sleep by the sounds of the cicadas outside and wake up very early to beautiful sunshine falling through the windows everywhere.

This is HYPERBOLE. The maximum of produce and of heat.

Everyone seems to be escaping to the mountains to eat their salads, and excessively praising winter — expressions of their grass-is-always-greener longings. There is refreshing watermelon, which strangely seems to arrive just at the right moment. There are tri-coloured capsicums and cucumbers, cos lettuces and potatoes which we will see in some gnocchi form or other in the following winter months. There are cannellini beans to be used now and dried for the months ahead. There are almonds, hazelnuts and even the chillies are at the peak of their heat, and wild, drying Middle Eastern-smelling fennel flowers.
There are still so many tomatoes.

Acciughe sotto pesto

Anchovies in parsley and olive oil

These can be eaten immediately or left to marinate for a while before serving them as an antipasto or as a snack with bread. You can use any leftover oil for dressing a salad, boiled potatoes or vegetables.

Serves 6–8

200 g (7 oz) anchovies preserved in salt, or about 24 fillets in oil, drained

about 250 ml (1 cup) olive oil

30 g (1/2 cup) chopped parsley

1 small, dried, red chilli, crumbled

3 garlic cloves, peeled and lightly crushed with the flat of a large knife blade

Clean the anchovies (see page 402).

Put them into a jar or a fairly narrow container, where they will remain covered with the oil. Add the parsley, chilli, garlic and olive oil. Gently mix through.

Store, covered, in a cool place or in the refrigerator. They will keep for about a month as long as they remain completely covered with the oil.

Insalata mista con mele e noci

Mixed salad with apple and nuts

This salad could be served as an antipasto or as a healthy side dish to accompany a simple, summery grilled fish or chicken. The mixed fresh salad leaves, in their differing tastes and textures, need only be lightly coated with the olive oil and vinegar dressing. You can substitute the juice of about half a lemon for the balsamic vinegar.

Serves 6–8

1 large or 2 small green apples (such as Granny Smith)

150 g (5¹/2 oz) red radicchio

150 g (5¹/2 oz) escarole

150 g (5¹/2 oz) rocket (arugula)

150 g (5¹/2 oz) oakleaf lettuce or soft, green lettuce

60 g (¹/2 cup) shelled walnuts, roughly chopped and lightly toasted

60 g (¹/2 cup) shelled pine nuts, lightly toasted in the oven or in a dry frying pan

8 tablespoons extra virgin olive oil

about 2 tablespoons balsamic vinegar

about 30 g (¹/3 cup) Parmesan cheese shavings

Prepare a bowl of lightly salted, cold water with a few drops of lemon juice. Wash, core and halve the apple, leaving on the skin. Slice each half finely — into about 9 pieces. Drop the slices into the water.

Trim off the hard stalk of the radicchio and the escarole, and any tough or damaged outer leaves and discard. Separate all the leaves and wash in cold water. Trim off the tough extreme ends of the rocket and wash. Spin dry or drain very well in a colander. Tear up the leaves into large, convenient pieces.

Divide the mixed leaves between the plates. Add the walnuts, the pine nuts and the drained apple slices.

Mix the olive oil with the vinegar in a small bowl. Season lightly with salt and pepper, and drizzle 1¹/2 tablespoons of the dressing over each salad. Adjust any seasoning to suit your personal taste. Scatter with the Parmesan cheese shavings and serve immediately.

insalata mista con
mele e noci

Spaghettini aglio, olio e peperoncino

Spaghettini with garlic, olive oil and chilli

This is a quick, simple sauce, ready in the time that it takes to cook the spaghettini. You can add more or less garlic and chilli to suit your taste. This pasta is not always served with Parmesan cheese. Naturally, you can decide.

Serves 6

500 g (1 lb 2 oz) spaghettini

about 125 ml ($\frac{1}{2}$ cup) extra virgin olive oil

3 small, dried red chillies, crumbled

3 garlic cloves, peeled and finely chopped

a small handful of chopped fresh parsley

grated Parmesan cheese

Put a large saucepan of salted water to the boil. When it comes to the boil, add the pasta and cook, following the packet instructions.

Put the olive oil, chilli and garlic into a saucepan large enough to hold all of the pasta. Heat until the garlic and chilli begin to sizzle, and colour and flavour the oil. Remove the saucepan from the heat.

Drain the pasta reserving about 125 ml ($\frac{1}{2}$ cup) of the cooking water. Add the pasta to the oil with the parsley and the cooking water, tossing quickly to coat all of the pasta strands. Serve immediately, with Parmesan cheese and an extra drizzle of olive oil, if you like.

Rigatoni ai peperoni

Rigatoni with capsicum

Certain sauces are served with specific types of pasta, and this seems to be an innate understanding amongst Italians, without them ever having been briefed on the subject. Here, the large rigatoni stand up well to the capsicum pieces in the sauce.

A dash of cream is added just to bring the sauce together and to keep it light at the same time. You can make this sauce ahead of time and heat it up gently to serve.

Serves 6

2 medium-sized red capsicums (peppers)

1 medium yellow capsicum (pepper)

4 tablespoons olive oil

1 medium red onion, peeled and finely chopped

3 garlic cloves, peeled and finely chopped

4 medium-sized ripe tomatoes, skinned and puréed

A handful of freshly chopped parsley

500 g (1 lb 2 oz) rigatoni, penne or similar pasta

4 tablespoons thick (single) cream

About 6 basil leaves, roughly torn

about 120 g (1 1/4 cups) freshly grated Parmesan cheese

Wash the capsicum. Halve them and remove the seeds and membranes. Cut them into small chunks.

Heat the olive oil in a large saucepan and add the onion and the garlic. Sauté for a few minutes until softened, then add the tomatoes. When they begin to bubble up, add the peppers, and half of the chopped parsley and season with salt and pepper. Add about 250 ml (1 cup) of water and simmer, covered for 30–40 minutes or until the capsicum is very soft. Add a few more drops of water to prevent the sauce from drying out, if necessary.

Meanwhile, bring a large saucepan of salted water to boil for the pasta.

Remove the saucepan from the heat. Purée half of the capsicum sauce (or pass through the fine disc of a food mill) and return to the saucepan, leaving the rest of the capsicum as they are. Add the cream and heat through.

Cook the pasta in the boiling water following the packet instructions. Drain and quickly toss into the sauce. Mix through the remaining chopped parsley and the basil, and serve immediately, sprinkled with Parmesan.

Pappardelle con melanzane e peperoni

Pappardelle with eggplant and capsicum

Pappardelle are flat noodles about 3 cm (1¹/₄ in) wide and are quite well suited to chunky, robust sauces.

Serves 6

1 quantity of fresh pasta*
(see page 368)

1 small eggplant (aubergine)

1 yellow capsicum (pepper)

1 red capsicum (pepper)

2 salt-packed anchovies,
rinsed and filleted, or
4 fillets in olive oil

3 tablespoons olive oil

2 garlic cloves, peeled and
chopped

5 medium-sized, fresh
tomatoes, skinned and
cut into chunks or
400 g (14 oz) tin of peeled
tomatoes with juice, cut
into chunks

1 tablespoon capers in
vinegar, drained

about 6 basil leaves,
roughly torn

about 120 g (1¹/₄ cups)
freshly grated Parmesan
cheese, to serve

Make the pasta. Cover and leave it to rest for about 30 minutes at room temperature. Preheat the oven to 200°C (400°F/Gas 6). Rinse the eggplant, quarter it lengthways and cut into 5 mm (¹/₄ in) slices. Put the slices into a colander, sprinkle with a little salt, and leave for about 30 minutes to let the bitter juices drain away. Rinse and pat dry with paper towels.

Meanwhile, put the capsicum onto a baking tray and into the oven — until they are soft and blistered and have darkened in places. Put them in a plastic bag, close the bag and leave the capsicum to sweat for about 10 minutes. Remove the skins, inner seeds and fibres, and cut the capsicum into 1 cm (¹/₂ in) strips.

Roll out the pasta dough following the instructions. Roll up the pasta strips along their length and cut noodles at 3 cm (1¹/₄ in) intervals with a knife. Toss the pasta through your fingers to separate and place on a tray, sprinkled with flour, until needed.

Roughly chop the anchovies and set aside. Heat the oil and garlic in a large saucepan. Add the eggplant and tomatoes and cook on a medium heat for about 10 minutes. Add the capsicum, capers, anchovies and basil. Season with salt and pepper, and cook for a few more minutes.

Cook the pappardelle in boiling salted water for 3 minutes. Drain, saving some water, and put the pasta and the sauce into a bowl and toss to evenly coat the pasta. Add some water if it seems dry. Serve with black pepper and Parmesan cheese.

Filetti di sogliola ai pinoli

Fillets of fish with pine nuts

The Tuscan coast provides a good variety of fish and seafood that people inland also rely on. This is a quick, simple yet full-flavoured dish that takes only a few minutes to cook. The mixture of pine nuts, garlic, parsley and breadcrumbs complements the delicate character of flounder wonderfully.

Serves 2

1¹/₂ tablespoons chopped parsley

1¹/₂ tablespoons breadcrumbs

1 garlic clove, peeled and chopped

1¹/₂ tablespoons pine nuts

4 tablespoons olive oil

1 anchovy, cleaned and filleted, or 2 fillets in olive oil

2 flounders (soles), filleted

about 30 g (¹/₄ cup) plain (all-purpose) flour for dusting the fish

about 60 ml (¹/₄ cup) white wine

Mix the parsley, breadcrumbs, garlic and pine nuts together with 1 tablespoon of the olive oil in a bowl. Roughly chop the anchovy fillets and mix through.

Heat the remaining olive oil in a saucepan. Season the fish lightly with salt and pepper and dust in flour. Add the fish fillets to the saucepan and pan-fry for a minute or two on each side on a medium heat, until the fillets are very lightly golden. Add the wine with 125 ml (¹/₂ cup) of water and when it bubbles up, spoon the herb mixture over the fish fillets. Cover with a lid and cook for a minute or so to mix the flavours. Serve immediately.

Seppia sulla griglia

Grilled marinated squid

This can be cooked on a barbecue or in a hot griddle pan. It can be served as a light main course as indicated here, or in smaller quantities as an antipasto. This dish can be prepared ahead and left to marinate in the refrigerator. In this case, bring it back to room temperature before serving. If you are using a barbecue, the tentacle part of the squid may be difficult to cook unless you have a special rack. If not, you can save the tentacles for a pasta or risotto.

Serves 4

1 kg (2 lb 4 oz) small to medium-sized squid

juice of 1 lemon

about 125 ml (1/2 cup) olive oil

about 15 g (1/4 cup) chopped parsley

1 small garlic clove, peeled and chopped

1 small dried red chilli, crumbled

To clean the squid, pull the tentacle part out of the body. From the inside of the body cavity, pull out the transparent bone and discard. Rinse out well under cold water. Hold the tentacles firmly with one hand squeezing out the hard beak part and cut off at this point. The tentacle part should now resemble a neat crown. Rinse under cold water. Pat dry with kitchen paper.

Heat a griddle pan to fairly hot. Cook the squid until it has grill marks on the underside and is opaque white. Turn over to cook the other side.

Meanwhile, make a dressing with the lemon juice, olive oil, parsley, garlic and chilli in a bowl and season with salt and pepper.

Mix the cooked squid through the dressing. Serve, or leave to marinate for a while. Serve with bread and a salad, to dress with the leftover olive oil marinade.

Trota in forno con peperoni

Baked trout with capsicums

Whole trout, which will require slightly longer cooking time, looks good for serving, although fillets will be easier to serve. This dish is good served at any temperature.

Serves 6

2 medium-sized, red capsicums (peppers)

2 medium sized, yellow capsicums (peppers)

2 medium sized, green capsicums (peppers)

7 tablespoons olive oil

2 medium carrots, peeled and thinly sliced

1 large onion, thinly sliced

Six fillets of trout, about 150–180 g (5^1/2–6 oz) each, or 3 whole trouts, about 350 g (12 oz) each, cleaned and gutted

about 60 g (^{1}/2 cup) flour for dusting the fish

3 medium, ripe tomatoes, sliced

about 10 basil leaves

250 ml (1 cup) white wine

125 ml (^{1}/2 a cup) white wine vinegar

Preheat the oven to 190°C (375°F/Gas 5). Halve the peppers vertically. Remove the seeds and fibres and discard and slice the peppers into fine strips.

Heat 5 tablespoons of the olive oil in a large saucepan and add the peppers, the carrots and the onion. Cook on a medium heat, covered for about 15 minutes until they have softened. Add a few drops of water if necessary and season with salt and pepper.

If you are using trout fillets, trim them and remove all bones. Season lightly with salt and pepper and dust in flour.

Spoon half of the cooked vegetables into an oven dish. Put the trout in a single layer on top and scatter the remaining vegetables over them. Add the tomato slices, the basil, the remaining 2 tablespoons of olive oil and pour in the wine. Sprinkle lightly with salt and pepper. Cover the dish with aluminium foil and put into the hot oven for about 25 minutes. Remove the foil, drizzle the vinegar over the fish and vegetables and return to the oven for 10 minutes more.

Serve hot, at room temperature, or even cold.

Trota in forno
con peperoni

Carpaccio

Carpaccio

Thinly sliced raw beef fillet with rocket

Serves 6

about 700 g (1 lb 9 oz) beef fillet, trimmed of fat

3 lemons

extra virgin olive oil

2 tender inner celery stalks, finely sliced

120 g (4^1/$_2$ oz) rocket (arugula), trimmed of any tough stalks

at least 50 g (^{1}/$_2$ cup) Parmesan cheese shavings, made with a small sharp knife or potato peeler

Carpaccio refers to very thin slices of raw meat or fish dressed with lemon juice and olive oil. The lemon juice marinates the meat which is considered as "cooked" by the acid of the lemon. This dish can be served as an antipasto or as a light main course. In Italy, carpaccio can be bought ready to serve from the butcher's or the supermarket.

The carpaccio should be served about 1–2 mm (less than ^{1}/$_8$ in) thick. Sometimes the piece of fillet is seared in a very hot frying pan on all sides for a few seconds before slicing, which adds a slightly different flavour to the meat. Put the meat in the coldest part of the refrigerator for a while before cutting to facilitate slicing.

Cut the beef into the finest slices possible with a sharp knife. If they need to be thinner, put them between 2 pieces of waxed baking paper and flatten gently with your hand.

Put a few slices, about 120 g (4^1/$_2$ oz) per person, onto large serving plates and squeeze the juice of half a lemon over each serving.

Drizzle with olive oil, sprinkle with salt and pepper and leave it for a few minutes. Scatter the celery over the carpaccio, top with a little rocket and the Parmesan cheese. Serve.

Verdure miste arrosto

Mixed roasted vegetables

This colourful baked vegetable dish could accompany any main course or could even be served as a meal in itself, perhaps together with a few other side dishes. You can add a couple of whole garlic cloves, and any fresh herbs such as basil, parsley, mint or thyme to this dish before cooking.

Serves 6

1 large eggplant (aubergine)

2 medium zucchini (courgettes)

1 red capsicum (pepper)

2 medium potatoes, peeled

3 medium tomatoes

1 large red onion, peeled

8 tablespoons olive oil

Preheat the oven to 200°C (400°F/Gas 6).

Halve the eggplants lengthways and cut into 3 mm ($1/8$ in) slices. Put them into a colander, sprinkle with a little salt and leave them for their bitter juices to drain away while you prepare the rest.

Trim the zucchini and slice them into thin rounds slightly on the diagonal. Trim the capsicum and cut into thin rings. Slice the potatoes into thin rounds and slice the onions into thinner rounds. Cut the tomatoes into thicker rounds of about 5 mm ($1/4$ in).

Drizzle 2 tablespoons of the olive oil into a 30 x 40 cm (12 x 16 in) oven dish.

Make individual rows of the vegetables, alternating the colour, running along the width of the tray. Drizzle with the remaining olive oil and 185 ml ($3/4$ cup) of water. Season with salt and pepper. Alternatively, you can put all the vegetables into a large oven tray, add the oil, water and seasoning, and mix through to ensure all the vegetables get a coat of oil. Put into the hot oven for about 50–60 minutes, or until the vegetables are soft and the top is golden. Serve warm.

Fagioli cannellini all'olio

Cannellini beans with olive oil

Serves 6

500 g (1 lb 2 oz) fresh or dried cannellini beans (soaked overnight in cold water if dried)

1 red onion, peeled and chopped

2 garlic cloves, peeled

1 large carrot, peeled and chopped

1/2 a celery stalk, trimmed and chopped

10 sage leaves

1 bay leaf

3 tablespoons olive oil plus extra for serving

You can use fresh or dried cannellini beans for these recipes. Dried beans, however, will need a minimum of 12 hours of soaking and will require double the cooking time of fresh beans.

If you are using fresh cannellini beans, wash them in cold water. If they are dried, drain the previously soaked beans. Put them into a large saucepan and cover completely with cold water. Bring to the boil and skim the surface with a slotted spoon to remove any scum.

Add the rest of the ingredients. Lower the heat slightly and cook uncovered, for about 40 minutes for the fresh beans and 1 1/2 hours for the dried beans. Add more water during this cooking time to ensure that the beans are covered. Season with salt in the last 10 minutes of this cooking time.

Test to see if the beans are soft, if not, cook for longer. Drain the beans and serve hot, or at room temperature, drizzled with olive oil and a grinding of black pepper.

Fagioli cannellini all'uccelletto

Cannellini beans cooked in tomato

500 g (1 lb 2 oz) fresh or dried cannellini beans (soaked overnight in cold water if dried)

2 tablespoons of olive oil plus extra for serving

Follow the method above and cook the beans for about 40 minutes if fresh and 1 1/2 hours for dried beans. Test to see if they are soft, if not, cook longer.

about 10 sage leaves

2 garlic cloves, peeled and crushed

300 g (10½ oz) tomatoes, skinned and chopped

½ a small, dried red chilli, crumbled

Meanwhile, in a separate large saucepan, heat the olive oil and add the sage leaves and garlic. As soon as it starts to sizzle, add the tomato and the chilli. Season with salt and pepper and simmer for about 10 minutes. Drain the cannellini beans, reserving about 250 ml (1 cup) of their cooking water. Add the beans and the reserved water to the tomato pan. Simmer for another 15 minutes. There should be a little sauce, but it should not be too liquid. Serve hot or at room temperature with a drizzling of olive oil.

Peperonata

Stewed capsicums

Serves 6

3 large, red capsicums (peppers)

3 large, yellow capsicums (peppers)

3 tablespoons olive oil

1 medium onion, peeled and chopped

2 garlic cloves, peeled and chopped

3 medium-sized, ripe tomatoes, skinned and cut into chunks

5 basil leaves, roughly torn

This side dish can also be served as part of a mixed antipasto platter. Capsicums always pair beautifully with roast or grilled meats and fish. You can also add chopped anchovies, baby capers and chopped parsley to the finished dish.

Wash the capsicums. Slice them vertically in half and remove the seeds and fibres. Cut them into strips.

Heat the olive oil in a saucepan and sauté the onion until it is lightly golden. Add the garlic and sauté for another minute before adding the capsicums. Cook on a medium heat for 10–15 minutes to soften. Add the tomato chunks, season with salt and pepper and add 375 ml (1½ cups) of water. Simmer for another 40 minutes more on a low heat, stirring the capsicums occasionally. Add a little water if necessary. Remove from the heat and stir in the basil. Serve hot or at room temperature.

Peperoncini rossi sott' olio

Red chillies in olive oil

For those who like their food somewhat *piccante* (spicy), it is worth making a good amount of seasoned oil which will last a long time.

A teaspoonful or so of the oil (and a bit of the chilli itself) can be drizzled onto pasta, and over grilled meats or salads. The oil will initially be very hot, but as it is used it can be topped up with more olive oil and will eventually lose some of its potency. The flavour of the oil will depend entirely on the chillies used. The chillies in Tuscany are about 4 cm (1³/₄ in) long, and are not excessively hot.

Be sure to wear rubber gloves when handling the chillies, as just a little on your hands can prove to be uncomfortable even a few hours later. The method here, is more important than the quantities of chillies used, so adjust the amounts to suit.

about 40 fresh red chillies

about 375 ml (1¹/₂ cups) olive oil

Cut the chillies into thin rounds of about 2 mm (less than ¹/₈ in). Put them into a colander in the sink and remove as many of the seeds by tapping the colander sharply on the side of the sink. Sprinkle generously with salt and put a plate that fits into the inside of your colander on top of the chillies Set aside for about 24 hours.

Still using gloves, squeeze the chillies with your hands to drain away the excess salt and moisture and pack them into a clean, sterilised jar. Cover them completely with olive oil. The oil will be ready in a couple of days, but will be better in a couple of weeks. Add more olive oil if the chilli oil is too strong.

Store in a cool place. The chillies must remain covered with the oil at all times.

Sorbetto di cocomero

Watermelon sorbet

This is about the most refreshing thing that can happen to you on a hot day in August. Sorbets are dificult to make without an ice-cream machine. You can, however, succesfully make a granita-type of dessert. If you have an ice-cream machine, pour the mixture in and follow the manufacturer's instructions.

Makes about 1.5 litres
(6 cups)

750 g (1 lb 10 oz) skinned and deseeded watermelon

300 g (10½ oz) caster (superfine) sugar

500 ml (2 cups) water

juice of 2 lemons

In a blender, purée the watermelon until completely smooth. Simmer the sugar with 250 ml (1 cup) of the water in a saucepan to just dissolve. Remove from the heat, mix in the remaining water, lemon juice and watermelon purée. Put into a plastic bowl, cover and put into the freezer.

After an hour or two, remove the bowl from the freezer and, using a fork or spoon, break down the ice crystals that have formed. Return the bowl to the freezer. Repeat after a couple more hours or until you have a soft, frozen slush.

Alternatively, pour the mixture into your ice-cream machine and freeze, following the manufacturer's instructions.
Remove from the freezer to soften very slightly before serving.

Macedonia di frutta

Mixed fruit salad

The idea of serving a fruit salad may seem quite dull and outdated to many people. But try this as a simple, quick dessert or snack for a beautiful, summer day. It shouldn't be necessary to add any more sugar than indicated if your fruit is ripe and of the best quality. You may add or use whichever fresh fruits are in season.

Serves 6–8

2 bananas

juice of 1 orange

juice of 1 lemon

2 apples, peeled and cored

2 pears, peeled and cored

1 kiwi fruit, peeled

2 ripe nectarines

2 red or black-skinned plums

2 white peaches

100 g (3¹/2 oz) blackberries, rinsed

2 tablespoons caster (superfine) sugar

Peel the bananas and slice them into a large bowl. Add the lemon and orange juice. Cut up the apples, pears and the kiwi fruit into fairly thick but easy-to-eat slices and add to the bowl. Leave the skins on the nectarines, plums and peaches. Cut in 1 cm (¹/2 in) slices towards the stone, then cut the slices away from the stone. Add the slices to the bowl, then toss in the whole blackberries. Add the sugar, mix through and refrigerate for at least an hour before serving.

Serve alone, or with a vanilla ice cream* (see page 139).

SEPTEMBER

What a relief. The month of cooler days and beautiful light. September is here with its shortened days offering gorgeous ripe figs and the grapes which draw groups of people into the fields with harvesting shears. This is the perfect weather month with its cool nights and apple-and-pear-coloured aura. There are pomegranates, dark spinach, pale fennel and escarole greens, and sudden wild mushroom browns sprouting up everywhere after the first rains. Mushroom pickers keep their source a secret, but everyone is cooking mushrooms in one way or another.

Crostone ai funghi

Grilled bread with mushrooms

September is suddenly the time when every restaurant's menu is spilling over with mushrooms. They are in gorgeous baskets on display everywhere. Serve this as an antipasto.

Serves 6

600 g (1 lb 5 oz)
chanterelles, porcini or
other wild mushrooms

1–2 sprigs of thyme

2 garlic cloves, peeled,
1 chopped, the other left
whole

3 tablespoons olive oil plus
extra for drizzling

6 thick, large slices of white
country-style bread

3 tablespoons chopped
parsley

Wipe the mushrooms with a damp cloth or rinse them if necessary and pat dry. Slice them into chunks or leave them whole if they are small. Put them in a saucepan with the thyme, the chopped garlic and the olive oil, and sauté on a medium heat for a few minutes. Season with salt and pepper. Lower the heat and simmer for about 15 minutes. Add a few drops of water, if necessary, to prevent the mushrooms from drying out.

Grill the bread on both sides and rub one side with the whole, peeled garlic clove and put onto individual plates. Spoon the mushrooms on top of the bread and serve scattered with parsley and drizzled with olive oil.

Crostini con pere, gorgonzola e miele

Crostini with pears, gorgonzola and honey

Serves 4

6 slices of country-style
bread

1½ large ripe, firm pears

3 tablespoons caster
(superfine) sugar

1 tablespoon butter

about 150 g (5½ oz)
gorgonzola dolce (sweet)

about 4 teaspoons of honey

This interesting mixture of ripe pears and the sweet, yet sharp, gorgonzola is served on a piece of grilled bread and drizzled with a little honey as an antipasto.

Heat an oven grill (broiler). Toast the bread lightly, just to dry it on both sides and remove from the oven.

Peel the pear and halve it vertically. Core and divide each half into six or eight thin slices.

Put the sugar and butter in a saucepan on a medium heat, and add the pear slices. Sauté until the sugar begins to caramelise lightly and the pears are soft, but still in their slices.

There should be a bit of syrupy liquid with the pears. Add a few drops of water if there is no liquid in the pan.

Divide the gorgonzola and spread roughly over the already toasted bread slices, and return them to the oven to heat through and to just melt the gorgonzola.

Remove from the oven and put the bread onto serving plates. Top each with a few slices of pear and thinly drizzle about a flat teaspoon of honey over each — making long, thin lines of it rather than thick blobs. Cut the bread in halves on the diagonal, if the slices are large, and serve them at once with a grinding of black pepper.

Prosciutto con fichi

Prosciutto with figs

The *prosciutto* serves as a garnish to the beautiful ripeness of figs, repeating the sweet-salty combination so appreciated in Tuscany. You can also serve *prosciutto* with ripe nectarines or melon* (see page 189).

Serves 4

16 ripe figs, cold from the refrigerator

about 24 thin slices of *prosciutto crudo*

Peel the figs if their skins are hard. If not, just remove the hard stem. Slice them in half vertically, not completely through. Open them up and divide between the plates. Drape with the *prosciutto* slices.

Zuppa di funghi

Wild mushroom soup

Wonderful wooden boxes at the markets contain the variously coloured, fresh mushrooms which become soups such as these.

Carefully rinse the mushrooms and dry them with paper towels. Trim away any hard stem and slice finely or cut into small chunks.

Heat the olive oil in a saucepan and add the onion. Sauté on a low heat until it is very soft. Add the wine and when it has evaporated add the mushrooms and the sage, and sauté for a few minutes to colour them lightly. Add the hot stock and simmer for about 25 minutes or until the mushrooms are soft. Season with salt and pepper. Coarsely purée about a third of the soup and return it to the pan.

Toast or grill (broil) the bread slices on both sides and put a piece into each individual soup dish. Ladle the soup over the bread. Sprinkle with Parmesan cheese and drizzle lightly with olive oil.

Serves 6

1 kg (2 lb 4 oz) mixed wild mushrooms, such as porcini, ovuli, chanterelles

4 tablespoons olive oil plus extra for serving

1 medium white onion, peeled and finely chopped

250 ml (1 cup) white wine

1 small sprig of sage

1.5 litres (6 cups) vegetable stock* (see page 389)

6 thick slices of white, country-style bread

about 100 g (1 cup) freshly grated Parmesan cheese, to serve

Malfatti gratinati

Baked spinach dumplings

Serves 6–8

1 quantity of béchamel 1
sauce* (see page 380)

250 ml (1 cup) fresh tomato
sauce* (¹/2 the quantity,
see page 382)

1.2 kg (2 lb 10 oz)
fresh spinach, or
500 g (1 lb 2 oz)
cooked spinach

500 g (1 lb 2 oz) fresh
ricotta cheese

2 eggs, lightly beaten

100 g (1 cup) freshly grated
Parmesan cheese

nutmeg

a little butter for greasing

60 g (¹/2 cup) plain
(all-purpose) flour

Malfatti means badly made, so don't worry if your dumplings
all look different — that's how they should be. This will make
about 30 dumplings.

Prepare the béchamel using only 60 g (2¹/4 oz) of flour and set
aside. Prepare a smooth, fresh tomato sauce, puréeing it if
necessary, and set aside.

Clean the spinach and cook in boiling salted water for about
5 minutes. Drain, and when it has cooled, squeeze out the water
very well with your hands. This is important as extra water will make
it difficult for the dumplings to hold their shape.

Chop the spinach finely. Add the ricotta cheese, the eggs,
half of the Parmesan cheese and a grating of nutmeg. Season
with salt and pepper, and mix with a wooden spoon to make a
soft mass.

Preheat the oven to 180°C (350°F/Gas 4). Liberally butter
a large oven dish of substantial height, that will accommodate
30 dumplings and the béchamel. Dollop a little of the béchamel
onto the bottom of the oven dish to just cover it.

Put the flour onto a flat plate and pat your hands in the flour.
Using a tablespoon and your hands, form dumplings the size of a
small egg, slightly elongated. Dust them very lightly in the flour and
put them onto the béchamel in neat rows.

Cover with the remaining béchamel. Splash the surface with
the tomato sauce and sprinkle with the remaining Parmesan
cheese. Bake for 30 minutes, or until the top is lightly golden.
Serve hot.

Ravioli di spinaci con burro e salvia

Spinach ravioli with butter and sage

This is probably the standard filling for ravioli found in most of the trattorias here. The recipe makes about 25 large or 50 small ravioli.

Serves 6–8

1 quantity fresh pasta*
(see page 372)

Filling

About 800 g (1 lb 12 oz) fresh spinach, washed and trimmed, or 350 g (12 oz) cooked spinach

1 tablespoon butter

450 g (1 lb) fresh ricotta cheese

2 eggs, lightly beaten

50 g (1/2 cup) freshly grated Parmesan cheese

nutmeg

To serve

160 g (5³/4 oz) butter

about 20 sage leaves

about 100 g (1 cup) freshly grated Parmesan cheese

Make the pasta dough. Cover and leave it to rest at room temperature for about 30 minutes.

To make the filling, cook the spinach in lightly salted, boiling water for about 5 minutes. Drain well and when it has cooled a little, squeeze out the excess water. Melt the butter in a frying pan and sauté the spinach to dry it out. When it has cooled a little, chop it finely on a wooden board. Put the ricotta cheese into a large bowl. Add the eggs, the Parmesan cheese, salt and pepper and a generous grating of nutmeg. Add the spinach and mix well with a wooden spoon to form a smooth mass.

Divide the dough into eight pieces. Work with one at a time, covering the dough you are not working with to prevent it from drying out. Roll out the dough following the instructions, to the last setting. If the pasta strip is too long to work with, divide it into half lengthways.

Lightly sprinkle your work surface with flour and lay the pasta sheets down. Place about 1 heaped teaspoon of the spinach mixture at about 5 cm (2 in) intervals, in the centre along the length of the pasta strip. (Leave a border around each teaspoon of filling to seal and cut around it.) Using a pastry brush, pat a little water around the filling, so the top layer of pasta will stick to the bottom layer, thus enclosing the filling.

Fold over the dough from top to bottom, enclosing the filling. If your pasta strips are not wide enough, or you are making large ravioli, lay down one sheet of pasta, with larger spoons of mixture at intervals along the centre. Brush around the filling with water, and lay another sheet of pasta over it. Press down gently with your fingers to seal the dough at the edges and around the filling. Cut into individual ravioli squares or rounds if you prefer. Make sure that the edges are sealed. If not, brush with a little more water and press down with your fingers or with the prongs of a fork. Don't worry if they look uneven, as home-made ravioli often do. Put them onto a lightly floured tray. If you are not cooking them immediately, keep them in the refrigerator, covered, for a few hours. They can also be frozen at this point, in a single layer on a tray, then stacked into a suitable freezing container once they are frozen.

Bring a large saucepan of salted water to the boil, with a tablespoon of oil to prevent the pasta from sticking together. Carefully add the ravioli and cook for about 5 minutes, testing one to see if it is done. The border of the ravioli should be quite soft, but if it is left too long, the inside will soften too much and leak out. Lift them out with a slotted spoon, draining the water well and put onto serving plates. In a frying pan lightly sauté the sage leaves with the butter, just crisping the leaves, but not burning the butter. Drizzle the butter over the ravioli and scatter with a few of the sage leaves. Sprinkle with Parmesan cheese and serve immediately.

Ravioli di spinaci con
burro e salvia

Risotto ai funghi

Wild mushroom risotto

Dried wild mushrooms are often used with fresh mushrooms as they have a very concentrated flavour. But, depending on the flavour of the fresh mushrooms, it may not be necessary to use dried ones.

Serves 6

20 g (³/₄ oz) dried, wild mushrooms (optional)

300 g (10¹/₂ oz) fresh wild mushrooms such as porcini and chanterelles or 300 g (10¹/₂ oz) Swiss Brown mushrooms

1.5 litres (6 cups) vegetable stock* (see page 389) or water

4 tablespoons olive oil

1 large white onion, peeled and finely chopped

2 garlic cloves, peeled and finely chopped

2 sprigs of thyme, leaves stripped off stalk

250 ml (1 cup) white wine

500 g (1 lb 2 oz) risotto rice

50 g (1³/₄ oz) butter

50 g (¹/₂ cup) freshly grated Parmesan cheese plus extra for serving

a handful of chopped fresh parsley

Soak the dried mushrooms in 250 ml (1 cup) of warm water for about 10 minutes. Drain and chop the mushrooms into pieces. Strain the soaking liquid to add to the risotto. Rinse the fresh mushrooms if necessary and wipe them with paper towels. Slice them finely.

Heat the stock or water in a saucepan.

Heat the olive oil in a separate large, heavy-bottomed saucepan and lightly sauté the onion on a medium heat. When it has softened slightly, add the garlic, thyme and the fresh and dried mushrooms. Season with salt and pepper, and sauté for a few minutes to soften. Add the wine and when it has evaporated, add the rice, stirring to coat. Cook for a minute, lower the heat and add a ladleful or two of the hot stock, stirring with a wooden spoon. Add the mushroom water or 250 ml (1 cup) stock or water. When the stock has been absorbed, add another ladleful and continue stirring, taking care to gently move all the rice at the bottom of the pan so it doesn't stick.

After about 20 minutes, taste the rice, and adjust the seasoning, if necessary. The rice may need another 5 minutes or so. It should have a creamy, slightly liquid consistency but still be slightly firm to the bite. Add the butter, the Parmesan cheese and the chopped parsley and stir. Serve immediately with extra Parmesan cheese if you like.

Pici alla boscaiola

Pici pasta with porcini

Serves 6

1 quantity of pici pasta*
(see page 374)

10 g (¹/₄ oz) dried porcini
mushrooms or 40 g (1¹/₂ oz)
Swiss Brown mushrooms

400 g (14 oz) fresh porcini
or other wild mushrooms or
400 g (14 oz) Swiss Brown
mushrooms

4 tablespoons olive oil

about 8 sage leaves

2 garlic cloves, peeled and
crushed

1 large white onion, peeled
and chopped

150 g (5¹/₂ oz) unsmoked
pancetta (belly bacon),
diced

250 ml (1 cup) white wine

800 g (1 lb 12 oz) tin of
peeled tomatoes with juice,
puréed

1 small dried red chilli,
crumbled

about 120 g (1¹/₄ cups)
grated mature pecorino or
Parmesaṅ cheese

Around this time of year, it is common to see women in the
countryside rolling out these long, egg-free pasta strings that
are typically served with chunky sauces, such as this one.
Naturally, you can serve any pasta you like with this sauce,
although making pici can be fun especially if you've got friends
helping. If you do use another type of pasta, then you may
need a little less sauce.

Fresh mushrooms are used here, along with dried
mushrooms for their intense, concentrated flavour.

Make the pici pasta dough, cover and let it rest for about
30 minutes at room temperature.

Soak the dried mushrooms in 250 ml (1 cup) of warm water
for about 10 minutes. Strain the water to use in the sauce and
chop the mushrooms. If using Swiss Brown mushrooms don't
soak them, simply chop them up.

Wipe the fresh mushrooms with damp paper towels, or
rinse if necessary, pat dry and slice finely. Heat 2 tablespoons of
the olive oil in a frying pan. Add the sage and the garlic, and the
fresh mushrooms. Season lightly with salt and pepper. Sauté until
the water from the mushrooms has evaporated and they are lightly
golden. Remove from the heat.

Heat the remaining 2 tablespoons of olive oil in a separate
saucepan. Sauté the onion with the pancetta until golden and
then add the dried mushrooms. Add the wine and cook until
it has evaporated. Add the strained mushroom water or

250 ml (1 cup) water, the tomatoes, the chilli, and season with salt.

Simmer on a low heat for about 25 minutes, adding only a little water if necessary. Add the cooked mushrooms to the pan and cook for another 5 minutes or so to blend the flavours. Meanwhile, roll out the pasta following the instructions. Put the pasta strings onto a tray sprinkled lightly with flour or semolina and set aside until you are ready to cook them.

Put a large saucepan of salted water to the boil. When it comes to the boil, add the pasta and cook for about 7 minutes, testing one strand to see if it is ready. Cook longer if necessary.

Drain and toss into the saucepan if they fit, or mix the sauce and pasta together in a bowl. Serve into individual pasta bowls, sprinkled with the grated pecorino or Parmesan cheese.

Pici alla boscaiola

Calamari ripieni

Calamari ripieni

Stuffed calamari

Serves 6–8

8 medium-sized calamari, about 15 cm (6 in) in length, about 120 g (4½ oz) each

6 garlic cloves, peeled and finely chopped

30 g (½ cup) chopped parsley

3 salt-packed anchovies, cleaned and filleted, or 6 fillets in olive oil, drained and roughly chopped

100 g (3½ oz) small peeled prawns (shrimp), roughly chopped

8 tablespoons olive oil

150 g (5½ oz) breadcrumbs

2 eggs, lightly whisked

250 ml (1 cup) white wine

Preheat the oven to 200°C (400°F/Gas 6). To clean the calamari, pull the tentacle part out of the body. From the inside of the body, pull out the transparent bone and discard. Rinse well under cold running water. Hold the tentacles firmly with one hand, squeezing out the little beak bone and cut it away, leaving the tentacles whole. They should resemble a neat crown. Rinse.

Chop up the tentacles and put them in a bowl. Add the garlic, parsley, the chopped up anchovy fillets and the prawns. Season lightly with salt and pepper, depending on the saltiness of the anchovies, and add 5 tablespoons of the olive oil and the breadcrumbs. Mix in the eggs.

Stuff each calamari with the mixture to a couple of centimetres (just less than an inch) from its opening, pushing it in firmly with your hands or a teaspoon. Secure closed the top open part with a toothpick.

Heat the remaining 3 tablespoons of olive oil in a wide saucepan, preferably an ovenproof one. (If you don't have one, transfer the cooked contents of the frying pan to an oven dish.) Lightly brown the calamari on all sides. Add the wine, season lightly and continue cooking for a few minutes more, until some of the wine evaporates. Add about 250 ml (1 cup) of water and transfer the dish to a hot oven.

Cook for about 30 minutes, turning them over halfway. The calamari should be soft. Serve hot or cold, whole or in slices, as they are, or with a few drops of lemon juice.

Filetto con porcini

Fillet of beef with porcini

In Italy, porcini can be fairly large. Medium-sized ones are used here as one mushroom is served per person — the cap of the mushroom should have roughly the same diameter as that of the beef fillet. You may use two or three smaller mushrooms instead.

Nepitella is a herb found growing around mushrooms in their season and can be substituted with wild mint, sage or thyme.

Serves 6

6 medium-sized porcini mushrooms or 6 medium-sized field mushrooms

6 tablespoons olive oil

2 garlic cloves, peeled and crushed lightly with the flat of a knife blade

2 sprigs of *nepitella*, roughly chopped

6 slices of white country-style bread

1.2 kg (2 lb 10 oz) beef fillet, trimmed and divided into 6 equal portions

If the mushrooms are very sandy, wash and dry them well with paper towels as they tend to absorb a lot of water. If they are not very sandy, wipe them clean with a damp cloth. Separate the stalks from the caps and roughly chop the stalks, leaving the caps whole.

Heat 3 tablespoons of the olive oil in a frying pan and sauté the stalks with the garlic and *nepitella* for about 10 minutes on a medium heat. Add the mushroom caps to the pan, (in batches if necessary) and cook for another 10 minutes or so, until they are cooked on both sides, and begin to crisp on the outside. Season with salt and pepper.

Grill (broil) the bread on both sides and set aside. Heat the remaining 3 tablespoons of olive oil in a separate large frying pan and when it is hot, pan-fry the fillet about 3 minutes on each side for rare, and 5–6 minutes on each side for medium. Put a grilled piece of bread onto each serving plate. Add the fillet to the bread and top with a mushroom cap. Scatter the stalks around.

Drizzle with extra virgin olive oil and serve immediately.

Coniglio in agro-dolce

Stewed rabbit

This is a rich, interesting dish which works equally well with skinned chicken. *Agro-dolce* translates as sour-sweet and often means that a combination of sugar and vinegar are used in the preparation of the dish.

Serves 4

1 rabbit, about 1.4 kg (3 lb 3 oz), cleaned and cut into 8 pieces

500 ml (2 cups) red wine

1 onion, peeled and chopped

4 garlic cloves, peeled and chopped

3 bay leaves

4 tablespoons olive oil

2 tablespoons flour

500 ml (2 cups) vegetable stock* (see page 389) or water

2 tablespoons sugar

60 ml (1/4 cup) white wine vinegar

2 tablespoons sultanas

1 tablespoon pine nuts

Put the rabbit pieces into a bowl. Put the wine, onion, garlic cloves, bay leaves and a few black peppercorns into a saucepan and heat slightly without boiling. Pour this liquid over the rabbit, cover with plastic wrap and leave to marinate for 1 1/2 hours in the refrigerator.

Heat the olive oil in a large saucepan or stockpot. Remove the rabbit pieces from the marinade and add them to the saucepan. Sauté on both sides to brown lightly and seal in the juices. Sprinkle with the flour, then add the marinade liquid (together with the onions, garlic and spices). Season with salt and cook on a medium heat to reduce some of the liquid. Stir to prevent the rabbit or sauce from sticking. Add the hot stock (or water) and cover with a lid. Lower the heat to a minimum and continue cooking for 1 1/2 hours, or until the rabbit is very tender and there is still quite a bit of thickened sauce in the saucepan. If it seems like it needs more liquid, add a little more stock or water. Stir in the rabbit from time to time to ensure it doesn't stick.

Melt the sugar with the vinegar in a small saucepan. Boil for a couple of minutes and remove from the heat. Stir the sultanas and the pine nuts into the vinegar and pour this sauce into the rabbit saucepan. Cook through for a couple more minutes to mix the flavours.

Serve the rabbit hot or at room temperature with the sauce spooned over.

Coniglio in agro-dolce

Caccincco

Cacciucco

Mixed fish soup with tomato

This dish, which is the Italian version of French bouillabaisse, can be prepared any time, depending on the availability of fish. Generally, it can be served as a meal in itself with a mixed green salad, and some bread. If you intend to serve other dishes as well, these quantities will serve more than six. The separate preparation of all the fish may seem daunting, but the end result is a worthwhile, beautiful bowl of mixed seafood.

Serves 6

200 g (7 oz) small clams

200 g (7 oz) mussels

1 kg (2 lb 4 oz) sliced fish such as turbot, monkfish, halibut or similar, cut in 2 cm (3/4 in) thick slices

6 scampi (langoustines)

300 g (10 1/2 oz) calamari

300 g (10 1/2 oz) squid or cuttle-fish

one small octopus, about 350 g (12 oz)

800 g (1 lb 12 oz) soup fish with bones such as red mullet, sea-hen or similar, scaled and gutted

about 12 tablespoons olive oil

Soak the clams in lightly salted water. Change the water a few times and drain in a colander to get rid of any sand. Rinse and drain well.

Wash the mussels carefully in cold water, discarding any that are open. Scrub the shells and remove the beards with an up and down motion to pry them loose. Keep the cleaned mussels in a damp cloth in the refrigerator if you are preparing them ahead of time.

Remove the skin of the fish slices and remove any visible bones. Rinse the scampi.

To clean the calamari, pull the tentacle part out of the body. From the inside of the body, pull out the transparent bone and discard. Rinse well under cold running water. Hold the tentacles firmly with one hand, squeezing out the little beak bone and cut it away, leaving the tentacles whole. They should resemble a neat crown. Rinse. Cut the body part into rings of about 1.5 cm (5/8 in).

To clean the squid, pull the tentacle part out of the body. From the inside of the body cavity, pull out the transparent bone and discard. Rinse well under cold water. Hold the tentacles firmly

1 red onion, peeled and chopped

1 large carrot, peeled and chopped

1 stalk of celery, trimmed and chopped

500 ml (2 cups) white wine

700 g (1 lb 9 oz) fresh tomatoes, skinned and chopped, or 500 g (1 lb 2 oz) tin of tomatoes, with juice, chopped

about 3 small dried red chillies, crumbled

3 garlic cloves, peeled and chopped

about 15 g (^{1}/$_4$ cup) chopped parsley

12 slices of white, country-style bread

with one hand squeezing out the hard beak and cut off at this point. The tentacle part should now resemble a neat crown. Rinse under cold water. Cut the body into rings of about 1.5 cm (^{5}/$_8$ in) and the tentacles into chunks.

If your fishmonger has not already cleaned the octopus, then cut a slit through the head. Open it out flat and remove the innards and eyes, and the beak part. Rinse.

Put the octopus in a saucepan, cover with cold water and season lightly with salt. Cover and cook on a medium heat until the octopus is soft. Remove from the heat, drain and discard the cooking water and keep the cooked octopus aside. When it has cooled, cut into 1.5 cm (^{5}/$_8$ in) slices.

Cut the whole cleaned soup fish into large chunks to fit into a large saucepan. Heat 5 tablespoons of the olive oil in a large saucepan. Add the onion, carrot and celery, and sauté for a few minutes to soften. Add the pieces of soup fish and sauté for another few minutes. Add 60 ml (^{1}/$_2$ cup) white wine and when it evaporates, add the tomatoes and chilli to taste. Add 1.5 litres (6 cups) of water and season lightly with salt. Cook on a medium heat for 15 minutes. Pass through the medium-holed disc of a food mill, working it slowly. If you do not push hard, the bones should not strain through. It should be a dense stock. Alternatively, you can strain the stock through a large-holed wire sieve, pushing down with a wooden spoon to extract all the flavour and even some of the fish flesh.

Return the stock to the pan, discarding the solids left behind in the sieve or food mill.

Heat 3 tablespoons of the olive oil in a saucepan. Add a third of the chopped garlic and about a tablespoon of the chopped parsley. Add the squid and calamari and sauté for a few minutes on a medium heat. Add 125 ml ($1/2$ cup) of wine and a little salt, and sauté for another 5 minutes until the squid and calamari are cooked and soft. Add the langoustines and cook for a further 5 minutes, until they are opaque and the shells are brighter.

Remove from the heat and add the cooked, sliced octopus to this saucepan. Set aside.

Heat another 3 tablespoons of olive oil in another saucepan. Add a third of the garlic and about a tablespoon of the chopped parsley. Add the fish slices and sauté for a few minutes before adding 125 ml ($1/2$ cup) of wine. Season lightly with salt and cook for about 15 minutes on a medium heat, turning them over halfway. Remove from the heat and set aside.

Heat $1/2$ tablespoon of olive oil in another saucepan. Add half of the remaining garlic and a small handful of parsley. Add the mussels to the pan, a pinch of salt and 60 ml ($1/4$ cup) of wine. Cover and cook for 6–7 minutes until they open. Transfer the mussels to a bowl with their liquid. Discard any that remain tightly shut.

Heat $1/2$ tablespoon of olive oil to the same pot. Add the remaining garlic and a tablespoon of parsley. Add the clams, 60 ml ($1/4$ cup) of wine and season lightly with salt. Cover and cook for about 5 minutes or until they open. Remove from the heat. Discard the ones that remain tightly shut.

Heat the stock. Grill (broil) the bread on both sides. Add a piece of grilled bread to the bottom of each soup plate. Divide the fish slices, the calamari and squid, the octopus, clams and mussels between the plates. Top each with a langoustine and add a ladleful of the hot stock into each soup plate. Sprinkle each with a little parsley and serve immediately with the extra grilled bread.

Patate al finocchio

Potatoes with dried wild fennel flowers

Serves 6

6 tablespoons olive oil

3 garlic cloves, peeled and crushed with the flat of a large knife blade

about 5 sage leaves

1.5 kg (3 lb 5 oz) potatoes, peeled and cut into 3 cm (1 1/4 in) cubes

1 litre (4 cups) hot water

1 teaspoon dried, wild fennel flowers or
1 teaspoon whole fennel seeds, crushed

Dried wild fennel flowers, collected around August, have a wonderful taste and smell, different from fennel seeds. You can, however, substitute dried whole fennel seeds if you cannot find the wild flowers. Cooked in this way, the potatoes are soft and creamy, and make an excellent companion to pork and fish dishes.

Heat the olive oil in a stockpot. Add the garlic and, when it begins to sizzle, add the sage leaves. Sauté for another minute, then add the potatoes. Season with salt and pepper, and mix through. Add the hot water or stock and, when it comes to the boil, lower the heat slightly, cover the pot and simmer for 20–30 minutes.

Add the fennel halfway through and mix with a wooden spoon. Remove the lid in the last 15 minutes or so of the cooking time. Make sure there is enough liquid to prevent the potatoes from sticking, adding a little more, if necessary. Adjust the seasoning. The potatoes should still be whole, but creamy and covered with a thick sauce. Serve hot or at room temperature.

Finocchi gratinati

Baked fennel

Serves 6–8

5 medium-large fennel bulbs, washed and trimmed

about 60 g (1/2 cup) flour for dusting the fennel

120 g (41/2 oz) butter

375 ml (11/2 cups) milk

nutmeg

60 g (2/3 cup) freshly grated Parmesan cheese

The liquid formed here with the milk, butter and flour makes a type of rough-looking béchamel that tastes delicious.

Heat the oven to 180°C (350°F/Gas 4). Boil the whole fennel in lightly salted water for about 15 minutes or until they are soft, yet firm. Drain well and divide each one in half lengthways. Cut each half into 3–4 pieces vertically, so the pieces remain attached at the stem. Pat the pieces in flour. Grease an oven dish with a little of the butter. Put the fennel into the oven dish in a single layer. Season with a little more salt and pepper, and add the milk. Dot with the remaining butter and sprinkle with the Parmesan cheese. Grate over some nutmeg and bake for about 35 minutes, or until the top is golden with a little thickened sauce. Remove from the oven and serve hot or at room temperature.

Spinaci alla fiorentina

Sautéed spinach

Serves 6–8

250 ml (1 cup) béchamel 1* (about 1/4 of the recipe, see page 380)

1.5 kg (3 lb 5 oz) fresh spinach, washed and hard stalks removed

3 tablespoons olive oil

2 garlic cloves, peeled and chopped

80 g (1/2 cup) pine nuts, lightly toasted

40 g (1/3 cup) freshly grated Parmesan cheese

Make the béchamel sauce and set aside. Cook the spinach in boiling salted water for about 5 minutes. Drain well and chop finely.

Heat the olive oil in a saucepan. Add the garlic and as soon as it begins to sizzle, add the spinach. Lower the heat and cook for 5 or 10 minutes.

Add the béchamel, the pine nuts and the Parmesan cheese and heat through. Add a grinding of black pepper. Serve hot.

Finocchi gratinati

Funghi sott'olio

Mushrooms preserved in olive oil

This is ideal to make when mushrooms are plentiful. You can use one type of mushroom here, or a combination. Serve them as part of a mixed antipasto. See note on preserving (page 400).

Makes about three 330 ml (11 fl oz) preserving jars

1 kg (2 lb 4 oz) fresh wild mushrooms such as porcini, chanterelles or ovuli

500 ml (2 cups) white wine vinegar

250 ml (1 cup) white wine

a few sage leaves

a few small sprigs of rosemary

3 garlic cloves, peeled and left whole

3 small dried red chillies, left whole

a few bay leaves

olive oil to cover the mushrooms in the jars

Rinse the mushrooms and pat dry. Cut them into slices or chunks.

Put the vinegar, wine, sage and rosemary into a saucepan. Season well with salt and bring to the boil. Add the mushrooms (in batches if necessary). When the liquid comes back to the boil, wait 3 minutes, then lift out the mushrooms with a slotted spoon. Put them onto a clean, dry cloth and pat dry. Pack them into clean, sterilised jars with the garlic, chilli, whole peppercorns and bay leaves divided between the jars.

Completely cover with oil. Push the mushrooms down with a fork to force out any air bubbles and close the lid tightly.

Store in a cool, dark place. They will be ready in about 3 weeks but will last many months, provided they remain completely covered with the oil. Once opened, store in the refrigerator and consume quickly. The remaining oil can be used to dress salads and vegetables.

Torta di mele

Apple cake

This cake, which also works well with pears, is very simple and quick to make, and can be thrown together in no time at all. You might like to add a couple of tablespoons of Vin Santo or another liqueur to the batter. It doesn't keep very well, so make the cake the day you will eat it. Serve it on its own, or with some fresh, slightly sweetened whipped cream.

Makes one 24 cm (9½ in) cake

3 medium-sized apples (golden delicious)

a little lemon juice

2 eggs

100 g (3½ oz) caster (superfine) sugar plus 25 g (1 oz) for sprinkling

1 teaspoon vanilla essence

200 g (7 oz) plain (all-purpose) flour plus a little extra for greasing the tin

2 teaspoons baking powder

125 ml (½ cup) milk

3 tablespoons olive oil

25 g (1 oz) butter plus a little extra for greasing

Preheat the oven to 180°C (350°F/Gas 4). Peel and core the apples. Cut them in half, and cut the halves into slices of about 5 mm (¼ in). Sprinkle them with a little lemon juice while you prepare the cake batter.

Whip the eggs with the 100 g (3½ oz) of the sugar and the vanilla in a bowl until thick and creamy. Add the sifted flour and baking powder, and mix to incorporate. Add the milk and the olive oil, and stir to make a smooth batter.

Butter and flour a 24 cm (9½ in) cake tin and pour in the batter, which will spread to cover the bottom. Pat dry the apple slices and arrange them on top of the batter. Sprinkle with the remaining sugar and dot with the butter.

Bake for about 45 minutes or until the top is golden. The cake inside will be moist and spongy.

Serve the cake warm or at room temperature.

Torta di mele in camicia

Baked apple tart

Makes one 24 cm (9¹/₂ in) tart

¹/₂ the quantity of sweet pastry* (see page 391)

3 medium-sized apples (golden delicious)

a little lemon juice

3 tablespoons apple, quince* (see page 309) or apricot* (see page 181) jam

1 egg yolk

1 teaspoon milk

As its name indicates, these apples are clothed in a sheet, or "shirt", of pastry. The jam provides the right amount of sugar. Eat this slightly warm, either plain or with whipped cream.

Make the pastry following the instructions. Cover and leave the pastry to rest for 30–60 minutes before rolling out.

Peel, halve and core the apples. Cut each half into about eight slices. Sprinkle with a little lemon juice if you are preparing them ahead of time.

Preheat the oven to 180°C (350°F/Gas 4). Lightly sprinkle a work surface with flour. Roll out two-thirds of the pastry into a 3 mm (¹/₈ in) thick round slightly larger than the diameter of your tart case. Line a 24 cm (9¹/₂ in) round cake tin, pressing the pastry gently onto the bottom and sides. Neatly cut away around the sides to leave a rim of about 4 cm (1³/₄ in).

Spoon the jam onto the bottom of the tart and spread it with the back of the spoon. Lay the apples flat over the jam, overlapping the slices in a neat outer circle, then finishing off the apples with an inner circle.

Roll out the remaining pastry into a disc of 3 mm (¹/₈ in) to cover the top of the tart. Cover the top with the pastry. Roll down the outer pastry edges over the top layer, rolling them over to seal the two together and pressing down gently with your fingers. Cut two thin slits out from the top in the middle of the pastry to allow the steam to escape. Whip the egg yolk lightly with the milk and brush it onto the pastry.

Bake in the hot oven for about 35 minutes or until the top is crisp and golden. Cool slightly before cutting into servings.

Pastine di ricotta e marmellata

Jam-filled ricotta pastries

The pastry for these tarts contains no sugar, so these triangles rely on the jam filling and the dusting of icing sugar for their sweetness. You can use one or more home-made or bought jams for these pastries, which are lovely for breakfast, as a snack, or after a meal.

Makes 20–25 pastries

Pastry

200 g (7 oz) butter, softened

300 g (10¹/2 oz) fresh ricotta cheese

300 g (10¹/2 oz) plain (all-purpose) flour

1¹/2 teaspoons of baking powder

1 teaspoon of vanilla essence

Filling

about 300 g (10¹/2 oz) jam (see index for cherry, plum, apricot, etc. jam recipes)

icing (confectioners') sugar, to serve

Using a wooden spoon, combine the softened butter with the ricotta cheese in a bowl. Add the sifted flour, a pinch of salt, baking powder and the vanilla essence. Transfer to a work surface, and knead together with your hands until the mixture comes together in a soft mass. Cover the pastry with plastic wrap and refrigerate for 30–60 minutes before rolling it out.

Preheat the oven to 180°C (350°F/Gas 4). Roll out the pastry with a rolling pin, on a lightly floured surface, to a thickness of about 3 mm (¹/8 in) and cut into 10 cm (4 in) squares. Pat your hands into flour as you work if the pastry seems very wet.

Put a heaped teaspoon of the jam into the centre of each square, varying the flavours. Fold over the pastry square into triangles, pushing the borders down firmly with your fingers, or with the prongs of a fork to seal them.

Line an oven tray with a sheet of baking paper. Arrange the triangles on the tray and bake for 20–30 minutes, or until they are golden. Remove from the oven and cool slightly before serving.

Serve warm or at room temperature, dusted liberally with icing sugar.

Marmellata di fichi

Fig jam

This wonderful Mediterranean fruit makes its yearly debut around September and doesn't last all that long, so home cooks always make sure that some of the fruit is preserved for later months. Figs require less sugar than other fruits, as they are very sweet. Giovanna boils her figs in a little water, cools them slightly, then presses the figs through a very fine sieve to eliminate almost all of the seeds before continuing with her jam. See note on preserving (page 400).

Makes about 1.5 litres
(6 cups)

2 kg (4 lb 8 oz) ripe figs

250 ml (1 cup) water

800g (1 lb 12 oz) caster
(superfine) sugar

zest of 1 lemon, coarsely
chopped

juice of 1 lemon

Cut away the hard stem of the figs and peel away any blemishes. Put the figs into a non-corrosive pan with the water and cook on a medium heat for about 15 minutes to soften. Add the sugar and the lemon zest. Simmer on a low heat for another hour or so, stirring frequently to prevent the jam from sticking. The liquid should have reduced and the figs will have melted with the sugar into a soft, sticky mass. Purée with a hand-held blender to the consistency that you like and put the jam into clean, sterilised jars and close the lids tightly. Put the jars upright into a large saucepan, cover with cold water and bring to the boil. Boil for 20 minutes, remove from the heat and leave the jars to cool in the water before removing them. Check the lid to ensure that a vacuum has been created.

Alternatively, close the lids tightly and turn the jars upside down. Cover the jars with a tea towel and leave them to cool completely. Check that a vacuum has been created on the lid.

Store the jars upright in a cool, dark place. The jam is ready to be consumed immediately, but will keep for up to a year. Once opened, keep in the refrigerator and consume quickly.

Giovanna

Mandorlata
con fichi

Mandorlata con fichi

Fig tart with almonds

You could use another fruit in place of the figs, such as apples, apricots or cherries, and substitute any nuts you like for the almonds. This tart is best eaten the day it is made.

Makes one 26 cm (10^1/$_2$ in) tart

^{1}/$_2$ the quantity of sweet pastry* (see page 391)

10–12 ripe, firm figs

5 tablespoons fig* (see page 279), or apricot* (see page 181) or plum* (see page 219) jam

155 g (1 cup) skinned almonds, halved lengthways

3 tablespoons sugar

1 egg yolk

2 teaspoons milk

Make the pastry following the instructions. Cover and put it in the refrigerator for 30–60 minutes before rolling it out.

Preheat the oven to 180°C (350°F/Gas 4). Roll out the pastry into a loose-bottomed tart case of 26 cm (10^1/$_2$ in), following the instructions, and bake the pastry (partially) blind.

Trim the figs of their stalks and cut away any tough skin, if necessary, then halve the figs. Spoon the jam over the bottom of the cooked pastry, spreading it with the back of a spoon. Lay the figs, cut-side-up, over the jam. Scatter with the nuts and the sugar. Whip the yolk lightly with the milk and brush onto the visible pastry. Bake for 20–30 minutes or until the nuts are golden and the figs are lightly golden and soft.

Serve warm or at room temperature, plain or with whipped cream, or vanilla ice-cream*.

Schiacciata con l'uva

Flat, sweetened bread with grapes

This is a simple and very typical dessert, snack or breakfast bread which may seem a little unusual in flavour at first. In Tuscany, small black, sweet grapes with very small seeds are sold in September, especially for this bread. The grapes keep the bread moist.

Dough

25 g (1 oz) fresh yeast

a pinch of sugar

about 310 ml (1¼ cups) tepid water

500 g (1 lb 2 oz) bread flour

Top

4 tablespoons olive oil

500 g (1 lb 2 oz) small juicy black grapes, rinsed and most stalks removed

4 tablespoons sugar

Put the yeast into a small bowl with the pinch of sugar and the tepid water to activate.

Put the flour into a large, separate bowl or onto a work surface. Add the yeast mixture and the pinch of salt, and stir to incorporate. Knead the mixture by hand for 5–10 minutes, or until you have a smooth, compact dough, adding a few more drops of water or a little flour, if necessary. Put the dough into a bowl and cover with a cloth. Leave it in a warm place for 1½ hours or until the dough has doubled in size.

Use a large 30 x 40 cm (12 x 16 in) oven tray, with a 3 cm (1¼ in) high rim. Lightly oil the tray and spread the dough into the tray. You can make a rough rectangular or oval shape, or stretch the dough to reach into the corners of the tray. Scatter the grapes over the dough and sprinkle with the sugar. Drizzle with the olive oil and leave to rise in a warm place, uncovered, for about 30 minutes or until it has risen slightly.

Meanwhile, preheat the oven to 200°C (400°F/Gas 6). Bake the bread for 30–40 minutes in the hot oven, until the top is crusty and the grape juice has trickled through the bread. Remove from the oven and cool slightly before serving. Serve in pieces, warm or at room temperature.

schiacciata con l'uva

OCTOBER

The change is sudden — from one warm, sunny day to a frosty, grey shock. Summer clothes are swiftly packed into summer boxes or wardrobes, and people revert to socks and jackets overnight. Through the morning fog there are beautiful autumn colours everywhere that look like they've been touched up with children's crayons. There are dark greens, cooked quince reds and warm walnut tones, mixed with deep, pumpkin orange. There are special walks in the woods on warm weekend afternoons, and the days are becoming even shorter. We are at the beginning of the hunting season, which supplies wild boar, hare and other meats less available in other seasons.

Pane alle noci

Walnut bread

This is a wonderful, crunchy bread that you can serve in place of, or together with, other breads. Topped with a fried egg and a side salad, it makes a light, yet filling meal. It is also very good toasted and spread with a dollop of jam.

This will make 1 large or 2 smaller loaves. You can also make small, individual rolls if you prefer. You might want to make more than the quantities given here, and freeze a couple of loaves for future use.

Makes 1 large or 2 smaller loaves

25 g (1 oz) fresh yeast

a pinch of sugar

310 ml (1¼ cups) tepid water

500 g (1 lb 2 oz) bread flour

2 tablespoons olive oil

about 150g (1½ cups) shelled walnuts, halved

Put the yeast into a bowl with the pinch of sugar. Stir in the water and leave it to activate. Put the flour into a large, wide bowl, or onto a work surface. Add the yeast, ½ tablespoon of salt and the oil, and mix to incorporate. Knead the dough for about 10 minutes, until you have a smooth, compact, elastic ball. Add a little more flour or water, if necessary.

Put the dough into a bowl, cover with a cloth and leave it to rise in a warm place for about 1½ hours, or until it has doubled in size. Lightly dust your work surface with flour. Divide the dough into half or leave whole and shape each into ovals or rounds, working the walnuts into the dough.

Dust a baking tray with flour and put the bread loaves onto the baking tray. Cover with a cloth and leave in a warm place for 30–60 minutes, or until they have risen.

Meanwhile, preheat the oven to 200°C (400°F/Gas 6). Put the bread into the hot oven and bake for 30–40 minutes until the top is crusty and lightly golden. The bottom should sound hollow when tapped. Remove to a rack to cool.

Cozze gratinate

Gratinéed mussels

These mussels on the half shell have beautiful colours and are an interesting, elegant-as-mussels-can-be antipasto dish. You can prepare it ahead of time and refrigerate the already-filled mussel shells in a baking dish. Take them out of the refrigerator a little while before you gratinée them so they are not too cold.

Serves 6

1 kg (2 lb 4 oz) fresh mussels

1 medium bunch of parsley, leaves chopped

4 garlic cloves, peeled and chopped

100 g (1 cup) breadcrumbs

4 tablespoons olive oil plus a little extra

lemon wedges, to serve

Preheat the oven grill (broiler). Carefully wash the mussels in cold water, discarding any that are open. Scrub the shells and remove the beards with an up and down motion to pry them loose. Keep the cleaned mussels in a damp cloth in the refrigerator if you are preparing them a few hours ahead of time.

Put the mussels into a saucepan, cover and put over a high heat for a couple of minutes, to open them up. Remove from the heat. Open up the mussels and discard the empty side of the shell. Discard any shells that have remained tightly closed.

Make a mix with the parsley, garlic, breadcrumbs and olive oil, and season with salt and pepper. Using a teaspoon, cover each mussel in the shell with the mixture and put them in an oven tray. Drizzle with a little extra olive oil and bake for 5–10 minutes, or until they are lightly gratineed. Put them onto a large platter and serve immediately with the lemon wedges.

Zuppa di cozze

Mussels with tomato

This is so simple to make, and a heap of shiny, black mussels with a tomato and garlic sauce is always appreciated. Be sure to serve extra grilled garlic bread for soaking up the sauce.

Serves 6

1.5 kg (3 lb 5 oz) fresh mussels in their shells

3 tablespoons olive oil

3 garlic cloves, peeled and finely chopped plus 1 extra clove, peeled and left whole

1 small red, dried chilli, crumbled

1 small bunch of parsley, leaves chopped

200 g (7 oz) tin of peeled tomatoes, with juice, puréed

6 thick slices of white country-style bread

Wash the mussels carefully in cold water, discarding any that are open. Scrub the shells and remove the beards with an up and down motion to pry them loose. Keep the cleaned mussels in a damp cloth in the refrigerator if you are preparing them a few hours ahead of time.

Heat the olive oil in a saucepan large enough to hold all the mussels. Add the chopped garlic, the chilli and half of the chopped parsley. When you begin to smell the garlic, add the tomato and simmer for 5–10 minutes. Season with salt and pepper. Add the mussels, turn up the heat and cook, covered, for about 6 minutes or until all the shells open. Remove and discard any shells that remain tightly shut. Sprinkle on the remaining parsley.

Toast or grill (broil) the bread slices on both sides and rub one side of each with the whole garlic clove. Lay each slice into a soup plate, spoon over the mussels and their stock and serve immediately.

Ravioli di zucca con burro e salvia

Pumpkin ravioli with butter and sage

This is a common filling for ravioli in the autumn and winter months.

The amaretto biscuits in this recipe give the ravioli a very particular bitter-sweet flavour. The amount used may be adjusted according to personal taste. This recipe makes about 25 large or 50 small ravioli.

Serves 6–8

1 quantity of fresh pasta*
(see page 372)

Filling

about 1.3 kg (3 lb) pumpkin

a little olive oil for greasing

2 Italian sausages, about
80 g (3 oz) each, skinned
and crumbled

2 eggs, lightly beaten

nutmeg

100 g (1 cup) grated
Parmesan cheese

50 g (1 3/4 oz) Italian
amaretto biscuits, crushed

To serve

160 g (5 3/4 oz) butter

about 20 sage leaves

about 100 g (1 cup) freshly
grated Parmesan cheese

Preheat the oven to 200°C (400°F/Gas 6). Make the pasta dough following the instructions and leave it to rest, covered, at room temperature for about 30 minutes.

To make the filling, slice the pumpkin into pieces of about 1 cm (1/2 in) and remove the seeds. Put into an oven dish greased with a little olive oil and bake for 45–60 minutes, or until it is cooked through and golden. Cool slightly.

Pan-fry the sausage bits with a drop of oil until they are golden brown, breaking them up with a wooden spoon.

Scrape out the pumpkin into the saucepan and discard the skins. Sauté — to dry out the pumpkin — for 5 minutes or so. Put into a bowl to cool. Add the sausage meat, eggs, a generous grating of nutmeg, the Parmesan cheese and the crushed amaretti. Season with salt and pepper. Mix with a wooden spoon until the mixture is smooth and consistent.

Divide the dough into about eight pieces. Work with one at a time, covering the dough you are not using to prevent it from drying out. Roll out the dough following the instructions, to the last setting.

If the strip is too long to work with, divide it into half lengthways. Lay the pasta sheets out onto your lightly floured work surface. Put about 1 heaped teaspoon of the pumpkin mixture at about 5 cm (2 in) intervals, in the centre along the length of the pasta strip. (Leave a border around each teaspoon of filling, to seal and cut around it.) With a pastry brush, apply a little water around the filling, so the top layer of pasta will stick to the bottom layer, thus enclosing the filling. Fold the dough over from top to bottom, enclosing the filling.

Brush around the filling with water, and lay another sheet of pasta over it. Press down gently with your fingers to seal the dough at the edges and around the filling. Cut into individual ravioli squares or rounds if you prefer. Make sure that the edges are sealed. If not, brush with a little water and press down with your fingers or with the prongs of a fork. Don't worry if they look uneven, as home-made ravioli often do.

Put them onto a lightly floured tray. If you are not cooking them immediately, keep them covered in the refrigerator for a few hours. They can also be frozen at this point, in a single layer on a tray, and stacked up into a suitable freezing container once they are frozen.

Bring a large saucepan of salted water to boil with a tablespoon of oil to prevent the pasta from sticking together. Carefully add the ravioli and cook for about 5 minutes, testing one to see if it is done. The border of the ravioli should be quite soft, but if it is left too long, the inside will soften too much and leak out.

Lift the ravioli out with a slotted spoon, draining the water off well and put onto serving plates. Lightly sauté the sage leaves in a frying pan with the butter taking care not to burn the butter and to just crisp the leaves. Drizzle the butter over the ravioli and scatter with a few of the sage leaves. Sprinkle with Parmesan cheese and serve immediately.

Penne con la zucca

Penne with pumpkin

Pumpkins are used in a variety of dishes, including breads, jams, soups and pasta. Because they keep well once harvested, they are often present on Tuscan tables during the winter months.

Serves 6

3 tablespoons olive oil

1 medium onion, chopped finely

1 Italian sausage, about 80 g (3 oz), skin removed and crumbled or 80 g (3 oz) of unsmoked *pancetta*, chopped finely

300 g (10¹/₂ oz) skinned, cleaned pumpkin, peeled and sliced finely

400 g (14 oz) tin of peeled and puréed tomatoes with juice

¹/₂ small dried red chilli

500 g (1 lb 2 oz) penne or other short pasta

about 120 g (1¹/₄ cups) grated Parmesan cheese, to serve

Heat the olive oil in a saucepan and sauté the onion until it has softened. Add the sausage or pancetta and sauté until it has browned lightly.

Cut the pumpkin slices into small pieces of about 2 cm (³/₄ in) and add them to the pan. Add the tomato and chilli, and season with salt and pepper. Add about 750 ml (3 cups) of water and simmer for 30–40 minutes. The pumpkin should melt into the sauce a little and there should be enough liquid to coat the pasta. Add a little more water, if necessary, to prevent the sauce from sticking.

Bring a large saucepan of salted water to the boil. Cook the penne according to the packet instructions. Drain and mix into the sauce, tossing quickly to coat evenly. Put into individual pasta bowls and sprinkle with Parmesan cheese. Serve immediately.

Risotto con la zucca gialla

Pumpkin risotto

Serves 6

70 g (2¹/₂ oz) butter

1 large white onion, peeled and finely chopped

2 garlic cloves, peeled and finely chopped

1 small carrot, peeled and finely chopped

1 small stalk of celery, trimmed and finely chopped

70 g (2¹/₂ oz) unsmoked *pancetta*, diced

600 g (1 lb 5 oz) skinned and cleaned pumpkin, cut into small squares

1.5 litres (6 cups) meat stock* (see page 388)

500 g (1 lb 2 oz) risotto rice

250 ml (1 cup) white wine

a small handful of chopped parsley

50 g (¹/₂ cup) freshly grated Parmesan cheese plus extra for serving

Using meat or chicken stock as your cooking liquid here gives depth to this simple risotto dish.

Warm your stock on the stovetop.

Heat 40 g (1¹/₂ oz) of the butter in a large, heavy-bottomed saucepan suitable for making risotto. Stir in the onion, garlic, carrot, celery and pancetta. Sauté on a gentle heat until lightly golden.

Toss in the pumpkin and 250 ml (1 cup) of the stock or water and sauté for another 10 minutes to soften the pumpkin a little.

Add the rice and stir to coat. Cook for a minute or two and then add the wine. Season with salt and pepper. When it has evaporated, add a ladleful of hot broth and stir.

When it has been absorbed, add another ladleful and continue in this way, stirring to prevent the risotto from sticking. The total cooking time should be 20–25 minutes. After about 20 minutes, taste the rice. It should be soft yet firm, and the texture should be creamy and slightly liquid. You may have to continue cooking it for a few more minutes. If you run out of broth you can add some hot water.

Stir in the remaining butter, the parsley and the parmesan cheese. Serve immediately with extra parmesan and a grinding of black pepper.

Risotto nero

Squid-ink risotto

Serves 6

1.5 litres (6 cups) fish stock* (see page 386)

700 g (1 lb 9 oz) squid with their ink, or about 10 g (¹/₄ oz) of separate squid ink

4 tablespoons olive oil

1 medium white onion, peeled and finely chopped

3 garlic cloves, peeled

250 ml (1 cup) white wine

500 g (1 lb 2 oz) risotto rice

1 tablespoon tomato passata

¹/₂ a dried red chilli

50 g (1³/₄ oz) butter

a small bunch of parsley leaves, chopped

This is definitely a surprise if you've never seen it. A beautiful, interesting and striking black dish which always seems to prompt a few questions. It really does have something special and elegant about it, and those who overcome their nervousness about trying it will understand its secure position. There is a general Italian consensus that cheese is not served with fish or seafood pastas and risottos, but naturally you may decide to serve freshly grated Parmesan cheese.

Heat the fish stock in a saucepan on the stovetop.

To clean the squid, pull the tentacle part from the body and pull out the transparent bone from the cavity, and discard. Rinse well under cold water. Hold the tentacles firmly with one hand, squeezing out the hard beak and cut off at this point, carefully reserving the ink sacs in a small bowl. The tentacle part should now resemble a neat crown. Rinse under cold water. Cut the body part into thin rings and divide the tentacles into four.

Heat the olive oil in a large heavy-bottomed saucepan. Sauté the onion with some of the whole garlic until soft, then add the squid. Season with salt and pepper, and sauté until the liquid from the squid has evaporated. Remove the garlic and discard. Pour in the wine and let it evaporate before adding the rice. Stir to coat and let the rice cook for a minute. Add the tomato passata, the chilli and a couple of ladlefuls of hot stock. When the liquid has been absorbed, add more stock and keep stirring, making sure you move the rice at the bottom of the saucepan to prevent it from sticking. Continue adding hot stock as it is absorbed.

After about 10 minutes, add the reserved squid ink and cook for another 5–10 minutes before tasting the rice. It should be soft yet firm, and the texture should be creamy and slightly liquid. Cook for longer if necessary, adding hot water if you run out of stock. Check the seasoning and adjust if necessary. Stir in the butter and serve immediately, scattered with the remaining parsley and grated Parmesan cheese, if you like.

Risotto nero

Pollo alla chiantigiana

Chicken with red wine, pine nuts and sultanas

Alla chiantigiana refers to the Chianti wine used to cook the chicken here. Use a good red wine, if not a Chianti.

Serves 4

3 tablespoons olive oil

1 chicken, about 1.5 kg (3 lb 5 oz), interiors removed, rinsed, dried and cut into 8 serving pieces

1 medium onion, peeled and very finely chopped

1 medium carrot, peeled and very finely chopped

1 stalk of celery, trimmed and very finely chopped

2 bay leaves

1 small dried red chilli, crumbled

750 ml (3 cups) red wine

80 g (1/2 cup) pine nuts

60 g (1/2 cup) sultanas

about 8 sage leaves, chopped

Heat the olive oil in a large stockpot. Add the chicken pieces and brown on both sides.

Add the onion, carrot and celery and bay leaves, and sauté for a few more minutes to soften. Season with salt and pepper, and add the chilli. Add the wine, lower the heat and cook, uncovered for about 40 minutes.

Towards the end of this time, a lot of the wine will have evaporated. Add about 375 ml (1 1/2 cups) of water to keep the chicken moist and to maintain a bit of sauce in the pot all the time. Turn the chicken over a couple of times during the cooking. Add the pine nuts and sultanas, and cook for another 10 minutes or so to blend the flavours. Add a little more water, if necessary, to keep about a cup of sauce in the pot all the time.

Scatter with the chopped sage and serve.

Spezzatino di vitello con mele cotogne

Veal stew with quince

You can use beef, pork or even wild boar instead of the veal. The quinces may be cooked together with the veal from the beginning if you prefer, although their colour will be less intense and the fruit will be softer.

Serves 6–8

4 medium quinces

375 ml (1 1/2 cups) white wine

3 tablespoons olive oil

1.5 kg (3 lb 5 oz) deboned veal shoulder or shank, trimmed and cut into chunks of 5 cm (2 in)

1 onion, peeled and chopped

2 garlic cloves, peeled and chopped

1 large carrot, peeled and chopped

1 celery stalk, trimmed and chopped

1 small bunch of parsley, leaves chopped

a few juniper berries

about 1.5 litres (6 cups) water

Preheat the oven to 160°C (325°F/Gas 3). Peel and core the quinces with a small, sharp knife, taking care as they are very hard. Cut them into 2 cm (3/4 in) slices and put them into a roasting dish. Add 125 ml (1/2 cup) of white wine and 125 ml (1/2 cup) of water. Cover the dish with aluminium foil and cook for about 2 1/2 hours, turning the quinces over once. Add extra water as necessary to prevent them from sticking. The quinces should start becoming a beautiful, deep, pinky red colour towards the end of this time. Leave them a little longer, if necessary.

Heat 2 tablespoons of the olive oil in a stockpot over high heat. Add the meat, and brown lightly on all sides. Season with salt and pepper. Transfer the meat to a plate and add the onion, garlic, carrot, celery and parsley with the remaining tablespoon of oil to the pot. Sauté on a medium heat for a few minutes until softened.

Return the veal to the pot and add the juniper berries with the 250 ml (1 cup) of wine. Cook until most of it evaporates, then add the water. Cover the pot with a lid, lower the heat to a minimum, and simmer for about 1 hour. Remove the lid and simmer for another hour or until the veal is very tender with a bit of a thickened sauce. Add a bit more water, if necessary. Add the cooked quince slices to the veal pot and simmer for another 5 minutes to mix the flavours. Serve warm.

Fritto misto di carne e verdure

Mixed fried meats and vegetables

Serves 8

Meat batter

about 125 g (1 cup) plain (all-purpose) flour for dusting

160 g (2 cups) breadcrumbs

5 eggs

Vegetable batter

2 eggs

185 g (1 1/2 cups) plain (all-purpose) flour

250 ml (1 cup) cold sparkling water

300 g (10 1/2 oz) chicken breast, skinned and boned and cut into 2 x 4 cm (3/4 x 1 3/4 in) strips

300 g (10 1/2 oz) veal escalopes, cut into 4 cm (1 3/4 in) pieces

300 g (10 1/2 oz) saddle of rabbit, with bone, cut into 3 cm (1 1/4 in) pieces

300 g (10 1/2 oz) deboned pork loin slices, 3 mm (1/8 in) thick, cut into 3 cm (1 1/4 in) squares

300 g (10 1/2 oz) skinned pumpkin, cut into 5 mm x 3 cm (1/4 x 1 1/4 in) chunks

Here is an autumn version of the spring fish and vegetable *fritto misto** (see page 133). Fried food always seems to be a big success with any generation. This is a feast of various meats and vegetables which you may vary according to the season and your tastes. Here, the meats are dipped into egg, then patted into breadcrumbs, and the vegetables are dipped into a batter. You may also simply pat the meat and vegetables into flour, then egg before frying. The pieces should be dry before being dipped, then fried in hot olive oil, until they are golden and crispy on both sides. The sooner you eat them after they are fried, the better they will be — and you will have worked up an appetite after all this frying.

To make the meat batter, put the flour onto a seperate flat plate, the breadcrumbs onto a flat plate and whip the eggs lightly in a shallow bowl. Season the egg with salt and pepper. Set aside. To make a batter for the vegetables, whip the eggs in a bowl, add the flour and water, and season with salt and pepper. Whip lightly to a smooth consistency.

Pour enough oil into a deep frying pan to come about 3 cm (1 1/4 in) up the side. Heat the oil on a medium heat. Dust the meat with the flour on both sides, then dip into the egg. Shake off excess and pat into the breadcrumbs, pushing down with your palms or fingers to ensure they stick. Put the meat into the hot oil in batches, taking care not to overcrowd the pan. Fry until the pieces are cooked through and golden and crispy on both sides.

3 large potatoes, peeled, halved lengthways and cut into 2 cm (³/4 in) chips

300 g (10¹/2 oz) porcini mushrooms, wiped with a damp cloth and cut into chunks

20 large sage leaves

20 sprigs or leaves of flat-leaf (Italian) parsley

If the pieces seem like they are browning too quickly, turn down the heat. Using a slotted spoon, transfer the cooked meat to a large plate or tray lined with paper towel to absorb the excess oil. (It may be necessary to change the oil at some stage, if the crumbs left begin to burn.)

Dip the pumpkin, potato and porcini into the batter, in batches. Shake off the excess batter, and fry in the hot oil until cooked through and golden and crispy on both sides. Transfer the cooked vegetables to a plate or tray lined with paper towel.

Lastly, dip the sage leaves then the parsley leaves into the batter which will cook very quickly. Pile the meats and vegetables onto a clean serving platter. Sprinkle with salt and serve with lemon wedges.

Ossobuco in gremolata

Braised veal shin with parsley and lemon zest

This dish may be cooked in a stockpot on the stovetop. Alternatively, the meat may be browned first in a frying pan, then transferred to an oven dish and completed in the oven. The cooked veal shins are served with their marrow and sprinkled with a mixture of chopped parsley, garlic and lemon zest.

Serves 6

2 medium carrots, peeled

1 medium onion, peeled

1 celery stalk, washed and trimmed

5 tablespoons olive oil

6 large slices of veal shin with bone marrow, each about 2 cm (3/4 in) thick

about 60 g (1/2 cup) plain (all-purpose) flour for dusting the veal

250 ml (1 cup) red wine

500 ml (2 cups) water

Gremolata

zest of 1 lemon, finely chopped or grated

30 g (1/2 cup) finely chopped parsley

1 garlic clove, peeled and finely chopped

Preheat the oven to 160°C (325°F/Gas 3). Put the carrot, onion and celery into a blender or food processor and pulse chop until they are almost minced (or chop up very finely by hand). Heat 3 tablespoons of the olive oil in a saucepan, add the vegetables and sauté to soften them.

With kitchen scissors, snip at the very rounded edges of each ossobuco to prevent them from curling during cooking. Dust each one with flour on both sides. Heat the remaining 2 tablespoons of olive oil in a large saucepan and add the meat in a single layer. Brown on both sides, and season with salt and pepper. Add the wine and cook until most of it has evaporated.

If the ossobuco pan is unsuitable for oven use, transfer to an oven dish in a single layer, with the sautéed vegetables and the water. Cover the dish with aluminium foil, put into the hot oven and cook for about 2 1/2 hours, or until the meat is very tender. Remove the foil for the last half hour of cooking. Add a little more water during the cooking time if necessary to keep the meat just moist.

To make the gremolata, mix the ingredients together in a bowl. Serve the ossobuco hot or at room temperature with the sauce from the pan spooned over, and sprinkled with the gremolata.

Torta di ricotta

Ricotta tart

Ricotta is a soft, delicate cream cheese used in savoury and sweet dishes. To this are added the colourful jewels of candied citrus peel, which is sold in large, wonderful chunks of orange, lemon, lime and grapefruit. It is quite different from the more commonly found mixed, syrupy, candied fruits.

Makes one 26 cm (10½ in) cake

½ the quantity of sweet pastry* (see page 391)

500 ml (2 cups) pastry cream* (see page 394)

500 g (1 lb 2 oz) fresh ricotta cheese

50 g (⅓ cup) pine nuts

2 tablespoons good-quality brandy

70 g (2½ oz) mixed candied citrus peel (available from Italian delicatessens), cut into small pieces.

Make the pastry and let it rest for 30–60 minutes before rolling out. Make the pastry cream and set it aside. Preheat the oven to 180°C (350°F/Gas 4).

Roll out the pastry following the instructions into a 26 cm (10½ in) or even a 28 cm (11 in) springform tin with 6 cm (2½ in) high rim. Roll pastry to slightly larger than your cake tin, then gently roll up the pastry in your rolling pin and lower it over the tart case. Gently push the pastry against the sides to ensure it doesn't roll down. Trim the pastry to come about two-thirds of the way up your tin. Patch up with a bit of pastry where necessary and put the cake tin into the refrigerator while you prepare the filling. You can make some biscuits with any leftover pastry.

Whisk the ricotta into the slightly cooled pastry cream, mixing well to incorporate. Stir in the pine nuts, brandy and the citrus peel. Pour the mixture into the tart case and, working quickly with your fingers, roll down the rim of the pastry just a little — or neaten it using your fingers to make an even border. Bake in the preheated oven for 30–35 minutes until the ricotta cream is lightly golden on the top and set. The pastry should be golden and cooked through, and the sides will have set thicker.

Cool slightly before removing the rim of the tart case and cutting into portions. Serve warm or cold.

Crema caramellata

Cream caramel

Different versions of this seem to be a universal item on restaurant menus, varying the amounts of eggs, sugar and swapping some cream for the milk.

You can add a little liqueur to the custard before baking, or various flavourings, such as cinnamon or citrus zest, to the milk while it is warming. If so, strain the custard before baking it in the mould. You can bake the cream caramel in a 26 cm (10^1/$_2$ in) bundt (ring) mould, with 8 cm (3 in) high sides, or in several small ramekins.

Serves 8–10

Caramel

200 g (7 oz) sugar

a few drops of water

Custard

1 litre (4 cups) milk

150 g (5^1/$_2$ oz) sugar

1 teaspoon of vanilla essence

6 eggs

Preheat the oven to 180°C (350°F/Gas 4). To make the caramel, put the sugar and water into a heavy-bottomed saucepan on a high heat. As soon as the sides start to colour, lower the heat and swirl the pan around to distribute the heat. Watch the sugar carefully as it can burn in a second.

When the caramel is a rich, deep golden colour, remove it from the heat and immediately pour it into your mould tin. Holding it with a cloth, swirl the tin around to quickly distribute the caramel all over the entire bottom and a little up the sides. Take care as it sets quickly. Set the mould aside while you make the custard mixture.

Put the milk, sugar and vanilla into a saucepan to heat. Whisk the eggs lightly in a bowl until they are well combined. (Do not mix too much as this will result in a lot of froth later.) Just before the milk comes to the boil, remove it from the heat. Add a ladleful to the eggs to acclimatise them, and whisk to prevent them from cooking. Continue adding more milk, incorporating it all.

Pour carefully onto the caramel and bake in a bain-marie for 50–60 minutes in the centre of the oven until the top is golden in parts, quite set but still a little wobbly. Remove from the oven and from the water bath, and leave to cool. Cover with cling film and refrigerate for a few hours or preferably overnight before serving.

Gently loosen the top sides of the cream caramel with the back of a spoon or your fingers. Put a large serving dish (with a slight rim to contain the caramel juice) upside down over your pudding. Holding the plate and cake tin firmly with your fingers, carefully and quickly flip them over, so that the plate is the right way up and the pudding plops gently down with the caramel sauce. Serve thick slices with the caramel spooned over.

Marmellata di zucca

Pumpkin jam

Makes just under 1 litre
(4 cups)

1 kg (2 lb 4 oz) cleaned,
skinned pumpkin

juice of 2 lemons

700 g (1 lb 9 oz) caster
(superfine) sugar

grated zest of 1 lemon

This is an unusual jam which you can spice up by adding some cinnamon or a couple of cloves, half a vanilla bean or perhaps a splash of brandy.

If you don't have a special jam saucepan, use a large heavy-bottomed, non-corrosive (stainless steel) pan. It is better to fill smaller jars with jam, since once opened they must be kept in the refrigerator and consumed as soon as possible. See note on preserving (page 400).

Cut the pumpkin into small pieces. Put them into a saucepan with the lemon juice and sugar. Cook for about 45 minutes on a low heat, stirring now and again to prevent the mixture from sticking.

Towards the end of this cooking time, purée the mixture with a hand-held blender. Add the lemon zest and simmer for another 20–30 minutes, or until you have a thickened jam. Stir frequently to prevent it from sticking.

Remove from the heat. You can check that the jam has reached the setting stage by dropping a teaspoonful onto a plate. Tilt the plate slightly. The jam should not run down, but should rather slide down with a little resistance. If it is not ready, return it to the heat for longer.

Pour the jam into clean, sterilised jars and close the lids tightly. Put the jars upright into a large saucepan, cover with cold water and bring to the boil. Boil for 20 minutes, turn off the heat and leave the jars to cool in the water before removing them. Check the lid to ensure that a vacuum has been created.

Alternatively, close the lids tightly and turn the jars upside down. Cover the jars with a tea towel and leave them to cool completely. Check the lid to see that a vacuum has been created.

Store upright in a cool, dark place. The jam is ready to be eaten immediately, but will keep, stored, for up to a year. Once opened, keep in the refrigerator.

Marmellata di mele cotogne

Quince jam

This gorgeous fruit makes any difficulty in handling it worthwhile. It is hard not to be charmed by quinces, once you have witnessed the magical colour transformation that occurs during the cooking process.

This jam includes a couple of pears to maintain a jam consistency, but not to render the flavour unrecognisable.

You can, however, use only quinces, substituting the pears with extra quinces, and make a firmer quince preserve.

A small heap of this jam served with a slice of very fresh ricotta cheese is worth trying. See note on preserving (page 400).

Makes 1 litre (4 cups)

900 g (2 lb) ripe quinces

250 ml (1 cup) red wine

400 g (14 oz) ripe pears (about 2 pears)

1 litre (4 cups) water

500 g (1 lb 2 oz) caster (superfine) sugar

juice of 1 lemon

zest of 1 lemon, chopped

Wash the quinces and dry them with a cloth to wipe away any fur. Cut them into quarters, taking care with the knife as they are generally hard. Leave the skins on but remove the cores. Put them into a non-corrosive saucepan with the wine and let it reduce a little. Peel and core the pears and add them to the pan with the water, the sugar and the lemon juice and zest, and bring to the boil. Lower the heat slightly and cook for about an hour, or until there is only a bit of thickened, syrupy liquid in the pan. Add 500 ml (2 cups) more of hot water and purée the quinces with a hand held blender. Return the pan to the heat and simmer for another 30–40 minutes, or until the jam has thickened, and is a deep red colour. Spoon a little jam onto a plate and tilt the plate slightly. The jam should slide down with a little resistance. If it is ready remove the pan from the heat.

Spoon into clean, sterilised jars and close the lids tightly. Put the jars into a large saucepan, cover with cold water and bring to the boil. Boil for 20 minutes, remove from the heat and leave the jars to cool in the water before removing them. Check the lid to ensure that a vacuum has been created.

Alternatively, close the lids tightly and turn the jars upside down. Cover with a tea towel and leave them to cool completely. Check the lid to see that a vacuum has been created.

Store the jars upright in a cool, dark place. The jam is ready to be eaten immediately, but will keep, stored, for up to a year. Once opened, keep in the refrigerator.

NOVEMBER

As it starts getting colder, the lessening of ingredients becomes noticeable — although this month still holds some beautiful gifts. There are chestnuts, sold roasted in small white paper packets in the streets. There are marvellous olives, brussels sprouts and the beautiful, rare elegance of truffles. There are cabbages, baby onions, cauliflowers and newborn bottles of jade and amber olive oil. This year's new wine is already on the table, and people are planning meals around November's few and special ingredients.

Crostone di cavolo

Grilled bread with braised cabbage

Different types of cabbages are used for this dish, ranging from red or pale green to the darker green of the typical *cavolo nero*. Boiling the cabbage for a few minutes helps to make it easier to digest.

Serves 6

1 medium cabbage, such as Savoy, about 800 g (1 lb 12 oz)

4 tablespoons olive oil

1 sprig of rosemary

3 garlic cloves, peeled, and 2 of them crushed with the flat of a large knife blade

1 small dried red chilli, crumbled

6 large, thick slices of white country-style bread

extra virgin olive oil, to serve

Bring a large saucepan of lightly salted water to boil. Wash and trim the cabbage, discarding any damaged leaves and cut into thin strips. Boil the cabbage in the water for about 5 minutes. Drain and discard the water.

Heat the oil in a large saucepan. Add the rosemary sprig and sauté for a few minutes to flavour the oil. Remove the rosemary and discard. Add the 2 garlic cloves and the chilli to the pan, then the cabbage. Season with salt and pepper. Add 750 ml (3 cups) of water, cover and cook on a low heat for an hour, stirring from time to time. Add a little more water if necessary to keep the cabbage moist, but not drowning in liquid.

Grill the bread slices on both sides and rub one side with the remaining peeled garlic clove. Cover each bread slice generously with the cabbage. Serve warm with a good drizzle of extra virgin olive oil.

Uova con tartufi

Eggs with truffle

Truffles discreetly find their way into the culinary market around November, and it's not difficult to be completely oblivious to their existence. They are definitely not front-row market items at bargain prices. Some people who love truffles are satisfied with a few drops of truffle oil as a dressing here and there. You can use black truffle in place of the white here. Serve this as an antipasto, or even as a light and special main meal.

If you don't have a special truffle slicer, then slice them with a knife as thinly as possible. You can make the eggs scrambled, poached, boiled or in an omelette instead to serve with the truffles.

Serves 2

about 25 g (1 oz) butter

2 eggs

about 10 g (¼ oz) white truffle

Heat the butter in a saucepan on a medium heat. Break the eggs into the saucepan and cook for a few seconds before covering the saucepan with a lid. Cook for about 30 seconds, or until the top part of the egg just turns opaque. The inside of the egg should remain soft. Remove from the heat and sprinkle with salt and freshly ground black pepper. Transfer to plates, add the pan butter, scatter with thin truffle slices and serve immediately with your favourite bread.

Focaccia con olive

Flat bread with olives

This is a lovely variation to serve with, or in place of, bread. You can also make this dough in a mixer using a dough hook.

Makes 1 oven tray of about 30 x 40 cm (12 x 16 in)

25 g (1 oz) fresh yeast

310 ml (1¼ cups) tepid water

a pinch of sugar

500 g (1 lb 2 oz) bread flour

2 tablespoons of olive oil plus extra for drizzling

500 g (2 cups) whole pitted olives

In a bowl, combine the yeast, the water and the sugar to activate.

Put the flour and 1 teaspoon of salt into a large, wide bowl or onto a surface. Add the yeast to the flour and mix in with a fork to incorporate. Add the oil and begin kneading with your hands for about 10 minutes until you have a compact, smooth dough. Add a little more flour or water if necessary. Put the dough into a bowl, cover with a cloth, and leave it to rise in a warm place for about 1½ hours or until it has doubled in size.

Punch down the dough and work in the whole olives. Using your fingertips, spread the dough into a lightly oiled oven tray with 3 cm (1¼ in) high sides. Drizzle the surface with olive oil and sprinkle with salt and a little pepper. Leave in a warm place for another 30–60 minutes, or until it has risen.

Meanwhile, preheat the oven to 200°C (400°F/Gas 6).

Bake in the hot oven for about 30 minutes until the top is golden and crusty. Cut into serving pieces and serve warm.

Conchiglie con olive

Pasta shells with olives

You can prepare this sauce ahead of time, and keep it covered by a thin layer of olive oil in the refrigerator. Bring it back to room temperature or warm very slightly before mixing into the just cooked pasta. You can chop up the olives very finely — even pulse purée them roughly for this sauce, if you prefer. This sauce, to which you can add a little more olive oil, could also be served as a topping for crostini — as an appetiser, or spooned over a grilled chicken breast or fish.

Serves 6

80 g (3 oz) each of pitted, good-quality black and green olives

4 tablespoons olive oil plus a little extra for serving

2 salt-packed anchovies, rinsed, cleaned and filleted, or 4 fillets in olive oil

2 garlic cloves, peeled and chopped

grated zest of 1 lemon

a small handful of freshly chopped parsley

500 g (1 lb 2 oz) short pasta such as penne, fusilli, shells

120 g (1^1/$_4$ cups) grated hard ricotta cheese or Parmesan cheese

Put a large saucepan of salted water to the boil. Chop up the pitted olives or pulse purée to tiny pieces.

Heat the olive oil in a saucepan. Add the anchovies, mashing with a wooden spoon to melt them into the oil. Add the garlic, and just when it begins to sizzle, add the lemon zest and the olives. Sauté for a few seconds, then remove from the heat and stir in the parsley.

Cook the pasta in the boiling water following the packet instructions. Drain, reserving about a cup of the cooking water, and toss the pasta into the olives. Add the water and a grinding of pepper, and mix through. Sprinkle with the ricotta and serve immediately with a splash of olive oil or chilli oil.

Minestra di legumi

Mixed bean soup

This is a lovely, hearty dish for a cold winter evening. Bean soups are particularly popular in Tuscany, flavoured lightly with a little *pancetta*, and served with a generous splash of extra virgin olive oil. Traditionally, this dish is served as a first course, followed by a grilled or roast meat and probably a side dish of sautéed greens — and, of course, a generous carafe of Chianti.

Serves 6

150 g (5¹/2 oz) of borlotti or kidney beans (soaked for 24 hours)

150 g (5¹/2 oz) barley

150 g (5¹/2 oz) split peas

150 g (5¹/2 oz) mixed lentils

3 tablespoons olive oil

1 medium red onion, peeled and chopped

1 large carrot, peeled and chopped

1 stalk of celery. trimmed and chopped

50 g (1³/4 oz) unsmoked *pancetta*, chopped finely

2 bay leaves

a few juniper berries

extra virgin olive oil, to serve

Rinse and drain the borlotti beans and put them into a large saucepan. Cover abundantly with cold water and bring to the boil. Lower the heat slightly and cook for 1¹/2 hours or longer, if necessary, until the beans are soft. Add more hot water during the cooking time, to keep the beans well covered. Season with salt towards the end of the cooking time.

Meanwhile, rinse the barley, split peas and lentils. Heat the olive oil in a large saucepan. Add the onion, carrot, celery and *pancetta* and sauté for 5 or 10 minutes to soften them. Add the rinsed pulses and the bay leaves and juniper berries. Cover with about 3 litres (12 cups) of cold water and bring to the boil. Skim the surface with a slotted spoon to remove any scum. Lower the heat and cook uncovered for about 40 minutes until all the pulses are soft. Season with salt and pepper towards the end of this cooking time.

When the borlotti beans are cooked, add them to the mixed pulse pan with about 500 ml (2 cups) of their cooking water, and cook for another 5–10 minutes. The consistency should be that of a thick soup. Serve hot or at room temperature with a generous drizzle of olive oil.

Tagliatelle al tartufo

Tagliatelle with truffle

White truffles from Alba are more expensive than the Umbrian black truffles. Tuscany has a limited supply of both white and black truffles. You can use black truffles in place of the white ones here, and vary the quantity to suit your taste, keeping in mind that only a couple of shavings per person will not be enough, yet too many may overpower the dish.

Serves 6

1 quantity of fresh pasta*
(see page 372)

200 g (7 oz) butter

about 120 g (1¼ cups)
freshly grated Parmesan
cheese

1 white truffle 60–90 g
(2¼–3¼ oz)

Make the pasta dough following the instructions. Cover with a clean cloth and leave it to rest for about 30 minutes. Roll out the pasta following the instructions, to the second last setting, following your machine instructions.

After the final rolling, dust the pasta strips lightly with flour to prevent them from sticking when you pass them through the cutters. If you are cutting the pasta by hand, roll the strip along the length. Cut into noodles at about 8 mm (1/3 in) intervals with a sharp knife. Toss the cut noodles through your fingers to separate them and put them onto a tray or large plate dusted with flour or semolina. Put a large saucepan of salted water with a tablespoon of olive oil to boil while you finish cutting the pasta.

Melt the butter in a small saucepan. Pour it into a large bowl that will eventually accommodate all of the pasta.

Add the pasta to the boiling water, testing to see if it is done after 3–4 minutes of boiling. Cook longer if necessary. Drain the pasta and mix into the butter bowl. Toss quickly to coat and serve onto individual plates. Sprinkle with the Parmesan cheese and shave thin slices of truffle on top. Drizzle with any remaining butter from the bowl and serve immediately.

Coniglio in umido con olive verdi

Rabbit with tomato and green olives

You may use chicken in place of the rabbit for this dish. If so, skin the chicken and cut it into serving pieces. Use good quality pitted or unpitted olives, as you prefer.

Serves 4

4 tablespoons olive oil

1 medium rabbit, about 1.4 kg (3 lb 3 oz), cleaned and cut into 8 serving pieces

1 sprig of sage

1 sprig of rosemary

3 garlic cloves, peeled and chopped

1/2 a small dried red chilli, crumbled

250 ml (1 cup) red wine

400 g (14 oz) tin of peeled tomatoes with juice, puréed

500 ml (2 cups) vegetable stock* (see page 389) or water

180 g (1 cup) green olives, drained of any liquid

Heat the olive oil in a large stockpot. Add the rabbit pieces and brown all over. Season with salt and pepper. Add the sage and rosemary sprigs, the garlic and the chilli, and sauté until you begin to smell the garlic. Add the wine and when most of it has evaporated, add the tomato. Simmer for a few more minutes, before adding the hot stock or water.

Lower the heat to a minimum and simmer for about 1 1/2 hours or until the rabbit is very tender. Shift the rabbit pieces occasionally to ensure they don't stick.

Add the olives in the last 10 minutes of the cooking time, turn the heat up, and cook uncovered to reduce the sauce a little. Serve hot or at room temperature.

Triglie alla livornese con olive e capperi

Red mullet with tomato, olives and capers

You can use any soft-fleshed fish, whole or in fillets, that will hold its shape in the pan for this recipe. While small, whole mullet tend to have many tiny bones, they look good and are extremely flavourful, and so are always popular. The olives often used for cooking are salted, sun- or oven-dried, and just coated in a little olive oil.

Serves 6

4 tablespoons olive oil

3 garlic cloves, peeled and finely chopped

400 g (14 oz) tin of peeled tomatoes with juice, puréed

2 salt-packed anchovies, rinsed and filleted or 4 fillets in olive oil

Six red mullets, about 200 g (7 oz) each, cleaned and left whole

about 60 g (1/4 cup) flour

80 g (3 oz) black olives, drained of any liquid

50 g (1 3/4 oz) capers in vinegar, drained

a small handful of chopped parsley

Heat the olive oil in a saucepan large enough to hold all of the fish. Add the garlic to the oil and just when you begin to smell the garlic, add the tomato and the roughly chopped anchovies. Add about 250 ml (1 cup) of water, a little salt and pepper, and cook for a few minutes to make a sauce.

Season the fish inside and out with salt and pepper, and pat lightly with the flour. Add to the pan and cook on a medium heat for about 5 minutes on each side, turning the fish over carefully. Towards the end of this cooking time, add the whole olives and capers, and heat through. Check the seasoning, adding a little salt or pepper, if necessary. Scatter with the parsley and serve.

Pollo con olive e salvia

Pollo con olive e salvia

Chicken with olives and sage

The olives used in this dish are sold in Tuscany as *tostate* (toasted) and, probably because of the way they have been sun- or oven-dried, result in a delicious dry yet almost chewy flavour. Try and find oven-dried or sun-dried olives from an Italian delicatessen, sold loose and shiny with hardly any olive oil, for this dish.

You can cook the dish entirely on the stovetop. If so, add the garlic and sage only towards the end of the cooking time to prevent them from browning too much, and add a few drops of water to the saucepan to prevent the chicken from drying out.

Serves 4

5 tablespoons olive oil

1 chicken, about 1.5 kg (3 lb 5 oz), insides removed, skinned and cut into 8 portions

200 g (7 oz) black olives in olive oil (drained)

4 garlic cloves, peeled and lightly crushed with the flat of a knife blade

about 20 fresh sage leaves

125 ml (1/2 cup) white wine

Preheat the oven to 200°C (400°F/Gas 6). Heat the olive oil in a large, wide saucepan or casserole dish suitable for oven use.

Add the chicken and brown on all sides (it should take 10–15 minutes). Season with salt and pepper on all sides. Add the olives, garlic cloves and sage leaves and cook for a couple more minutes to blend the flavours.

Pour in the wine and transfer the dish to the hot oven. Cook for 30–40 minutes. The chicken should be moist and golden, and the sage leaves and olives should be crisp and there should be only a little thickened sauce. Remove from the oven.

If you would like a little more sauce, transfer the chicken, sage, garlic and olives to a serving plate, add 60 ml (1/4 cup) of water to the pan and put the dish onto the stovetop. Scrape up the bits with a wooden spoon, mixing them into the sauce, let it bubble for half a minute or so and serve over the chicken.

Stracotto di manzo

Beef braised in red wine

Stracotto means overcooked, and the beef in this recipe is in fact cooked for a very long time, resulting in a deliciously tender piece of meat that could almost be eaten with a spoon. Use a large round (not flat) piece of meat for this dish.

Serves 6

3 tablespoons olive oil

1.5 kg (3 lb 5 oz) deboned shoulder of beef, trimmed of fat

2 medium onions, peeled and chopped

3 medium carrots, peeled and chopped

1 stalk of celery, trimmed and chopped

1 sprig of sage

500 ml (2 cups) good-quality red wine (such as Chianti)

1 tablespoon tomato paste (purée)

Heat the olive oil in a stockpot on a medium heat. Add the meat, turning over to brown on all sides. Season with salt and pepper. Add the onion, carrot, celery and sage sprig around the meat, and continue cooking until the vegetables are softened and lightly golden. Add the wine together with 250 ml (1 cup) of water and the tomato paste.

Lower the heat to a minimum and cook, covered, for about 3 hours, turning it over a couple of times. There should be a lot of sauce, at least 500 ml (2 cups), so add a little more water while it's cooking, if necessary. The meat will be very tender. Transfer the meat to a cutting board.

Pass the vegetables through the medium-holed disc of a food mill back into the pot, or roughly purée the vegetables and add them back to the pot with the sauce.

Cut the meat into thick slices and serve warm, with the vegetable sauce spooned over.

Petto di pollo
con tartufo

Petto di pollo con tartufo

Chicken breasts in butter with truffle

If you don't have a truffle slicer, use a sharp knife to slice the truffles very finely. If possible, use a pan that is suitable for oven use as well. You can use white truffle instead of black. This dish is also good without the truffles — simply squeeze some lemon juice into the pan butter just before serving.

Serves 4

4 individual chicken breasts, skinned and boned (not flattened)

about 60 g (1/2 cup) flour for dusting

80 g (3 oz) butter

1 tablespoon olive oil

1 black truffle, about 25–30 g (1–1 1/4 oz)

Preheat the oven to 200°C (400°F/Gas 6). Rinse the chicken breasts and pat dry with paper towels. Trim off any fat. Season with salt and pepper, and dust with flour on both sides.

Heat half of the butter with the tablespoon of olive oil in a frying pan. Add the chicken breasts and fry for a few minutes on each side to seal until they are lightly golden.

If your frying pan is not ovenproof, transfer the chicken breasts to an oven dish. Add the rest of the butter to the pan and put into the hot oven for about 20 minutes, or until the chicken is cooked through, juicy, tender and golden, crispy brown.

Remove from the oven. Scatter a few very thin slices of truffle over each piece, and serve immediately with the pan butter spooned over.

Olive verdi sott'olio

Green olives preserved in olive oil

Untreated, dark green or purple-black olives can be bought —
or in Tuscany picked directly off a tree — for preserving. They
must be soaked in water for several days to reduce their
bitterness. See note on preserving (page 400).

This quantity will make slightly more than 1 litre (4 cups).
If you use smaller jars, make sure that each jar gets a garlic
clove or two, a chilli and is completely covered with olive oil.

Makes over 1 litre (4 cups)

1 kg (2 lb 4 oz) untreated, green olives

a small handful of fine salt

about 750 ml (3 cups) white wine vinegar, or enough to cover

about 3 small dried red chillies

about 6 garlic cloves, peeled

olive oil to cover the olives in the jars

Crack the olives by pressing down firmly on them with the flat of a
large knife blade using the palm of your hand. Remove the pits,
(keeping the olives whole) and rinse the olives. Put them into a
bowl of cold water to soak for 4–5 days, changing the water every
day until the bitterness of the unripe olives subsides. The olives will
probably darken slightly.

Drain and firmly squeeze out the excess water from the
olives. Put them into a bowl and sprinkle with salt. Cover with a
plate or a weight pressing down onto the olives, and leave them
for 24 hours. Squeeze the olives firmly with your hands to remove
the moisture.

Transfer the olives into a bowl, cover with the vinegar and
put a plate or weight on the olives to keep them submerged. Set
aside for 24 hours. Drain well and squeeze out firmly to drain away
all the liquid. Pack the olives into sterilised jars with the chilli and
garlic, and completely cover with olive oil. Use a special weight, if
necessary, to keep the olives completely submerged in the oil.

They will be ready to eat within a couple of weeks but will
improve with time. Store in a cool place. They will last for many
months, provided they remain completely covered in the oil.

Olive nere agli agrumi

Black olives with orange and lemon

This can be served as part of an antipasto, or as a side dish to accompany a roast. Use good-quality, black dried olives tostate, or toasted — as they are sold in Tuscany — or drained, black olives in brine or olive oil. Seasoned, they will only last a couple of days in the refrigerator, as they are not immersed in any liquid. The orange and lemon zest bits look lovely against the shiny black olives.

500 g (1 lb 2 oz) dried black olives

about 2 tablespoons olive oil

1 tablespoon balsamic vinegar

1/2 a dried red chilli, crumbled

zest of 1 lemon, cut into thin strips with a knife or lemon zester

zest of 1 orange, cut into thin strips with a knife or lemon zester

juice of 1/2 an orange

Mix all the ingredients together in a bowl and season with salt and pepper, depending on the saltiness of the olives.

Leave for at least an hour to marinate, mixing them through. Keep any left-over olives covered in the refrigerator.

Cantuccini

Cantuccini

Almond biscotti

These biscuits are twice-cooked (bis-cotto) and fill the house with a wonderful smell while baking. They are normally served with and dipped into a small glass of Vin Santo. You could even serve them with a bowl of *zabaglione** (see page 398) and fresh fruit slices, or dunk them into morning coffee. You can use other nuts in place of, or together with, the almonds.

Makes about 45 biscuits

60 g (2^1/$_4$ oz) butter, softened

250 g (9 oz) caster (superfine) sugar

grated zest of 1 lemon or orange

2 eggs

400 g (14 oz) plain (all-purpose) flour

1^1/$_2$ teaspoons baking powder

150 g (1 cup) whole almonds with skin

3 tablespoons Vin Santo

Preheat the oven to 180°C (350°F/Gas 4). Mix the butter and sugar in a bowl with a wooden spoon until smooth. Add the zest and eggs, and beat well. Mix in the sifted flour, baking powder and a small pinch of salt. Stir in the whole almonds and the Vin Santo.

Line a large baking sheet with baking paper. Lightly dust your work surface and hands in flour. Form about three whole salami shapes with your hands — slightly shorter than the length of the tray — of about 3 cm (1^1/$_4$ in) high and 5 cm (2 in) wide. Put them onto the baking sheet, allowing for enough space between each for spreading while they cook. Bake for about 20 minutes until they are golden and dry. They will still seem a little soft. Remove from the oven and while still hot, cut about 2 cm (^{3}/$_4$ in) slices at an angle with a sharp knife, sawing the surface lightly to just pierce through, then chopping through cleanly once, rather than sawing through the biscuits. Handle them carefully as they will be fragile before their second baking.

Lay the slices cut-side-up onto the baking sheet and return to the oven for 5–10 minutes to lightly toast the biscuit. They should be cream coloured on the inside and golden brown on the rim. Cool before storing in an airtight container, where they will keep for a couple of weeks.

Ciambellone all'olio

Sponge cake with olive oil

Makes one 26 cm (10^1/$_2$ in) cake

4 eggs, separated

300 g (10^1/$_2$ oz) caster (superfine) sugar

1 teaspoon vanilla essence

250 ml (1 cup) olive oil

400 g (14 oz) plain (all-purpose) flour

2 teaspoons baking powder

250 ml (1 cup) milk

icing (confectioners') sugar, to serve

You can elaborate on this simple sponge cake by adding various ingredients — orange or lemon zest, pine nuts, cinnamon or a splash of Vin Santo.

Preheat the oven to 180°C (350°F/Gas 4). Grease a 26 cm (10^1/$_2$ in) bundt (ring mould) or springform cake tin with sides of about 8 cm (3 in).

Whip the egg yolks in a bowl with the sugar and vanilla until they are thick and creamy. Whisk in the olive oil. Add the sifted flour and baking powder, and whisk to incorporate. Add the milk and mix well.

Whip the egg whites to soft peaks and fold them into the yolk mixture. Scrape the batter out into the cake tin. Bake for about 45 minutes, or until a skewer inserted comes out clean. Turn out onto a cake rack to cool. Dust with icing sugar, or serve in slices with a few caramelised apple or pear chunks and cream. The cake will keep for a few days stored in an airtight container.

Mele o pere caramellate

Caramelised apples or pears

Serves 6

4 medium-sized apples or pears

8 tablespoons caster (superfine) sugar

2 tablespoons butter

Peel, core and cut the fruit into fairly thick slices. Put the sugar, butter and fruit into a saucepan over a medium heat. As soon as the sugar dissolves and begins to colour on the sides, swirl the pan around to distribute the heat.

Lower the heat slightly. Cook until the sugar and butter have made a caramel sauce and the fruit has softened and darkened in places with the caramel. Serve a small heap next to a slice of sponge cake with a dollop of whipped, unsweetened cream. These can also be served alone with vanilla ice cream* (see page 139).

Castagnaccio

Chestnut flour cake

Originally, this cake was made in December once the November chestnuts had been dried and made into flour. Nowadays, chestnut flour and this rather unusual cake are both sold in November. As with all their traditional goods, the local people love this cake which they have grown up with.

Makes one 24 cm (9^1/$_2$ in) flat cake

80 g (3 oz) sultanas

400 g (14 oz) chestnut flour

8 tablespoons olive oil

about 450 ml (16 fl oz) water

80 g (^{2}/$_3$ cup) shelled walnuts, broken up into pieces

80 g (^{1}/$_2$ cup) pine nuts

2 sprigs of rosemary, leaves stripped off stalk

butter for greasing

breadcrumbs for lining the cake tin

Preheat the oven to 200°C (400°F/Gas 6). Soak the sultanas in a little warm water to soften them. Put the chestnut flour into a bowl with 4 tablespoons of the olive oil, a pinch of salt and the water. Mix in with a wooden spoon to make a smooth and fairly liquid batter.

Drain off the water from the sultanas and add half of them to the mixture. Add half of the walnuts, pine nuts and rosemary leaves, and mix into the batter.

Butter a 24 cm (9^1/$_2$ in) round or square cake tin and sprinkle with breadcrumbs to cover the bottom, shaking away the excess. Pour in the cake mixture. Scatter the remaining rosemary, walnuts, sultanas and pine nuts over the surface of the cake. Drizzle with the remaining olive oil.

Bake for about 50 minutes or until the top has a rich golden, yet soft crust. Remove from the oven and when it has cooled slightly, cut into small squares. This is best served warm.

Montebianco

Whipped snow-capped chestnut mountain

The end result of this delicious dessert should look like a mountain with snow draped over its peak.

It is fairly rich, so small portions might be appreciated depending, of course, on personal tastes.

Serves 4–6

500 g (1 lb 2 oz) chestnuts

1 tablespoon fennel seeds

about 60 ml (1/4 cup) warm milk

2 tablespoons caster (superfine) sugar

2 tablespoons good-quality brandy or rum

400 ml (14 fl oz) thick (single) cream

1/2 tablespoon icing (confectioners') sugar

Score the chestnuts underneath, making a slit with a sharp knife. This will make them easier to peel. Boil the chestnuts in water with the pinch of salt and the fennel seeds, for about an hour or until they are tender. Drain, and when cool enough to handle, peel, taking care to remove all of the skin.

Pass the still warm chestnuts through the fine-holed disc of a food mill into a bowl. Add the warm milk and mix in the caster sugar and the liqueur. Add a little more milk if it seems very stiff. Pass the mixture through the food mill once again, this time through the largest holes and onto your serving plate, leaving the long threads to form a mound.

Whip the cream lightly with the icing sugar. Spoon the soft snow over the mountain top and serve spoonfuls immediately.

Pane co' santi

Saint's bread

This typical sweet bread is generally found around the beginning of November for All-Saints' Day. One explanation of its name, is that it was fit only for a saint. Another version refers to the ingredients — the olive oil, walnuts and sultanas — as being the saints themselves. Serve after a meal with a glass of Vin Santo or port, or simply with morning coffee.

25 g (1 oz) fresh yeast

310 ml (1¼ cups) tepid water

2 tablespoons plus a pinch caster (superfine) sugar

about 500 g (1 lb 2 oz) bread flour

4 tablespoons olive oil

60 g (½ cup) sultanas

125 g (1 cup) shelled walnuts, cut into large chunks

1 egg yolk

2 teaspoons milk

Put the yeast, water and a pinch of sugar in a bowl. In a separate bowl, combine the flour and sugar. Add the yeast and mix in well. Knead by hand for about 10 minutes, until you have a smooth, elastic dough. Add a little more flour or water, if necessary. Cover the bowl with a cloth and leave it to rise in a warm place for about 1½ hours, or until it has doubled in size.

Sauté the sultanas and walnuts in the oil in a pan on a low heat, until the ingredients begin to colour lightly. Remove from the heat to cool. Mix in 1 teaspoon of salt and 1 teaspoon of pepper.

Put the bread dough onto a lightly floured work surface and flatten it out slightly. Add the sautéed mixture and knead gently to incorporate the ingredients. Divide the dough into two and form each into flattened ball shapes. Put them onto a baking tray lined with baking paper and leave to rise in a warm place, covered with a cloth, for another 30 minutes, or until the loaves have risen slightly.

Meanwhile, preheat the oven to 180°C (350°F/Gas 4). Mix the egg yolk with the milk in a small bowl and brush onto the bread. Bake in the oven for about 50 minutes, or until golden brown. The bottom should sound hollow when tapped. Remove to a cake rack to cool. Serve warm or at room temperature.

Pane co' santi

DECEMBER

This just seems to mean Christmas. The nearer it gets, the colder and darker it is and the brighter the lights seem to become. The city is beautiful. Most people who have a garden have their beautiful decorated Christmas tree outside.

A chosen real tree, draped with a few simple eccentricities of tradition, and magnificently lit up at night. It makes me want to shout with enthusiasm — why hadn't I thought of that before? The ground is fairly bare. The odd carrot, cardoon and other few winter vegetables — like silverbeet and the faithful rosemary and sage. This time of year is compensated for by these ever-present produce, by their friends which were cultivated in the months before, and by tradition.

Crostini neri

Chicken liver crostini

400 g (14 oz) chicken livers

3 tablespoons olive oil

1 small white onion, peeled and chopped

125 ml (1/2 cup) Marsala

one strip of lemon zest, about 6 cm (2 1/2 in)

1 small apple, peeled, cored and chopped

100 g (3 1/2 oz) salted anchovies, rinsed and filleted

100 g (3 1/2 oz) capers in vinegar, drained

2 tablespoons butter

2 tablespoons chopped parsley

1 loaf white, country-style bread, sliced and halved

These *crostini* are very typically Tuscan and show up at just about every occasion. Often, the bread is also grilled and dipped into hot stock and served warm, spread with the chicken liver. The crostini are good both ways.

Clean the chicken livers thoroughly, removing any filaments or green bile bits which could make the livers bitter.

Sauté the onion in olive oil or until lightly golden. Add the chicken livers, the Marsala, lemon zest and the apple. Cook for about 20 minutes on a medium heat, crushing the livers with a wooden spoon until the mix is fairly dry. Add the anchovies and capers to heat through. Season with a little salt, if necessary, and black pepper. Put into a food processor or blender, add the butter and process until smooth. Put into ramekins or small bowls. Sprinkle with the parsley.

Grill or toast the bread on both sides. Pile into a basket and serve warm.

Crostini di acciughe e burro

Crostini with butter and anchovies

Allow for enough bread per person. Generously add small pieces of unsalted butter to each. Break up a few salted filleted anchovies (or fillets in olive oil) and add a few pieces onto each piece of bread. Top with one or two baby capers and serve with the chicken liver crostini.

Salmone in carpaccio

Salmon carpaccio

This elegant dish is prepared ahead of time and refrigerated, which makes it quite convenient to prepare even for a large group. The herbs render a delicious flavour — if you can't find fennel flowers, use some coarsely crushed fennel seeds or even fresh fennel leaves.

Serves 10

one fillet of fresh salmon, about 1 kg (2 lb 4 oz)

1 1/2 tablespoons fine salt

2 tablespoons caster (superfine) sugar

2 tablespoons fresh thyme

2 tablespoons chopped fresh tarragon

2 tablespoons dried, wild fennel flowers (or seeds), crumbled

juice of 2 lemons

250 ml (1 cup) olive oil

freshly ground black pepper

2 tablespoons capers, chopped, to serve

Clean and skin the salmon fillet removing any bones using your fingers or even with a pair of tweezers. You can run your hand along the salmon fillet in the opposite direction of the bones to place them. Put the salmon fillet into a dish with a rim, where it fits compactly in a single layer, keeping it in one piece, if possible, or two.

Make a mix with the salt, sugar and herbs, and sprinkle over both sides of the salmon. Pour over the lemon juice and olive oil, and grind on some black pepper.

Cover the dish with plastic wrap and refrigerate for at at least two days and up to four or five before serving. Turn the salmon over twice each day.

To serve, remove the salmon from its container. Shake off the excess liquid and put onto a cutting board. Using a long, unserrated slicing knife, start from the tail end and cut very thin slices away from you, slightly on the diagonal. Put them flat onto a large serving dish, with some overlapping, if necessary.

Whisk the remaining liquid to form a thickened oil, and spoon over the salmon. Scatter over some chopped capers if you like, a grinding of black pepper, and serve with bread or with a side salad of rocket.

Tagliolini in brodo di gallina

Tagliolini in hen stock

Often for an occasion such as Christmas lunch, meat is boiled for its stock, in which the first course of pasta is served. The boiled meat is then eaten as a second course, or served that evening with *salsa verde** (see page 378) and *acciugata** (see page 379), accompanied by boiled vegetables.

Serves 6

1 hen, about 1.8 kg (4 lb)

1 stalk of celery, roughly chopped

1 large carrot, peeled and roughly chopped

a few stalks of parsley

1 large white onion, peeled

3 or 4 whole cloves

1/2 the quantity of fresh pasta* (see page 372)

about 80 g (3/4 cup) freshly grated Parmesan cheese, to serve

Rinse the boiling fowl and put it into a large saucepan. Cover with 3 litres (12 cups) of cold water and bring to the boil, skimming the surface with a slotted spoon to remove any scum. If your pan is not big enough you can add more water once the liquid has reduced a little. Add the celery, carrot, parsley stalks and the onion studded with a few cloves. Season lightly with salt and add a few black peppercorns. Lower the heat and simmer for about 2 hours.

Make the pasta dough following the instructions. Cover with a clean cloth and leave it to rest for 30 minutes. Roll out the pasta dough, to the second-last setting (following the manufacturer's instructions). Dust with flour and pass the pasta strips through the tagliolini cutters. If your pasta machine does not have this cutter, then roll up each pasta strip along its length and cut at 3 mm (1/8 in) intervals with a sharp knife. Toss the noodles through your fingers to separate them and put them onto a tray, lightly dusted with flour. Meanwhile, put a large saucepan of salted water to boil.

Remove the fowl from the pan, strain the stock and discard the vegetables. Boil the tagliolini in the boiling, salted water for about 3 minutes, or until cooked. Put a ladleful of hot stock into each soup bowl and add a serving of tagliolini. Sprinkle with Parmesan cheese, black pepper and serve immediately.

Gnocchi di
patate

Gnocchi di patate

Potato dumplings

These should be soft and moist little cushions of dough and are best made just before serving. However, you can also prepare them beforehand — keep them in a buttered dish, then before serving, drop them for a few seconds into boiling water. You can also serve them with a tomato sauce* (see pages 382–383), or with butter, sage and Parmesan cheese.

Make the ragù following the instructions.

Wash the potatoes and boil them with their skins in lightly salted water for about 20 minutes, taking care not to overcook them. Drain and when cool enough to handle, peel them.

Pass the potatoes through a food mill, into a wide bowl. Add a little salt and just enough flour to make a soft and elastic dough, kneading with your hands. The dough should be soft and slightly sticky, but it shouldn't stick onto your work surface.

Meanwhile, bring a large saucepan of salted water to the boil. Dust your hands and work surface lightly with flour. Working quickly, break off pieces of the dough, and roll out into long cylindrical strands of about 1 cm (1/2 in) in diameter. Cut these strands into pieces at about 2 cm (3/4 in) intervals with a sharp knife. Put onto a lightly floured tray until you are ready to cook.

Cook the gnocchi in batches in the boiling water. When they float to the surface they are ready. Lift them out with a slotted spoon or a wire strainer, allowing the water to drain off well. Keep the gnocchi in a hot, buttered oven dish until you are ready to serve them. Transfer to pasta bowls, and add a few tablespoons of hot ragù and a nut of butter. Sprinkle with Parmesan cheese and serve immediately.

Serves 6–8

1 quantity of simple ragù* (see page 384) or Tuscan ragù* (see page 385)

1.3 kg (3 lb) waxy potatoes

about 350 g (12 oz) plain (all-purpose) flour

about 50 g (1³/4 oz) butter

about 120 g (1¹/4 cups) freshly grated Parmesan cheese

Lasagne

Lasagne

This internationally popular dish is normally saved for special occasions. It is often made with slight variations to the meat sauce and the consistency of the béchamel. This version uses a rich Tuscan meat sauce. Make this in an oven dish about 30 x 40 cm (12 x 16 in). This quantity should make about five layers of pasta in the dish.

Serves 10

1 quantity of Tuscan ragù*
(see page 385)

1 quantity of fresh pasta*
(see page 372)

1 quantity of béchamel 1*
(see page 380)

about 80 g (3/4 cups) freshly grated Parmesan cheese

Make the ragù, making sure it is fairly liquid, and set aside. Make the pasta following the instructions. Cover and let the dough rest for about 30 minutes. Make the béchamel sauce and set aside.

Roll out the pasta to sheets of 40 x 10 cm (12 x 4 in) — the second last setting (following the manufacturer's instructions).

Meanwhile, preheat the oven to 180°C (350°F/Gas 4). Put a large saucepan of salted water to boil with a tablespoon of olive oil, to prevent the pasta sheets from sticking together.

Boil the lasagne sheets, a few at a time, for about 4 minutes or until they have softened. Lift them out with a slotted spoon and lay them out separately onto a dry cloth.

Spread a little béchamel onto the bottom of a deep oven dish (long enough to contain the lengths of the pasta). Put a layer of the lasagne sheets onto the bottom, overlapping slightly if necessary. Cover with a few splashes of ragù, then a few spoons of béchamel and a sprinkling of Parmesan cheese. Repeat this method until all the ingredients are used, or the dish is filled, finishing with a sprinkling of Parmesan cheese.

Bake for about 30 minutes in the hot oven, until the top is golden but not dried out. Remove from the oven and let it cool slightly before cutting into servings.

Fagiano arrosto

Roast pheasant with pancetta

Pheasant is enjoyed for its unusual flavour and is most often eaten on special occasions during the hunting season. The slow addition of stock here keeps the meat moist. You may use chicken or guinea fowl instead — the cooking time, however, will be less.

Serves 4

1 pheasant, about 1.2 kg (2 lb 10 oz), cleaned and insides removed

about 8 sage leaves

150 g (5½ oz) thinly sliced unsmoked *pancetta*

40 g (1½ oz) butter

3 tablespoons olive oil

2 bay leaves

3 garlic cloves, peeled

125 ml (½ cup) Vin Santo

about 750 ml (3 cups) vegetable stock* (see page 389)

Preheat the oven to 190°C (375°F/Gas 5).

Rinse the pheasant in cold water. Pat dry with paper towels. Season the inner cavity with salt and pepper, and insert a few sage leaves and a couple of slices of *pancetta*. Sprinkle a little salt and pepper onto the outside and wrap the *pancetta* slices around the pheasant to completely enclose it. Tie up with kitchen string to secure it.

Heat the butter and olive oil in a large ovenproof stockpot. Add a few sage leaves, the bay leaves and garlic cloves to the pot. Add the pheasant and brown lightly for about 10 minutes on each side. Add the Vin Santo and when most of it has evaporated, add 250 ml (1 cup) of hot stock, cover the pot and put it into the oven.

Cook for 1–1½ hours, until the pheasant is tender, adding another 250 ml (1 cup) of stock halfway through. Remove the lid, add another cup of stock and cook for another 10–15 minutes on each side to brown.

Remove the pheasant from the pot and remove the string. Cut into serving portions with poultry shears. Serve with the pan juices.

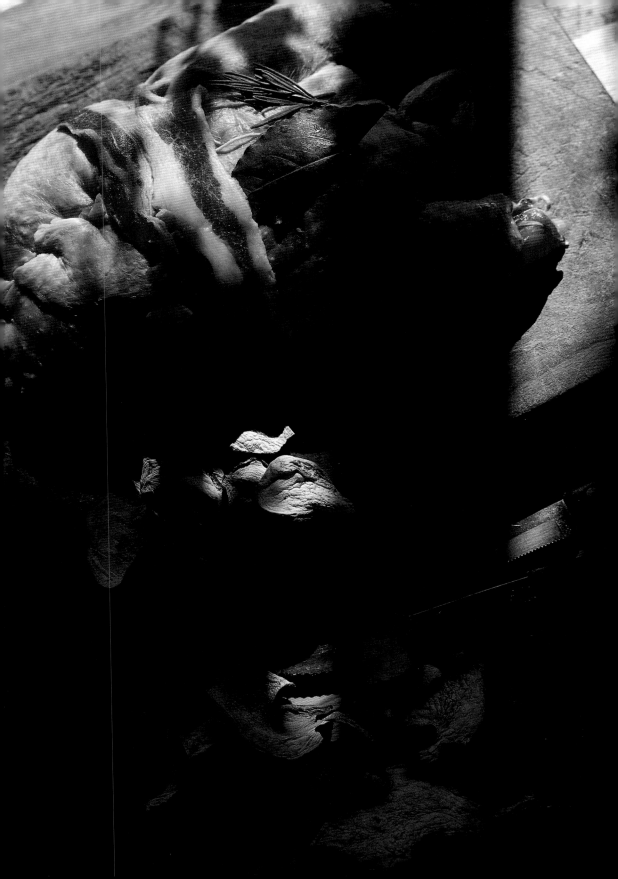

Fagiano
arrosto

Piccione al crostone

Pigeon on grilled bread

Pigeon is considered a rare and precious treat for its flavourful dark meat. Pigeon is also often made with risotto, or roasted together with a variety of other meats. Here, the pigeons are stuffed with a simple mix of sausage and sage, and simmered on the stovetop. You may use any stuffing you like.

Serves 6

3 medium-sized pigeons, about 400 g (14 oz) each, cleaned and insides removed

about 10 sage leaves

2 sprigs rosemary

3 Italian sausages, about 80 g (3 oz) each

5 tablespoons olive oil

2 garlic cloves, peeled

250 ml (1 cup) red wine

250 ml (1 cup) vegetable stock* (see page 389) or water

60 g (1/2 cup) good-quality olives, drained of any liquid

6 thick slices of country-style white bread

Clean the pigeons well. Rinse, drain away the water and pat dry with paper towel. Lightly season the insides of the pigeon with salt and pepper, then the outsides. Finely chop up six of the sage leaves. Remove the rosemary from its stem and chop up finely. Mix the sausage meat together with the chopped sage and rosemary, and divide this between the pigeons, stuffing it into their cavity.

Put the olive oil, garlic cloves and remaining sage leaves into a saucepan that will accommodate the pigeons snugly, and heat up. Add the pigeons and on a medium heat, brown them all over. It should take about 10 minutes on each side. Add the wine, and continue cooking uncovered until some of it has evaporated. Pour in the hot stock or water, lower the heat, cover the pan, and continue cooking for another 30–40 minutes, until the pigeon is cooked through and tender. Turn the pigeons over a couple of times during the cooking process to ensure they cook evenly. Make sure there is a little sauce in the pan, if not add a bit more water or stock. Add the olives and simmer for another 5 minutes.

Meanwhile, grill (broil) or toast the bread on both sides and put onto individual serving plates. Transfer the pigeons to a cutting board and divide each one lengthways in half. Put a pigeon half over each piece of grilled bread, spoon over the sauce with a few olives and serve immediately.

Tessa

Arrosto misto

Arrosto misto

Mixed roast

This is a typical dish served for an occasion such as Christmas. You will probably need two oven dishes that will fit into your oven simultaneously, to accommodate all the meats and potatoes. The end result is a beautiful heaped platter of roast meats with potatoes and herbs.

Serves 10

about 4 tablespoons
aromatic salt*
(see page 378)

1 chicken, about 1.5 kg
(3 lb 5 oz), cleaned and
insides removed

1 kg (2 lb 4 oz) piece of
pork loin

1 guinea fowl, about 1.5kg
(3 lb 5 oz), cleaned and
insides removed

1 rabbit, about 1.4 kg
(3 lb 2 oz), cleaned and
insides removed

125 ml (1/2 cup) of olive oil

500 ml (2 cups) white wine

2 kg (4 lb 8 oz) potatoes,
washed, peeled and cut
into chunks

10 Italian sausages

Preheat the oven to 200°C (400°F/Gas 6). Put the chicken and pork loin into one oven dish and the guinea fowl and rabbit into another. Drizzle the olive oil over the meats and scatter the aromatic salt onto the outside of the pork and lightly into the inner cavities and outsides of the chicken, guinea fowl and rabbit.

Put both oven dishes into the oven and brown the meats, turning them over. It should take 10–15 minutes on each side. Add 250 ml (1 cup) of wine to each dish and divide the potatoes and sausages between the dishes. Mix with a wooden spoon to coat the potatoes with the pan oil. Roast for another 1 1/4 hours or so, turning over to brown evenly. Check to see if the meats are done. The juices from the thickest part of the chicken should run clear when pierced with a skewer. All the meats should have a crisp, golden exterior and be well cooked throughout. The potatoes should also be golden and crispy. If one or more of the meats cook before the others, remove from the oven and transfer to a plate while you continue cooking. Remove the trays from the oven.

When the meats have cooled slightly, cut the pork into slices. Cut up the rabbit, chicken and guinea fowl into small serving portions with a pair of poultry shears. Sprinkle potatoes with salt, if necessary. Pile all the meats up with the potatoes onto a serving platter, drizzle with some of the pan juices and serve immediately.

Anatra arrosto con cipolle, olive e marsala

Roast duck with baby onions, olives and marsala

Once a traditional and rustic way of serving duck, this dish is now reserved for festive occasions. The Marsala in this recipe lends the sweet flavour so well suited to this meat.

Serves 4

400 g (14 oz) baby onions, peeled

1 duck, about 1.4 kg (3 lb 2 oz), cleaned and insides removed

30 g (1 oz) butter

250 ml (1 cup) Marsala

800 g (1 lb 12 oz) potatoes, peeled and cut into chunks

2 bay leaves

250 g (9 oz) black (oven- or sun-dried) olives

2 sprigs sage

2 sprigs rosemary

2 garlic cloves, peeled

Preheat the oven to 200°C (400°F/Gas 6). Bring a small saucepan of slightly salted water to the boil, add the onions and boil for a few minutes. Drain, keeping the onions aside.

Prick the skin of the duck in a few places with a fork. Put the duck into a large roasting dish. Rub the skin with the butter and season with salt and pepper. Put into the hot oven, breast side down, and roast for about 30 minutes, or until the top is golden brown.

Remove from the oven, turn the duck over and pour over the Marsala. Add the onions, potatoes, bay leaves, olives, sage, rosemary and garlic. Mix them through with a wooden spoon. Add 125 ml ($1/2$ cup) of water.

Return the dish to the oven for another $1^{1}/4$ hours or so, turning the duck over again halfway through cooking, and shuffle the potatoes with a wooden spoon.

There should only be a little liquid left with a crispy duck, which should be well cooked throughout. Remove from the oven and check the potatoes to see if they need salt.

Cut up the duck with poultry shears, carve some of the meat and serve hot, together with the potatoes, onions and pan juices.

Sformato di spinaci

Baked spinach pie

This dish can be prepared ahead of time and warmed up to serve.

Make the béchamel and set aside. Preheat the oven to 180°C (350°F/Gas 4).

Cook the spinach in boiling salted water for about 5 minutes. Drain well, squeezing out the excess water and chop up finely.

Melt the butter in a frying pan. Add the garlic and sauté for a minute. Add the spinach and sauté to dry it out for a few minutes. Remove from the heat and put into a large bowl. Let it cool slightly before adding the béchamel, eggs, Parmesan cheese and a little extra freshly grated nutmeg.

Butter a high oven dish or 30 cm (12 in) loaf tin. Sprinkle with half of the breadcrumbs to line the tin. Pour in the mixture and sprinkle with the rest of the breadcrumbs. Bake for 30–40 minutes or until the top is golden and a bit crusty, and feels set.

Cool slightly before cutting into thick slices or serve at room temperature.

Serves 6

500 ml (2 cups) béchamel 2* (see page 380)

1.2 kg (2 lb 10 oz) fresh spinach, washed and hard stalks removed

50 g (1¾ oz) butter

1 garlic clove, peeled and finely chopped

4 eggs, lightly beaten

100 g (1 cup) grated Parmesan cheese

nutmeg

about 2 tablespoons breadcrumbs

Scarola in padella

Sautéed escarole

Here, escarole is filled with an anchovy, caper and olive mixture and gently sautéed to soften it. It is a delicate, simple dish that could be served with any meat or fish main course, and elegant enough to stand next to any celebration roast. You can use witlof, curly endive or any similar head of leaves.

Serves 8

4 small heads of escarole, about 1 kg (2 lb 4 oz)

80 g (3 oz) pitted black olives

4 salted anchovies, rinsed and filleted or 8 fillets in olive oil, drained

60 g (2 1/4 oz) small capers (in vinegar) drained

4 tablespoons olive oil

2 garlic cloves, peeled and lightly crushed with the flat of knife blade

1 small dried red chilli, crumbled

1 tablespoon butter

Wash the heads of escarole carefully, leaving them whole and discard any damaged outer leaves.

Cut up the olives into thin rings and put them into a small bowl. Chop up the anchovy fillets and add them to the olives. Add the whole capers and a tablespoon of olive oil, and mix through.

Gently open out the heads of escarole a little and divide the olive mixture between the four, spooning it into the centre of each and also between some leaves. Close up the escarole and tie up securely with kitchen string towards their centre, so the filling doesn't come out during cooking.

Put the garlic, chilli, the remaining olive oil and the butter into a large saucepan and heat up. Add the escarole bundles, cover the saucepan with a lid, and simmer gently for 15–20 minutes. Remove the lid, turn the bundles over and continue cooking, uncovered, for another 5–10 minutes. There should be very little liquid in the pan. If it looks too dry during the cooking process, add a few drops of water to prevent the escarole from sticking. Serve them whole, or carefully divide the bundles vertically into halves.

Ricciarelli

Almond cakes

These small, soft cakes are found in every shop in Siena along with the traditional panforte. They are baked on sheets or individual discs of rice paper, which is trimmed around the cake when it is cooked and eaten with the small cake. If you do not have rice paper, line your baking tray with a piece of baking paper. When cooled, simply transfer from the baking paper to a tin.

Makes about 20 biscuits

300 g (10^1/$_2$ oz) almond flour (or very finely ground almonds)

280 g (10 oz) caster (superfine) sugar

150 g (5^1/$_2$ oz) icing (confectioners') sugar

1 teaspoon baking powder

grated zest of 1 orange

2 egg whites

1 sheet of rice paper (or about 20 small rounds) to line the baking tray

Line a flat baking tray with baking paper.

Mix the ground almonds with the caster sugar, 100 g (3^1/$_2$ oz) of the icing sugar, the baking powder and the orange zest in a bowl.

Whisk the egg whites to soft peaks and combine with the almond mix, using a wooden spoon. Mash the mixture together to make a sticky, wet mass.

Mould oval shapes to 6 cm (2^1/$_2$ in) long x 4 cm (1^1/$_2$ in) wide x 2 cm (^{3}/$_4$ in) thick onto a spoon. Slide the ovals off the spoon carefully with your thumb, and reshape any indentations. Put them onto the baking tray, allowing room for them to spread. Sprinkle the tops with 25 g (1 oz), or half of the remaining icing sugar. Leave the biscuits on the tray for 2–3 hours at room temperature to dry them a little before baking.

Preheat the oven to 140°C (275°F/Gas 1). Bake for about 30 minutes or until they are lightly golden and a little firm on the outside. The insides will still be soft. Remove from the oven. Cool slightly before sprinkling with the remaining 25 g (1 oz) of icing sugar. Cut the rice paper around the bottom of the cakes. They will keep for about a week stored in an airtight container.

Cavallucci

Christmas spiced biscuits

Candied citrus peels are sold in beautiful large chunks of orange, lemon, lime and grapefruit. They have an unmistakably sweet, citrus taste and are often used in desserts. These homemade biscuits have a wonderful chewy, delicious texture.

Makes about 15 biscuits

300 g (10¹/₂ oz) caster (superfine) sugar

185 ml (³/₄ cup) water

350 g (12 oz) plain (all-purpose) flour

2 teaspoons baking powder

100 g (1 cup) shelled walnuts, cut into chunks

50 g (1³/₄ oz) candied citrus peel (available from Italian delicatessens), cut into small dice

1 tablespoon ground anise

2 teaspoons ground cinnamon

Preheat the oven to 150°C (300°F/Gas ¹/₄). Put the sugar into a heavy-bottomed saucepan with the water. Bring to the boil and cook on a medium heat for about 5 minutes or until it becomes a pale syrup. Remove from the heat. Carefully stir in the sifted flour, baking powder, the nuts, citrus peel, the anise and the cinnamon. Mix with a solid spatula or wooden spoon, to make a sticky, consistent dough.

Line a large baking tray with baking paper. Dollop heaped tablespoons of dough about 6 cm (2¹/₂ in) in diameter onto the tray, placing them apart from each other, with the help of another tablespoon. They will look like small heaps of wet sand. Bake for about 45 minutes or until they are very lightly golden, slightly firm and a little puffed up.

These biscuits will keep for about a week stored in an airtight container. If they become very dry and hard after a few days, put them back into a hot oven for a few minutes to soften them before eating.

Pere al cioccolato

Pears with chocolate

Serves 6

6 ripe firm pears

1 litre (4 cups) water

350 g (12 oz) caster (superfine) sugar

2 bay leaves

3 or 4 whole cloves

Cream

200 ml (7 fl oz) milk

200 ml (7 fl oz) thick (single) cream

1 vanilla pod, halved lengthways

3 egg yolks

1 tablespoon plain (all-purpose) flour

80 g (3 oz) caster (superfine) sugar

150 g (5 1/2 oz) quality unsweetened, dark chocolate

6 small amaretti biscuits (available from Italian delicatessens), coarsely crushed

6 teaspoons good-quality brandy

These cooked pears are presented on a pool of vanilla cream, drizzled lightly with brandy or another liqueur, then with melted chocolate and sprinkled with amaretti biscuit crumbs.

Peel the pears carefully, leaving the stem intact. Hollow out the bottom with a melon baller or a teaspoon and remove the pips.

In a large saucepan make a syrup with the water, the 350 g (12 oz) sugar and the bay leaves and cloves. When it comes to the boil, lower the heat to a gentle simmer and add the pears. Cook them for 10–15 minutes, turning them over a couple of times. Remove from the heat and leave them to cool, before transferring them to a bowl with a slotted spoon.

To make the cream, heat the milk and the cream with the vanilla pod in a saucepan. Lightly whip the eggs in a bowl with the flour and the 80 g (3 oz) of sugar. Just before the milk mixture comes to the boil, remove it from the heat and add a ladleful to the egg mixture, whisking to avoid cooking the eggs. Add all the egg mixture back to the milk pan and return it to a very low heat, stirring continuously with a wooden spoon until it thickens. When bubbles begin to appear on the surface, remove from the heat and pour into a clean bowl, whisking to ensure that it remains smooth. Remove the vanilla pod and save it for your vanilla sugar*.

Melt the chocolate in a small saucepan over another saucepan of simmering water, stirring to ensure a smooth mixture.

Spoon the cooled cream onto individual serving plates and sprinkle with the amaretti crumbs. Put a pear onto the custard and spoon a teaspoon of brandy over each pear. Drizzle the melted chocolate over the pears and serve immediately.

Pere al cioccolato

Datteri con mascarpone e noci

Datteri con mascarpone e noci

Dates filled with mascarpone cream and walnuts

These may be served after dinner or as an antipasto, even though they are sweet. They are rich and delicious. The quantities given here are estimated at three dates per person. You may adjust this to suit your personal taste. Although dates are not grown in Tuscany, they are often served for festive occasions.

Serves 8

at least 12 shelled whole walnuts

110 g (1/2 cup) mascarpone

125 g (1/2 cup) ricotta cheese

6 tablespoons caster (superfine) sugar

2 tablespoons good-quality brandy, rum or grappa

24 fresh dates

Toast the walnuts lightly in an oven or a dry frying pan.

Put the mascarpone and ricotta cheese into a bowl with the sugar and liqueur. Mix gently but thoroughly. Divide each walnut in half, lengthways across its seam.

Slit the dates vertically down one side with a sharp knife, leaving them whole. Remove the stone. Fill each date with a teaspoonful or so of the mascarpone mixture. You can pipe the mixture in if you prefer. Add a walnut half to each date and gently close them up a little. Refrigerate for about an hour before serving.

Basics

Pasta all'uovo

Fresh egg pasta

Making the dough

The proportions given in this recipe can vary slightly and depend
on the flour and the size of the eggs. The method given to produce
the pasta dough is by hand and rolled out with a pasta machine
which clamps onto a work surface. It is also possible to make
the dough in a food processor. This recipe makes about 650 g
(1 lb 7 oz).

    Put the flour and 1 teaspoon of salt into a large, wide bowl
or in a mound on your work table, and make a well in the centre.
Break the eggs into the well and begin mixing them in with a fork,
incorporating the flour into the eggs. When the mixture starts to
come together, begin kneading the dough with your hands on the
work surface. It will seem very dry at first. Firmly push down onto the
dough with your palms, then away from you with the heel of your
palms. After about 10 minutes of kneading, the dough should be
shiny, smooth and compact. Cover it with a clean, dry cloth and
leave it to rest at room temperature for about 30 minutes. It may be
frozen at this point, wrapped tightly in plastic wrap. If you will not be
rolling out the pasta dough immediately, it may be refrigerated for a
few hours wrapped in plastic wrap. Remove the dough from the
refrigerator and knead it a little to soften before rolling it out.

Rolling out the dough

Divide the dough into 4 equal pieces. Begin working with one
piece, covering the others with a slightly damp cloth to prevent
them from drying out. Flatten the piece of dough roughly into a
rectangular shape to fit through the widest setting of the pasta

450 g (1 lb) strong flour

4 eggs

1 tablespoon olive oil

machine. Roll the dough through — it should emerge longer and flatter. Fold the length of the dough in half and roll it through the same setting again. Repeat a few more times, as this helps to render a smooth dough. Lower the setting by one from the widest, and pass the pasta strip through once. (It may be necessary to cut the strips lengthways into two or three to be able to manage them more easily.) Lower the setting by one again and pass the strip through. Continue lowering the setting and passing the pasta through once, until the second last or even the last setting is reached, depending on the required thickness. Dust with a little flour if the dough seems a bit sticky.

For *fettuccine*, *pappardelle*, *tagliolini* and *lasagne*, roll the pasta to the second-last setting. For *ravioli*, *tortellini* and other stuffed pastas, roll the pasta to the last setting. However, as each machine is different follow the manufacturer's instructions.

Cutting the dough

Dust the pasta sheet with flour before passing it through the cutters to prevent the noodles from sticking together. If you don't have the required cutter sizes, roll up the pasta sheet along its length and cut strips with a sharp knife. Sprinkle fine semolina flour or ordinary flour onto a tray, gently toss the pasta noodles through your fingers to separate and lay them onto the floured tray while you cut the remaining dough.

Cooking fresh pasta

For 500 g (1 lb 2 oz) of pasta, use a large saucepan and bring about 2 litres (8 cups) of water to the boil with 1 tablespoon of salt. Add 1 tablespoon of olive oil, to prevent the pasta from sticking together. Add the fresh pasta. Depending on its thickness, it should take 3–4 minutes to cook. Test a noodle to see if it is ready. Cook for longer if necessary. Lift out the pasta with a slotted spoon, pasta spoon or wire strainer.

Cooking dry pasta

For 500 g (1 lb 2 oz) of dry pasta use a large saucepan with about 2 litres (8 cups) of water. Add 1 tablespoon of salt. When the water comes to the boil, add the dry pasta to the pan. As soon as it comes to the boil again, begin timing the pasta following the packet instructions. Give a quick swirl with a pasta fork to ensure the pasta doesn't stick together. When the pasta is ready, lift it out of the water with a slotted spoon, pasta spoon or wire strainer and tip directly into your pan or bowl containing the sauce. Alternatively, drain the pasta using a colander, but reserve 1 or 2 cups of the pasta cooking water. Mix in the sauce and toss through. If the sauce seems a bit dry, add a little of the cooking water. Serve immediately with freshly grated Parmesan cheese.

Pici

Pici pasta dough

This is a pasta dough made without egg and rolled out by hand into long thin noodles.

Serves 6

600 g (1 lb 5 oz) plain (all-purpose) flour

1 tablespoon olive oil

300 ml (10¹/₂ fl oz) water

Put the flour into a wide bowl or onto your work surface. Add ¹/₂ teaspoon of salt and the olive oil. Begin adding the water and mixing with your hands to form a dough. Knead the dough for about 10 minutes, pushing down with the palms of your hands, then pushing the dough away from you with the heel of your palms. It should be a smooth and compact mass. The amount of water needed may vary. Cover the dough with a clean, damp cloth and leave it to rest for about 30 minutes at room temperature.

Break off pieces of the dough and begin rolling out long, thin ropes by hand, if possible working on a wooden surface.

It may be easier to flatten out the pasta dough on a lightly floured surface, into a roughly rectangular shape of about 1 cm (1/2 in) thick, and divide this rectangle into thin strips. Roll each strip between your palms to achieve long, thin strings or roll them out on a flat, wooden surface. They should look like thick very long hand-made spaghetti. These are just perfect even if they don't look so.

Pane bianco

White country-style bread

A typical loaf of Tuscan bread has a good crust, is rough-textured and unsalted (it is said to balance the saltiness of Tuscan *prosciutto* and other cold meats).

Makes 1 large, or 2 smaller, loaves

25 g (1 oz) fresh yeast

a pinch of sugar

310 ml (1¼ cups) tepid water

500 g (1 lb 2 oz) bread flour

1 tablespoon of olive oil

Put the yeast into a bowl with the pinch of sugar. Stir in the water and leave it to activate. Put the flour in a large, wide bowl, or onto a work surface. Add the yeast, a pinch of salt and the oil, and mix in to incorporate well. Knead the dough for about 10 minutes, until you have a smooth, compact, elastic ball. Add a little more flour or water if necessary. Put the dough into a lightly floured bowl, cover with a cloth and leave it to rise in a warm place for about 1½ hours, or until it has doubled in size.

Dust the work surface lightly with flour. Divide the dough in half or leave whole and shape into ovals or rounds. Put the dough onto one or two lightly floured baking sheets, leaving space between each to allow for rising. Cover with a cloth and leave in a warm place for 30–60 minutes, or until risen. Meanwhile, preheat the oven to 200°C (400°F/Gas 6). Put the bread into the oven and bake for 30–40 minutes, until lightly golden and crusty. The bottom should sound hollow when tapped. Transfer to a rack to cool.

Smicca

Herbed olive oil

It is worth making a fairly large amount as this keeps for a long time if the herbs remain covered with the oil. It is extremely useful to have this on hand. For a roast chicken, or 1.5 kg (3 lb 5 oz) of roast potatoes, you could use 2–3 tablespoons plus a little extra olive oil.

Makes 1 litre (4 cups)

120 g (4^1/$_2$ oz) rosemary sprigs

100 g (3^1/$_2$ oz) sage sprigs

4 garlic cloves, peeled

about 750 ml (3 cups) olive oil

Rinse the rosemary stalks and sage. Put them onto paper towels to dry — even overnight. Strip the rosemary leaves off the sprigs and remove any tough stalks from the sage sprigs.

Chop the sage, rosemary leaves and the garlic very finely by hand, or pulse-chop in a blender. Season lightly with salt and cover with the oil. Stir through. Leave it overnight to settle, then check that the herbs are completely covered with oil. Add a little more oil if necessary. Store in a closed jar in a cool, dark place or in the refrigerator. This will keep for several months — just keep topping it up with olive oil.

Sale aromatico

Aromatic salt

Makes 390 g (13$\frac{1}{2}$ oz)

120 g (4$\frac{1}{2}$ oz) rosemary sprigs

100 g (3$\frac{1}{2}$ oz) sage sprigs

4 small dried red chillies

4 bay leaves

zest of 1 lemon

6 garlic cloves, peeled

15 g ($\frac{1}{2}$ oz) black peppercorns

500 g (1 lb 2 oz) salt

It is worth making a fairly large amount of this seasoning. It keeps well, stored in an airtight container in the fridge, and is delicious as well as extremely convenient.

Rinse the rosemary and sage and put them onto paper towels to dry overnight. Strip the leaves off the rosemary stalks and remove any tough stalks from the sage sprigs. Cut a slit down the chillies (wearing gloves), and remove some of the seeds.

Put the bay leaves, rosemary, sage, lemon zest, chillies and garlic into a food processor and pulse-chop until they are in tiny pieces. Transfer to a suitable container with a lid. Grind the peppercorns and add to the mixture with 500 g (1 lb 2 oz) salt. Mix through thoroughly. Keep refrigerated in an air-tight container.

Salsa verde

Green sauce

This sauce is typically served as an accompaniment to boiled meats and vegetables, alongside an anchovy sauce*. Sometimes, eggs are added to the sauce. If you like, add 3 finely chopped, hard-boiled eggs to the sauce and mix through. You can also add chopped anchovies directly to this sauce and serve without an anchovy sauce alongside. The ingredients can be chopped by hand, or in a food processor.

Makes about 375 ml
(1 1/2 cups)

300 g (10 1/2 oz) parsley

3 garlic cloves, peeled

100 g (3 1/2 oz) capers in
vinegar, drained

310 ml (1 1/4 cups) extra
virgin olive oil

Often, a thick slice of white bread is added to this recipe, soaked in a little white wine vinegar, squeezed out and added with the rest of the ingredients.

Pulse-chop the parsley with the garlic and the capers in a food processor. They should be specks in the sauce and not a paste, so don't chop them up too finely. Transfer to a bowl. Season with salt and pepper, and add the olive oil. Mix through. If you are not using the sauce immediately, store in an air-tight container in the refrigerator.

Acciugata

Anchovy sauce

This sauce is particularly good served warm with boiled meats and boiled vegetables. It can be used as a dressing for raw vegetables and salads as well — in which case serve it at room temperature.

Makes 375 ml (1 1/2 cups)

150 g (5 1/2 oz) salt-packed
anchovies, filleted

50 g (1 3/4 oz) capers in
vinegar, drained

310 ml (1 1/4 cups) olive oil

Clean the anchovies following the instructions (page 402).

Chop them up finely and put them in a bowl. Chop the capers finely and add them to the anchovies.

Heat the olive oil in a saucepan until it is quite hot. Remove from the heat and quickly stir in the anchovy-caper mix, mashing them into the oil with a wooden spoon to make a rough-textured sauce. Add a little freshly ground black pepper.

If you are not using the sauce immediately, keep it covered in the refrigerator and warm through gently to serve.

Besciamella 1

Béchamel 1

This is a fairly thin béchamel used, for example, in the lasagne*. When a thicker béchamel is required, use the amounts given for béchamel 2.

Makes about 1 litre (4 cups)

1 litre (4 cups) milk

100 g (3¹/₂ oz) butter

80 g (3 oz) plain
(all-purpose) flour

freshly grated nutmeg

Heat the milk in a saucepan. In a separate wide saucepan, melt the butter, then add the flour. Stir with a wooden spoon and cook for a minute or two until it is lightly golden. Add a ladleful of the warm milk and stir energetically so that it does not form lumps. Continue adding the milk in ladlefuls and stirring all the time until all the milk has been incorporated. Season with salt and pepper, and a generous grating of nutmeg. Continue cooking and stirring on a low heat for another 10 minutes to thicken. It should be very smooth.

Remove from the heat. If you are not using it immediately, give a good whisk before you do use it.

Besciamella 2

Béchamel 2

Makes about 1 litre (4 cups)

1 litre (4 cups) milk

100 g (3¹/₂ oz) butter

120 g (4 oz) plain
(all-purpose) flour

freshly grated nutmeg

This is a thicker béchamel which will give consistency to certain dishes, like savoury tarts.

Follow the method above.

Maionese

Mayonnaise

This can also be made in a food processor.

Makes 500 ml (2 cups)

3 egg yolks

about 500 ml (2 cups) light olive oil

juice of ¹/₂ lemon

Put the yolks into a bowl and whip them with a whisk or electric mixer for a couple of minutes, until they fluff up a bit. Begin adding the oil, a few drops at a time, whisking steadily to incorporate it. Once the mayonnaise begins to take on its thickened consistency, continue adding the oil in a thin, steady drizzle, whisking continuously with the other hand. The amount of oil needed may vary slightly. Add the lemon juice and season lightly with salt and pepper, and whisk in. The mayonnaise should be thick and fluffy.

If the mayonnaise curdles, you can begin the process again, by breaking 1 new yolk into a separate bowl and adding a spoonful of the curdled mayonnaise to it instead of olive oil. Sometimes, a few drops of hot water and an energetic whisk will return your mayonnaise to its correct consistency.

Cover and refrigerate if not using immediately.

Pomarola semplice

Simple tomato sauce

If you are using tinned tomatoes, the cooking time will be slightly less — about 15 minutes from when the tomatoes begin to boil.

Makes about 700 ml (24 fl oz)

3 garlic cloves, peeled and lightly crushed with the flat of a large knife blade

6 tablespoons olive oil

1.2 kg (2 lb 10 oz) of ripe fresh tomatoes, skinned and chopped or 900 g (2 lb) tin of peeled tomatoes with juice, chopped

about 12 basil leaves, roughly torn

Put the garlic and olive oil into a saucepan on a medium heat. When the garlic begins to sizzle, add the tomatoes. Season with about a teaspoon of salt and a little pepper. When the tomatoes begin to boil, lower the heat and simmer for about 20 minutes, depending on how much water the tomatoes contain. Break up the tomatoes with a wooden spoon and cook until the tomatoes have melted into a thick, smooth sauce. Take care not to dry out the sauce — it should have a thick, soft consistency. If you prefer a completely smooth sauce, pass through a food mill or purée roughly in a blender. Add the basil towards the end of the cooking time.

If you will not be using the sauce immediately, store in a jar in the refrigerator. Cover the tomato sauce with a thin layer of olive oil. The sauce can also be frozen for future use.

To preserve a fresh tomato sauce: See note on preserving (page 400). If you will be preserving a sauce, you will probably be using a larger quantity of tomatoes. If you will be using 6 kg (13 lb 8 oz) of tomatoes for example, do not multiply the garlic and olive oil accordingly. Rather, for an increased quantity, add a few more tablespoons of olive oil, a few more basil leaves and one or two more garlic cloves.

Pack the sauce into clean, sterilised glass jars and close the lids tightly. Put the jars upright into a large saucepan, cover with water and bring to the boil. Boil for 20 minutes and remove from the heat. Leave the jars to cool completely before removing them from the water. Check that a vacuum has been created on the lids. Store in a cool, dark place. They will keep for many months. Once opened, keep in the refrigerator and consume quickly.

Pomarola con gli odori

Tomato sauce with herbs

Makes about 700 ml (24 fl oz)

6 tablespoons olive oil

1 red onion, peeled and chopped

1 small stalk of celery, trimmed and chopped

1 medium carrot, peeled and chopped

2 garlic cloves, peeled and roughly chopped

1.2 kg (2 lb 10 oz) ripe, fresh tomatoes, skinned and chopped or 900 g (2 lb) tin of tomatoes with juice, chopped

a few parsley leaves, roughly torn

about 6 basil leaves, roughly torn

If you are using tinned tomatoes, the cooking time will be slightly less — about 15 minutes from when the tomatoes begin to boil.

Heat the olive oil in a large saucepan. Add the onion, celery, carrot and garlic, and sauté on a gentle heat until they have softened. Add the tomatoes and the parsley, and season with a teaspoon of salt and a little pepper. Simmer on a medium heat for about 20 minutes or until the tomatoes have melted into a thick sauce.

Add the basil leaves towards the end. Roughly purée the sauce in a blender. If you will not be using the sauce immediately, store it in a jar in the refrigerator. Cover the tomato sauce with a thin layer of olive oil. The sauce can also be frozen for future use.

To preserve a fresh tomato sauce: See note on preserving (page 400). If you are preserving a sauce, you will probably use a larger quantity of tomatoes. Do not multiply the onions and carrots, etc., accordingly. For an increased quantity, add another onion, carrot and piece of celery, etc., and a few more tablespoons of olive oil.

Pack the sauce into clean, sterilised glass jars and close the lids tightly. Put them upright into a large pot and cover with water. Bring to the boil and boil for 20 minutes. Remove from the heat and let the jars cool completely before removing them from the water. Check that a vacuum has been created on the lids and store in a cool, dark place. They will keep for many months. Once opened, store in the refrigerator and consume quickly.

Ragù

Quick ragù (meat sauce)

Makes about 850 ml (30 fl oz)

4 tablespoons olive oil

1 large onion, peeled and chopped

400 g (14 oz) minced (ground) veal or beef

2 garlic cloves, peeled and finely chopped

125 ml (1/2 cup) white wine

400 g (14 oz) tomato passata

1 bay leaf

1 sprig of fresh thyme or marjoram

2 strips of lemon zest, about 6 cm (2 1/2 in) each

This is a sauce eaten frequently, spooned over pasta and gnocchi — a staple of Tuscany and generally all over Italy. The lemon zest here is optional. It can also be added to the Tuscan ragù* (see opposite page) if you like the flavour. When making ragù, it is a good idea to make double the amount you will need and freeze it for future use. This amount will be enough for 6–8 portions.

Heat the olive oil in a wide saucepan. Add the onion and sauté until it has softened and is lightly golden. Add the meat and the garlic, and cook until the water has evaporated completely and the meat begins to brown. Add the white wine and when that has evaporated, add the tomato, the bay leaf and the thyme or marjoram. Season with salt and pepper.

Lower the heat and simmer for about 30 minutes, adding only 125–250 ml (1/2–1 cup) of water at a time as it thickens. It should be a thick, rich, deep golden sauce. Add the whole lemon zest pieces and simmer for another 10 minutes.

If you like a smooth sauce, you can pass half or all of the ragù through the medium-holed disc of a food mill, directly back into the pan.

Ragù alla toscana

Tuscan ragù (meat sauce)

Makes over 1 litre (4 cups)

10 g (¹/₄ oz) dried mushrooms

5 tablespoons olive oil

1 medium onion, peeled and finely chopped

2 garlic cloves, peeled and finely chopped

a small bunch of parsley, leaves chopped

1 medium carrot, peeled and finely chopped

1 stalk of celery, trimmed and finely chopped

500 g (1 lb 2 oz) minced (ground) beef

2 Italian sausages, about 80 g (3 oz each), skinned and crumbled

750 ml (3 cups) red wine

100 g (3¹/₂ oz) tomato passata

2 tablespoons tomato paste (purée)

This is a rich, delicious, full-flavoured sauce used for lasagne, and to spoon over pasta and gnocchi. The amount will be enough for about 10 portions.

Soak the mushrooms in a cup of warm water for about 10 minutes to reconstitute them. Squeeze out the water and finely chop the mushrooms. Strain the water to use in the ragù.

Heat the olive oil in a wide saucepan. Add the onion, garlic, parsley, carrot and celery. Sauté for about 10 minutes, mixing with a wooden spoon until softened and lightly golden.

Add the meat and the sausage meat and sauté on a medium heat until all the moisture from the meat has evaporated and the meat begins to brown. Add the red wine and cook until a lot of it has evaporated. Add the tomato passata and the paste, the mushrooms and the strained mushroom water. Season with salt and pepper. Cover and simmer for 2–2¹/₂ hours on a low heat. Add a little water when necessary to prevent the sauce from sticking and to maintain a good sauce consistency. Stir frequently to prevent the sauce from sticking.

Brodo di pesce

Fish stock

This is a light stock used for making seafood risottos or for adding to fish dishes which require longer cooking time and a fuller flavoured cooking liquid than water.

Makes 1.5 litres (6 cups)

about 1 kg (2 lb 4 oz) fish bones and soup fish

1 large white onion, peeled and quartered

1 leek, roughly chopped

1 celery stalk with leaves, roughly chopped

1 large carrot, peeled and chopped

a small bunch of parsley stalks and leaves, left whole

4 or 5 whole cloves

2 bay leaves

2 garlic cloves

When using fish heads, many cooks remove the eyes and the gills, as these can make the stock bitter. Rinse the fish bones and put them into a large saucepan with all the other ingredients and add a little salt. Cover with about 2 litres (8 cups) of cold water and bring to the boil.

Lower the heat and simmer for 30 minutes, skimming the surface with a slotted spoon to remove any scum. You can add a couple of thyme or tarragon sprigs and thick lemon slices, and leave them to infuse for 5–10 minutes. Strain through a fine sieve. A fish stock is best used the day it is made. It can be frozen when cooled for future use.

Brodo di pollo

Chicken stock

Makes about 1.5 litres
(6 cups)

1 medium-sized chicken

1 large white onion, peeled
and quartered

1 small leek, roughly
chopped

1 celery stalk with leaves,
chopped

2 carrots, peeled and
chopped

a small bunch of parsley
stalks and leaves, left whole

a few black peppercorns

Chicken stock is used very often, and is made with chicken meat as well as the bones. If you are using only bones, add a couple of extra chicken wings as they make a tasty stock. Boiled chicken is often eaten on its own or with a sauce and serves as a very convenient, quick meal to have on hand.

Rinse the chicken and put into a large saucepan. Cover with about 3 litres (12 cups) of cold water and bring to the boil. (If all the water doesn't fit into the pan at once, add the rest later once the stock has reduced a little.) Skim the surface of any scum with a slotted spoon and add the rest of the ingredients. Season with a little salt.

Lower the heat and simmer for about 1 1/2 hours. Strain the stock through a fine sieve, remove the chicken meat from the bones and set aside. Discard the rest. If you are not using it immediately, it may be cooled and refrigerated for up to two days. You can remove the layer of fat that solidifies on the surface. The stock may also be frozen when cooled for future use.

Brodo di carne

Meat stock

This is a light stock used for cooking risottos and serving pasta in broth. It is also used in place of water for adding to long-cooked meat dishes, for a more concentrated flavour. Tougher cuts of meat can also be used in place of the bones, as they soften after a long cooking time. The meat can be served with green herb sauce* and anchovy sauce* (see pages 378 and 379).

Makes about 1.5 litres
(6 cups)

800 g (1 lb 12 oz) veal or beef bones (and meat or meat off-cuts)

1 large white onion, peeled and quartered

1 leek, roughly chopped

1 celery stalk with leaves, cut into large chunks

1 large carrot, peeled and cut into large chunks

1 tomato, quartered

about 6 whole parsley stalks

2 bay leaves

a few black peppercorns

Rinse the bones and put them into a large pot with the meat or meat off-cuts. Cover with about 3 litres (12 cups) of cold water and bring to the boil. Skim the surface of any scum with a slotted spoon. Add the rest of the ingredients and simmer for about 2 hours. Strain through a fine sieve and discard the solids. If you are not using the stock immediately, cool before transferring to a suitable container and refrigerating. Remove and discard any fat that solidifies on the surface of the stock in the refrigerator. The stock will keep for a couple of days in the refrigerator. It can also be frozen when cooled, for future use.

Brodo di verdure

Vegetable stock

Makes 1.5 litres (6 cups)

1 large onion, peeled and quartered

1/2 a small leek, roughly chopped

2 carrots, peeled and cut into large chunks

1 celery stalk with leaves, cut into large chunks

1 large tomato, halved

2 garlic cloves, peeled

6 whole parsley stalks

1 bay leaf

a few black peppercorns

This stock is very light and is used for cooking risottos, serving pasta in broth and for adding to long-cooked meat, poultry, fish or vegetable dishes for a fuller flavour rather than adding water.

Put the ingredients into a large saucepan and cover with about 3 litres (12 cups) of cold water. Add a little salt. Bring to the boil and skim the surface of any scum with a slotted spoon. Lower the heat and simmer for 1 hour.

Strain through a fine sieve. If you are not using the stock immediately, cool before storing in a suitable container in the refrigerator. It will keep for about two days in the refrigerator. It can also be frozen when cooled, for future use.

Pasta brisée

Savoury pastry

Makes two 26 cm (10 1/2 in) tarts of about 2.5 cm (1 in) high

250 g (9 oz) butter

500 g (1 lb 2 oz) bread flour

1 tablespoon olive oil

5 tablespoons ice cold water

This pastry can also be made in a food processor.

Cut up the butter into pieces and put into a wide bowl. Add the flour and 1 flat teaspoon of salt and mix in, sifting and working it through your fingers until it looks like large crumbs.

Add the oil and water, and knead it gently and quickly with your hands just until the dough comes together in a mass. (Do not work it a lot as you would a bread dough.)

Divide the pastry into 2 parts, wrap up individually in plastic wrap and refrigerate for an hour before rolling it out. The pastry can be frozen at this point — if you will not be using it immediately.

To roll out the pastry: Sprinkle your work surface with a little flour. Using a rolling pin, roll out the disc of pastry to a thickness of about 3 mm ($^1/_8$ in) and slightly larger than the diameter of your tart case. Roll up the pastry carefully around the rolling pin, and lower it into a loose-bottomed tart case. Unroll it, pressing the bottom and sides down gently with your fingertips, patching up anywhere if necessary. Roll the rolling pin sharply across the rim of the tart case to cut away the excess pastry. Press your fingertips again across the sides of the pastry so that it is pushed out slightly above the rim to allow for a little shrinking when it cooks. The tart case may now be filled for baking or baked blind before filling.

To bake blind: Line the pastry in its tart case with baking paper or heavy aluminium foil. Fill with baking beans, or baking weights, and bake in a preheated oven at 180°C (350°F/Gas 4) for about 20 minutes, or until the visible pastry is lightly golden brown. Remove the beans and the paper, prick the bottom of the pastry in a few places with the prongs of a fork and return the tart case to the oven for 5–10 minutes more (for a partially baked crust), until the bottom is cooked and quite dry. If not, the tart risks tasting soggy and a little uncooked. For a fully baked tart crust, the filling of which will not require any oven time, remove the beans and bake for another 20 minutes or until the pastry is golden and cooked. Remove from the oven.

Pasta frolla

Sweet pastry

You can leave out the lemon zest if it doesn't complement the flavour of the filling, or substitute it with orange zest, or a little powdered cinnamon, etc. This pastry is different from bread or pasta and should not be kneaded, but gently, yet thoroughly worked to incorporate the ingredients. The tart should be 2.5 cm (1 in) high and have enough pastry for a lattice crust or topping.

Makes two 24 cm (9^{1}/$_{2}$ in) tarts

250 g (9 oz) butter, slightly softened

250 g (9 oz) caster (superfine) sugar

500 g (1 lb 2 oz) cake flour

a pinch of salt

grated (yellow only) zest of 1 small lemon

2 whole eggs and 1 yolk

Put the butter into a bowl or onto a work surface with the sugar and mix to incorporate with a wooden spoon. Mix in the flour, salt and lemon zest and sift the crumbly flour through with your fingers. Add the eggs and using your hands, gently mix until the mixture comes together and you can shape it. Add a little more flour if it seems too wet or a couple of drops of cold water if it seems too dry. Separate the pastry into 2 equal parts and flatten lightly with your palm to form discs. Cover with plastic wrap and leave the pastry to rest for 30 minutes to an hour in the refrigerator before rolling it out. If you won't be using the pastry immediately, it will keep for a couple of days refrigerated. You can also freeze the pastry at this point (it can be quite handy to have kept some in the freezer).

To roll out the pastry: Sprinkle your work surface with a little flour. Using a rolling-pin, roll out the disc of pastry, to a thickness of about 3 mm ($1/8$ in) and slightly larger than the diameter of your tart case. Roll up the pastry carefully around the rolling pin and lower it onto the tart case. Unroll it, pressing down on the bottom and sides and patching it up in places if necessary. Roll the rolling pin sharply across the rim of the tart case to cut away the excess pastry, which can be used for a lattice crust, if required. The tart case may now be filled with jam, pastry cream or fruit for baking, or it may be baked blind, partially or completely, before filling.

To bake blind: Line the pastry in its tart case with baking paper or heavy aluminium foil. Fill with baking beans, or baking weights, and bake in a preheated oven at 180°C (350°F/Gas 4) for about 20 minutes, or until the visible pastry is lightly golden brown. Remove the beans and the paper, prick the bottom of the pastry in various places with the prongs of a fork and return the tart case to the oven for 5–10 minutes more, for a partially-baked shell, until the bottom is lightly golden and quite dry. (If not, the tart risks tasting soggy and a little uncooked.) For a fully baked tart crust, (the filling of which will not require any oven time) remove the beans and bake for another 20 minutes or until the pastry is golden and cooked. Remove from the oven.

Crema

Crème anglaise

If you prefer a sweet custard crème, add a little more sugar.

Makes about 1.2 litres
(42 fl oz)

1 litre (4 cups) milk

**125 g (4¹/₂ oz) caster
(superfine) sugar**

**1 vanilla bean, halved
lengthways**

10 egg yolks

Put the milk, half of the sugar and vanilla bean into a saucepan
to boil.

　　Whip the egg yolks with the remaining sugar in a bowl until
they are creamy. Just before the milk comes to the boil, remove
the saucepan from the heat. Add a ladleful of hot milk to the eggs,
to acclimatise them slowly, whisking to prevent them from curdling.
Add another ladleful, then add the whole mixture back to the milk
saucepan. Return to a very low heat for a few minutes, stirring
continuously with a wooden spoon. Take care not to let it get too
hot as the eggs will curdle. The crème is ready when it coats the
spoon or when your finger leaves a path if you trace it through the
crème on the spoon. Remove from the heat and strain into a
suitable container for storage or serving.

　　Scrape out some seeds from the vanilla bean with a
teaspoon and add to the container. Keep the bean for your vanilla
sugar* (see page 397). Stir the custard as it cools. Serve warm or
cold. The crème may be refrigerated for a couple of days and
warmed gently through to serve (or served cold).

Crema pasticcera

Pastry cream

Makes about 1.2 litres
(42 fl oz)

1 litre (4 cups) milk

1 vanilla bean, halved
lengthways or 1 teaspoon
of vanilla essence

8 egg yolks

250 g (9 oz) caster
(superfine) sugar

120 g (4½ oz) plain
(all-purpose) flour

2 tablespoons butter

Put the milk into a saucepan with the vanilla and bring it to the boil.

Whip the yolks in a bowl with the sugar until pale and creamy.

Add the sifted flour and whisk to incorporate. Just before the milk comes to the boil, remove it from the heat. Add a ladleful of the hot milk to the yolk mixture, whisking continuously. Slowly incorporate all the milk, then return all the mixture back to the pan and reduce to a very low heat to cook the mixture through. Stir constantly with a wooden spoon for a few minutes, until the mixture thickens. If you notice any lumps, give an energetic whisk with a wire whisk. Vacuum-type bubbles will begin to appear on the surface when the cream is ready.

Remove from the heat and pour into a suitable container. Whisk in the butter and let it cool, whisking occasionally to keep the cream smooth. Put a piece of plastic wrap directly onto the surface of the cream to prevent a skin from forming. It will keep for 2–3 days in the refrigerator. Whisk again to smooth it out before using.

Torroncino

Praline

This is very convenient to keep on hand to scatter over ice cream or desserts. It will keep stored, covered in a glass jar in a cool place for a few weeks. You can use any nuts you like — alone or mixed.

Makes about 1 litre (4 cups)

400 g (14 oz) caster (superfine) sugar

200 g (7 oz) skinned almonds or hazelnuts

a little butter or light olive oil

Lightly grease a little butter or oil in a thin layer onto a large baking tray or, ideally, onto a marble work surface so the caramel can be poured directly onto it to cool.

Put the sugar into a heavy-bottomed saucepan and add a few drops of water. Cook the sugar on a medium heat until it is a deep, rich golden colour, taking care as it can burn in a second. Remove from the heat and stir the nuts into the sugar with a wooden spoon.

Carefully pour the caramel to spread onto the oiled surface. When it has cooled and set, break off chunks and bash with a heavy mallet, or pulse-blend in a food processor to reduce it to coarse crumbs.

Caramello

Caramel syrup

This is a convenient sauce to have, as it remains liquid and stores well. Apart from being very good served spooned over pannacotta* (see page 216), you can serve it simply over sautéed fruits.

Makes about 375 ml
(1 1/2 cups)

300 g (10 1/2 oz) caster
(superfine) sugar

375 ml (1 1/2 cups) hot water

Put the sugar into a small saucepan with 185 ml (3/4 cup) of hot water and stir it to dissolve. Put it over a medium heat until it begins to caramelise. Swirl the pot around to distribute the heat evenly. Watch the caramel closely, as it can burn in a second. When it is a rich, deep golden colour, remove it from the heat and quickly pour in the remaining 185 ml (3/4 cup) of hot water, standing back as it will bubble and splash up. Return to a low heat for a few minutes, stirring. Make sure it is completely melted. Pour the caramel into a clean, slightly warm jar and let it cool before closing the lid. Store in a cool place.

Pan di spagna

Sponge cake

For lining cake moulds, etc. with the sponge, bake in a flat, large oven tray, so you can easily cut it into strips. If you want a cake filled with jam, fruit or pastry cream, bake it in a smaller, round or square cake tin to make a higher cake.

Makes one tray of
30 x 40 cm (12 x 16 in)

6 eggs

225 g (8 oz) caster
(superfine) sugar

280 g (10 oz) plain
(all-purpose) flour

1 teaspoon of vanilla
essence

Preheat the oven to 180°C (350°F/Gas 4).

Beat the eggs in a bowl with the sugar until they are pale, very thick and creamy. This will take quite a while. Add the sifted flour bit by bit, mixing in well after each addition. Add the salt and the vanilla, and whisk in to incorporate.

If you are using a large, flat baking tray, line it first with baking paper, as it will make it easier to remove it from the tray when cooked. If not, you can simply butter and flour the cake tin or baking tray. Pour the batter into the tin and bake in the preheated oven for 30–40 minutes, or until the top is lightly golden and springs back gently when you touch it. The cake will have come away from the sides slightly. Turn out onto a rack to cool.

Zucchero alla vaniglia

Vanilla sugar

After you have used vanilla pods, dry them, pack them into a jar and cover with sugar. In a couple of weeks, the sugar will have a lovely vanilla smell and flavour. You can keep topping up the jar with sugar, and add another bean or two to the jar as you use them.

Crema di mascarpone

Mascarpone cream

Makes about 500 ml (2 cups)

250 ml (1 cup) cream

2 tablespoons caster (superfine) sugar

1 teaspoon vanilla essence

250 g (9 oz) mascarpone

This is a lovely, thick and rich cream to serve with dessert. You can add a little more sugar if you prefer a sweeter cream.

Put the cream into a bowl with the sugar and the vanilla, and whip lightly until it just begins to thicken. Gently whisk in the mascarpone, taking care not to overbeat it. You may adjust the consistency by adding more cream or mascarpone. Use immediately or cover, and store in the fridge, but give another whisk before serving.

Zabaglione

Sabayon

This can be served warm, to accompany a dessert or cake, or with a few cantuccini biscuits to dip into the sabayon. You can use Vin Santo instead of the Marsala.

Serves 6

3 egg yolks

100 g (3½ oz) caster (superfine) sugar

125 ml (½ cup) Marsala

Half-fill a saucepan with water and bring it to the boil.

Whip the eggs with the sugar in a wide, stainless steel bowl until slightly thickened. Beat in the Marsala. Lower the heat of the water to minimum and set the egg bowl over the water. Continue whisking until the mixture is thick, voluminous and fluffy, taking care that the eggs do not cook and become scrambled. Remove from the heat and serve.

How to...

Making risotto

The quality of the rice is probably the most important factor in making a risotto. Use Italian arborio, carnaroli or similar risotto rice.

Have the stock (or water) you are using on a gentle simmer on the stovetop next to a heavy-bottomed risotto saucepan. Melt the butter or olive oil in the risotto pan. Add the chopped onion and the other base vegetables you will be using such as celery, carrot or garlic, and sauté them until they have softened and are very lightly golden. Add the rice, stirring to coat it, and cook for a minute or two. Add the wine, if using, and when it has evaporated, add a couple of ladlefuls of hot stock. Stir with a wooden spoon. Season with salt and pepper, and any other seasonings. Continue to add more hot stock as it is absorbed by the rice, stirring all the time to prevent it from sticking. If the stock is used up before the risotto is ready, continue adding hot water. The total cooking time of the rice should be about 25 minutes. After the risotto has been cooking for about 20 minutes, taste it to check the seasoning and the texture. It should be soft, yet quite firm and have a fairly liquid, creamy texture. Add a generous nut of butter and freshly grated parmesan cheese. This will hold the risotto loosely together. Add any chopped, fresh herbs and serve sprinkled with extra Parmesan cheese.

If the risotto, at any point, gets lightly stuck to the bottom of the pan, remove the pan from the heat and let it stand for a few minutes before stirring. This should help to unstick the rice.

Making preserves

Although much of Tuscan cooking relies on produce brought directly to the table, cooks also utilise preserves which, in themselves, add variety to a menu, and make out-of-season produce available.

The recipes in this book use products collected from home-grown fields a couple of hours before they were preserved.

There are a few rules to observe when preserving foods:

✣ The products should be very fresh and unblemished.

✣ The glass jars in which they are to be preserved, must be thoroughly cleaned, sterilised and dried.

✣ The tops or lids used should always be new and fit tightly.

✣ The fruit or vegetables should be tightly packed into the jars, sealed, then processed (brought to the boil and boiled for at least 20 minutes) in their sealed jars. If they are not to be processed, any air-bubbles should be removed by pushing the ingredients down with a fork. They should then remain covered with their preserving liquid (oil, vinegar, syrup etc.).

✣ Clean cutlery should always be used in extracting the contents of the jars.

✣ The jars should be kept in a cool, dark place and once opened, stored in the refrigerator and consumed fairly quickly.

✣ It is better to make more jars of smaller quantities, which can then be consumed relatively quickly instead of leaving opened jars in the refrigerator for a long time.

✣ If at any time the contents of a jar look or smell suspicious, the jar should be discarded.

When making jam, I have seen many Tuscan homecooks spoon the hot jam into clean, sterilised jars, close the lids tightly and turn the jars upside down. They are left there, covered with a tea towel to cool completely. This creates a vacuum, which can be seen on the lid, ensuring that no air remains in the jars. The jars are then stored upright in a cool, dark place for up to a year. While it is safer to boil the jars, this is a quick and effective method.

Note: Botulism can be very dangerous. It can be present in tiny quantities and is therefore difficult to detect. Homemade preserves which are not preserved in vinegar or salt and have no preservatives are more susceptible to bacteria, as they lack the acidity which blocks the development of the bacteria. Boiling the foods in jars neutralises the toxins as they are sensitive to heat. However, preserves are not always boiled. The making of preserves must therefore be carried out under very strict and careful conditions.

Cleaning salt-packed anchovies

Rinse the anchovies in cold water with a little vinegar to remove the salt. Fillet them, by cutting off the head and making a slit all along the underside with a small, sharp knife. Remove the central bone by pulling it away by the tail with your one hand, while holding the anchovy in the other. You will be left with two attached fillets.

Skinning fresh tomatoes

Bring a saucepan of water to boil. Have a bowl of cold water ready. Make a cross with a sharp knife on the bottom part of the tomato. Plunge the tomatoes into the boiling water for a few seconds — until the skins wrinkle slightly. With a slotted spoon, transfer them to the cold water bowl. This will help to loosen the skins. Drain off the water and peel away the skins.

A quick way of removing the skins for sauces is to cut a cross on the bottom of the tomato. Push that side against the large holes of a grater and grate through, holding the tomato with the palm of your hand. You should be left with most of the tomato skin in your palm.

Cooking in a bain-marie

Make the pudding cream, cake or savoury mixture required, and put it into its cake tin. Set this tin comfortably into a larger oven dish with adequate sides. Pour enough hot water into the larger oven dish to come about halfway up the sides of the smaller cake tin. Transfer carefully to the preheated oven to bake for the required time. You can add a few drops of lemon juice to the larger oven dish to prevent it from discolouring.

Glossary of ingredients and techniques

This is not a detailed guide, rather a simple description of the Italian ingredients used in the recipes which may not be known to everybody. Many Italian delicatessens stock these items.

Anchovies - Are used salt-packed or preserved in olive oil and are generally of very good quality.

Bake blind - Pre-bake the pastry case with baking beans or weights. After removing the beans, the pastry will either be filled and served as it is, or returned to the oven for further baking.

Balsamic vinegar - Originating from Modena, it is aged from one year up to 50 years, and can range in price like a good bottle of wine. It has a very definite taste and is most often used in salad dressings, but also for cooking.

Blanch - Drop into boiling water for a minute or so to soften slightly or loosen skins. Cooked in this way, the colour of vegetables is maintained.

Butter - Is almost always unsalted.

Candied citrus peel - These are chunks of orange, lemon, grapefruit and peels, which have been poached, and dry-preserved in a sugar syrup. They are used chopped up in desserts before baking.

Capers - Small berries which grow on creeper-like shrubs in a warm, dry season. They are preserved in salt or vinegar. The salt-preserved capers should be rinsed before they are used. They are eaten raw with salads or used in cooked sauces.

Capocollo - This cured meat is eaten mainly with bread — forming part of the many *affettati misti* (mixed, sliced cold meats) so popular in Tuscany.

Chillies - Are used fresh and dried, crumbled up or in flakes or powder form. They can be substituted by red pepper flakes, the quantity depending on their strength and your personal taste.

Cotechino - A coarsely ground pork mince speciality from Reggio-Emilia which is well seasoned and stuffed into large sausage-like skins. While it is sold fresh and pre-cooked, the pre-cooked version is usually called for in recipes. Fresh cotechino requires a much longer cooking time.

Cream - There are two types: one for cooking and the other for whipping. Use regular thick (single) cream in sweet and savoury dishes, unless you prefer to substitute a heavy (double) cream, for example, in the ice-cream recipes, some tarts, or for serving with desserts.

Dice - Cut up into small, uniform cubes.

Finocchiona - This very typical Tuscan salami made with fennel seeds, is fairly large in diameter. Its flavour is subtle, yet distinct.

Gorgonzola - This is a cow's milk, blue cheese. There are two types — one sweeter and the other with a sharper tang. They are suitable for eating with bread, and with certain fruits such as pears and apples. Gorgonzola is also used for pizza toppings, and with sauces for pasta, gnocchi and polenta dishes.

Grana Padano - Is a less mature and less expensive cheese than Parmesan cheese, and is also suitable for grating or eating in chunks.

Gratinée - Put under a hot grill (broiler) or in a hot oven to melt or brown the surface lightly.

Herbs - Are generally always used fresh. Bay leaves are used fresh and dry. Oregano is most often used dry — other than in a few preserves made with vinegar.

Marsala - A sweet wine made from dried, fermented grapes, quite similar to port, and is also added to desserts before baking, and used in roasts etc.

Mascarpone - This fresh thick, rich, and slightly sweet versatile cream cheese is most often used in desserts, but is also delicious stirred into a sauce at the last minute in place of cream.

Mozzarella - A soft, white cheese sold packed in its own whey, which is best eaten as fresh as possible. It is indispensable for pizza, is often used for baked vegetable dishes and is also eaten in a salad with tomato and basil, dressed with olive oil. The most superior type is made from buffalo milk which is not always readily available outside of Italy.

Olive oil - A lighter, later pressing of the olive pulp, which is less expensive than extra virgin and is suitable for sautéeing and frying foods.

Olive oil extra virgin - Comes from the first, cold pressing of the olives. There are many varieties to choose from, which are perfect for drizzling over salads, vegetables and cooked foods to serve.

Olives - Both green and black olives are widely used. They are available preserved in brine and drained before using, and also in olive oil. They are often sold loose — in hardly any liquid, or just a coating of olive oil after having been sun- or oven-dried. These olives are particularly good for cooking.

Pancetta - Cured belly bacon, both smoked and unsmoked, which is used chopped up in many pasta dishes and also in slices for wrapping around meats during roasting, to flavour and prevent the meat from drying out. It is also called Rigatino in Tuscany.

Parmesan cheese - An essential ingredient for grating over pasta or slicing very thinly over salads, or simply eaten in chunks. It comes from Parma in Reggio-Emilia and is aged for between one to three years. It is referred to as "mature" from 12 to 18 months; "old" from 18 to 24 months and "very old" at two to three years. It is priced according to age, the older being more expensive.

Pasta - Dry pasta is available in many shapes. Ranging from the long spaghetti types to short pasta stars, shells, etc. Fresh pasta with egg is also available from Italian speciality shops.

Pecorino cheese - There are two types of this sheep's milk cheese produced in Tuscany: an aged, firmer, stronger-tasting one — referred to as *stagionato*, which is suitable for grating over pasta, and goes well with certain fruits, such as pear, and the softer, milder type of pecorino referred to as *fresco*, which is unsuitable for grating, and is eaten in slices with cold meats and salads, such as broad beans.

Polenta - A maize flour used for making thick potato-like purée which can be cut into thick slices when cooled and grilled (broiled), fried or gratinéed.

Prosciutto crudo - Tuscan cured ham is saltier than the well-known Parma ham and is said to be the reason why Tuscan bread is unsalted. The ham is used in cooking to add flavour, and is also eaten simply with bread.

Rice - For risotto, a plump, almost round short grain rice, is used. It always remains slightly al dente (firm to the bite). Some typical ones include arborio, and carnaroli. Long-grain rice is used for rice salads and for stuffing tomatoes, etc. Short-grain rice is used for soups as well as for baking in puddings, etc.

Ricotta - Is a soft sheep's or cow's milk cheese, often used in desserts and for fillings in stuffed pastas. There is also a mature, salted type suitable for grating over pasta.

Robiola - A soft goat's cheese which is delicate, yet distinct in flavour. It is eaten with bread, and sometimes can be stirred into cooked foods to add a little richness.

Salsiccia - These Italian sausages are made from minced and spiced pork and are generally quite flavourful and salty. They are also available with chilli, although the ones used for cooking are normally plain.

Saute - Pan-fry in olive oil or butter on a fairly steady, medium heat, until lightly golden.

Semolina - Is an unrefined wheat flour, which can be finely or coarsely ground. It is used for cooking, baking and also for sprinkling onto a surface in place of flour.

Simmer - Cook on a low, steady heat — normally for quite a long time.

Vin Santo - A sweet, dessert wine made from dried, fermented grapes. It is served often as a dessert wine accompanied by cantuccini biscuits, but is also used for cooking desserts and roast meats.

Zampone - This speciality comes from Reggio-Emilia, and is a mixture of coarsely ground and seasoned pork, which is stuffed into a deboned pig's shin and trotter. It is generally served with a variety of boiled meats and also cooked with tripe. It is appreciated for its rich, gelatinous texture.

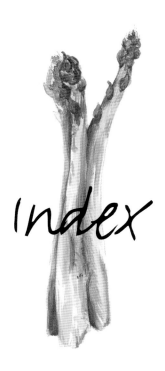

Index